Writing Black Scotland

Writing
Black Scotland

Race, Nation and the Devolution of Black Britain

JOSEPH H. JACKSON

EDINBURGH
University Press

Edinburgh University Press is one of the leading university presses in the UK. We publish academic books and journals in our selected subject areas across the humanities and social sciences, combining cutting-edge scholarship with high editorial and production values to produce academic works of lasting importance. For more information visit our website: edinburghuniversitypress.com

Edinburgh University Press Ltd
The Tun – Holyrood Road
12(2f) Jackson's Entry
Edinburgh EH8 8PJ

First published in hardback by Edinburgh University Press 2020

Typeset in 11/13 Adobe Garamond by
Servis Filmsetting Ltd, Stockport, Cheshire,
and printed and bound by CPI Group (UK) Ltd,
Croydon, CR0 4YY

A CIP record for this book is available from the British Library

ISBN 978 1 4744 6144 3 (hardback)
ISBN 978 1 4744 6145 0 (paperback)
ISBN 978 1 4744 6146 7 (webready PDF)
ISBN 978 1 4744 6147 4 (epub)

Contents

Acknowledgements

Over the long period over which this book has reached some sort of maturity, I have accrued social and intellectual debts at a frenetic rate. The enthusiasm and kindness of Gail Low started me on this path at the University of Dundee. David Dabydeen and Michael Gardiner have overseen my development from a know-nothing to a know-something in black British studies and in Scottish literature respectively, and have exerted a greater shaping influence over my thinking than anyone else. Graeme Macdonald and Alan Riach engaged deeply and critically with my ideas. Scott Hames and Alex Thomson have provided me with peerless editorial feedback and moral support. Michelle Houston and Ersev Ersoy at Edinburgh University Press have been wonderful, and Jane Burkowski has greatly helped me to improve the manuscript.

I have a long list of extremely supportive friends and interlocutors. I'd like to say thanks to everyone, and in particular people who have either read my writing and offered generous and thoughtful feedback from its earliest stages, or helped me keep it together at various points: Yoon Sun Kyoung, Claire Westall, Máté Vince, Katie Vickers, Vicky Smith-Majdoub, Christian Smith, Adam Slavny, Andrea Selleri, Michael Morris, Siân Mitchell, Malachi McIntosh, Alice Leonard, Sam La Vedrine, Kirri Hill, Sorcha Gunne, Letizia Gramaglia, James Christie, Lucy Ball and the Very Hungry Caterpillars. The imprint of their friendship is everywhere in what follows.

The institutional research leave I was granted in 2017–18 by the University of Nottingham allowed me to complete a great deal of writing, without which I would likely not have been able to finish the book. My colleagues at Nottingham have also provided a great deal of encouragement and insight. I would like to thank particularly Nicola Royan,

Dominic Head, Pete Kirwan, and Sean Matthews, who have all read draft work, helping me to improve my writing and my reasoning, and Lynda Pratt for her mentoring and guidance. Special mention must go to Steven Morrison, a great friend to me, who has read every word twice over and given me some excellent ideas. My students have taught me too, from 'Devolutionary British Fiction' at Warwick to 'Dependency Culture', 'Contemporary Fiction' and 'One and Unequal' at Nottingham, and I'd like to say thanks to all of them, singling out Chris Griffin, Zara-Jane Apau and Chloe Ashbridge as those with whom I could talk about this project specifically. There may be mistakes, but without the advice and generosity of all these people, there would be far more.

My friends in Nuneaton have kept me in good spirits. I have promised them I will start another book right away. They tell me they are already missing the composition of this one.

Finally, to my family, whose constant support means I have never had far to fall, and to Carina, for absolutely everything else.

Series Editors' Preface

After two decades of devolution in Scotland, where might the energies of critical intellectuals find purchase or engagement today? Critics celebrate a renewal of artistic and literary confidence; but the polarisation of constitutional debate often treats cultural production as a proxy for political identity. It is more urgent than ever to understand how the historical and contemporary construction of Scottish identities intersects with questions of race, gender and class: yet Scottish cultural studies are dispersed across conflicting traditions of ethnographic, sociological, historical and aesthetic enquiry. Despite repeated calls for more cosmopolitan perspectives, Scottish literary studies remain embedded in a conservative and belated approach to tradition: animated politically by the need to articulate a distinctive cultural identity, too often dependent on a limited set of historiographical frames, neglectful of broader critical and disciplinary contexts. The Engagements series aims to respond to the dynamism of recent cultural and political debate, without being bound by these familiar limits. We hope to publish work which analyses modern and contemporary Scottish literature, culture and society, drawing on interdisciplinary, transnational, comparative and theoretical frameworks. As we write, it seems certain that what the legal theorist Neil Walker has described as the UK's 'constitutional unsettlement' will continue for another decade, attended by economic crisis and political struggle on cultural terrain. Some humanities scholars have argued for a move beyond critique. We disagree: Scotland's past and present continue to demand critical analysis, the detachment of the scholar combined with the commitment of the activist. They call, we believe, for engagements.

Edinburgh — Glasgow — Stirling
2020

On Blackness and Makars: What is a Black Scotland?

What does it mean to speak of a 'black Scotland'? One definition might draw on the significant presence of black people in Scottish history. In the sixteenth century, the Scottish Makar William Dunbar's 'Of Ane Blak-Moir' is reputedly the first literary representation of a black Scottish woman, which suggests that black Scots lived and worked in the court of King James IV (1488–1513).[1] In the eighteenth and nineteenth centuries, in the era of plantation slavery, black people such as Joseph Knight were brought to Scotland as slaves, Robert Wedderburn and Mary Seacole were born from the Scottish diaspora in the Caribbean, and skilled workers like 'Black' Peter Burnet emigrated to Scotland from the United States.[2] Frederick Douglass, who travelled extensively in Scotland campaigning against slavery, chose his own surname from Walter Scott's *The Lady of the Lake*.[3] Hugh MacDiarmid's slogan, 'Back to Dunbar!', did not urge a retrospective of the black dialect poet Paul Laurence Dunbar, born to former slaves in Ohio in 1872, but the name that he shared with the early Makar stands as evidence of Scotland's part in the genealogy of slave-holding in the Americas, or, in Hannah Lavery's elegant formulation, 'the Scotland beyond Scotland'.[4] Gilbert Heron, the father of the American poet Gil Scott-Heron, was the first black football player to play for Celtic FC, one example among many: post-war black migration to Scotland is registered across public life, in politics, civil society, business, sport, music and literature.[5] With the reinvention of the Makar tradition, Jackie Kay, a black Scottish woman, was announced as the new national Makar in 2016. These individual examples are only a small part of a much larger social history.

However, the notion of a black Scotland demands more than a record of individual black lives. Taking the example of black Britain as a larger conceptual antecedent, it implies a critical practice: a way of viewing and reading cultural texts. In this sense, we encounter all the figures listed thus far as part of a larger literary and cultural historiography: as embedded in processes of retrieving, representing and reinterpreting black experience in and beyond Scotland. The more established field of black British cultural studies attends to a range of analytical areas, among them historiography, colonial and postcolonial discourse, the politics of race and representation, racism and anti-racism, black collectivity and the critical interrogation of black expressive culture.[6] These co-ordinates can also be plotted in Scottish terms. Scottish physicians, scholars, philosophers and writers produced many of the key racialising texts of the British Empire. Scotland was a disproportionately large part of Britain's imperial and slave-holding project, where fortunes made in Caribbean plantations echo in present-day street names and dynastic wealth. Edinburgh was once the pre-eminent intellectual environment for the eighteenth- and nineteenth-century invention of race, and Glasgow has seen its own 'Race Disturbances' in the twentieth century – events that belie its anti-racist mythologies.[7] Even without formal powers over migration and citizenship, which under devolution remain reserved at Westminster, Scotland has its own public political culture of race.

Under 'Scotland' in *The Oxford Companion to Black British History*, Michael Niblett points out that in the aftermath of the 1997 referendum on a devolved Parliament, 'black Scots identity [became] an issue within discussions over the construction of a "postcolonial" Scottish identity'.[8] In these terms, a critical approach to blackness and Scotland is part of a process of constant re-evaluation that maintains the primacy of the civic over the ethnic in the contemporary nation, with an emphasis on the new political conditions of devolved government. The most acute application of such an approach would be to address what, in *No Problem Here: Understanding Racism in Scotland*, Neil Davidson et al. call the 'entrenched narrative of an absent racism' in Scotland, and the commensurate lack of critical attention to the 'structuring power of racism' in the devolved nation.[9] That narrative has been entrenched for a very long time: Robert Miles and Leslie Muirhead, writing about racism in Scotland in 1986, noted that the absence of critical work in the field had allowed 'the widespread commonsense view that Scotland has "good race relations because there is no racism here" to go unquestioned'.[10] There is, after all, credible evidence that incidents of racist abuse and violence are proportionally more, rather than less, common in Scotland compared to England and Wales.[11] *No Problem Here* tracks racism as a structuring force in Scotland across various racialised groups, highlighting the 'memory hole' of a Scottish imperial and slave-holding past; that 45 per cent of 'Black African Caribbean' respondents agreed that they had 'experienced discrimination in Scotland in the last five years'; that the 'position of Scotland's Black and minority ethnic communities in [. . .] the labour market continues to remain bleak, and in some cases is even getting worse'; and that black and minority ethnic people in Scotland 'still face serious disadvantages including higher rates of poverty, lower rates of employment and a range of health inequalities'.[12]

A black Scotland, then, encompasses the ongoing critical and representational practices that take as their object a national history of race, racism and racialised experience. *Writing Black Scotland* offers a race-critical approach to Scottish literature, addressing what Liam Connell has criticised as a tendency within the discipline 'to preserve the national – and often "racial" – particularity of Scotland'.[13] In this expanded frame, black Scotland might have the same operation in a Scottish context as black writing in England has had in regional, national, state-national and transnational scope: resisting racism and imperialism, analysing and re-analysing race signifiers and a public political culture of race, to 'remain alive to the disjuncture between elite discourse on migration and the lived reality of racialised minorities in Scotland'.[14] Underlying all of these varied critical and historical registrations is the contingent character of the black signifier itself. As Stuart Hall describes, '[black] has always been an unstable identity, psychically, culturally, and politically. It, too, is a narrative, a story, a history. Something constructed, told, spoken, not simply found'.[15] Hall's emphasis on narrative and storytelling reflects the way that literature has historically been a vehicle for the transmission of racial meanings, including in the body of works coded 'black British', a taxonomy rooted in the Caribbean Artists Movement in the 1960s, and an active critical designation fifty years later.

Crucially, however, blackness in Scottish writing is not simply a subset of blackness in British writing. Just as contemporary Scottish literature has never translated cleanly into a shared 'British' literature, the late twentieth-century prominence of 'writing blackness' in a Scottish national frame troubles a unitary 'black Britishness'. In a 2006 interview with Gail Low and Marion Wynne-Davies, Femi Folorunso offers an observation about black Britain and nationhood, that '[i]t is precisely because of the differences between England and Scotland in the post-mortem response to empire and imperialism that it becomes crucial to negotiate national distinctions in terms of black British identity'.[16] For Folorunso, this question of national differentiation is rooted in a qualitatively different relationship with imperial history, a 'need to explore what Empire meant for Scottish national culture' in a context where even 'high-minded English intellectuals [. . .] have a difficulty in separating England from Britain'.[17]

But Folorunso's moderate call for recognition of national specificity within 'black British identity' contains the seed of a more fundamental problem. Any unitary narrative of 'Britishness' cannot be politically anodyne in a historical period marked by ongoing constitutional challenges to the integrity, and even the continuity, of the Union – what Tom Nairn in *The Break-Up of Britain* termed the 'twilight of the British state'.[18] The elaboration of a 'black Scotland' pursued here militates against the direction of travel for black British literary studies, which, since New Labour, has been associated less with an antagonistic critique of Britain, and more with a revitalising national energy that has contributed to the renegotiation and reinvention of the category of 'Britishness'. This disciplinary tendency has correlates in British governmentality, where the ready-made concept 'black British' has been co-opted into the larger cultural refurbishment of Britishness that has accompanied the constitutional and legislative reforms of devolution and political multiculturalism.[19] 'Black Britain' is an uneasy component of a state-nation still deeply inscribed with structural racism: racially discriminative public policies on immigration and policing, a national economy leveraging neo-colonial economic and cultural relationships, and a British national narrative still oscillating between postcolonial melancholy and periodic celebrations of the benevolence of Empire. The critical and interrogative national dimension of black Scotland, meanwhile, stands against any attempt to deploy a unitary and undifferentiated black Britain in defence of the Union. Instead, literary attempts to imagine a black Scotland demand a reconceptualisation, or even the complete 'break-up', of black Britain.

Writing Black Scotland examines a historical conjuncture in which questions of race, nation and citizenship took on new dimensions in the literary-cultural milieu of Scotland. For my purposes, such a 'devolutionary' period of time, spanning the referendum of 1979 to the early years of the Scottish Parliament, marks the intersection of four related historical developments which underpin this milieu. Accelerated post-war decolonisation had unwound the tight binding of Empire wrapped around the home nations and replaced it, in Tom Devine's words, with a promise of '[s]tate support from the cradle to the grave'.[20] In spite of a national 'indifference' to the end of Empire, the context of postcolonialism, including a suite of intellectual tools focused on decolonisation and racialisation, had a significant impact at a cultural level in Scotland.[21] At the level of the British state, a new politics of race was being developed, a 'culturalist' orientation that started to redefine Britain more explicitly as a pluralist or 'multi-ethnic' nation, and which was key in adjusting and preserving the constitutional integrity of the state. Commonwealth migration to Scotland in the 1980s meant, as Jan Penrose and David Howard describe, the expansion of the '*racialisation* of Scottish society and politics'; race discourses that had, in the colonial era, been exported from Scotland became a pressing question within its territorial limits.[22] Finally, the ethnic dimensions of Scotland came into sharper focus as a consequence of new conditions for a national politics and culture after the referendums in both 1979 and 1997, new conditions which found an acute registration in the literature of the period.

Power tools: devolutionary Scotland

Despite attempts by pro-Union commentators to cast the Scottish National Party as a collection of anti-English racists, nationalist party politics in Scotland remain mostly civic and civil.[23] As David McCrone observes, there is 'no sustained political movement or party which desires to restrict immigration, no "little Scotland" movement'.[24] Self-declared racist organisations in Scotland, such as the Scottish Defence League or Scottish Dawn, usually adapt and espouse the ethno-purist British nationalism of the English Defence League, Britain First or National Action. Outspoken Scottish ethnic nationalism and white supremacist Celticism remain politically marginal, but are extant in Scotland and abroad in the form of Sìol nan Gàidheal or the neo-Confederate imaginary of the Ku Klux Klan.[25] Nevertheless, any examination of Scotland as a national constituency, its sovereignty and prospective statehood, encounters race and racism as necessary negotiations, an ethno-cultural shadow of Scotland's vaunted civic national project. Any vision of Scotland's 'post-ethnic potential' must simultaneously guard against the depoliticising, celebratory multiculturalism often instrumentalised by the British state, and a complacent return to egalitarian exceptionalism, the 'Scottish Myth' critiqued eloquently by McCrone in *Understanding Scotland*.[26] Powers over immigration and equal opportunities legislation are reserved to Westminster, but the Scottish Government retains devolved powers that make up a larger politics of race, such as education and policing, and conducts promotional campaigns such as the 'One Scotland' initiative. Meanwhile, some European social democracies invoked as prospective models for an independent Scotland show an increasing propensity for 'neo-racism': nativist political parties, inflammatory rhetoric directed at non-white 'others', and moral panics around migration.[27] While the racism of contemporary Scotland is inseparable from imperial histories and postcolonial nostalgia, a growing clamour for ethno-cultural protections in the contemporary European political landscape, structured around racialised discourses of immigration and manifested in social democracies with less exposure to colonial racism, suggests that 'post-British' independence is unlikely to be a panacea.

The period following 1979 in Scottish literary studies has been shaped by the contestation of the literary-cultural relationship to political devolution, and the situation of Scotland within a 'postcolonial' paradigm. In his examination of the literary politics of Scottish devolution, Scott Hames has offered two competing visions of devolutionary culture, 'one determinedly Scottish, the other inescapably British'.[28] One vision is of 'The Dream', a restorative cultural-political process, spearheaded by writers and artists, leading inexorably towards self-determination.[29] The cause of 'cultural devolution' has been championed by critics like Cairns Craig, for whom literature responded to Scotland's 'stalled history' and 'stalled political reality', which had been brought into even more acute relief by the interregnum that followed the perplexing referendum of 1979. Galvanised by political stasis, writers focused on exploring a 'variety of routes into alternative ontologies where the imaginary' – Scotland's deferred self-determination – 'can become real'.[30] This cultural politics was also to carry the burden of democratic representation for Scotland – the so-called 'Parliament of Novels' phenomenon – lasting at least until a new referendum became a manifesto commitment for the Labour Party in the run-up to the 1997 general election. In this equation, Scottish literature 'operates as a direct analogue for statehood', affirming not only the integrity and cultural health of the distinct nation, but in a teleological sense its destiny 'to be the nation again' – or in a modern sense, an independent state.[31]

As a check on this literary politics, Hames offers a vision of 'The Grind'. This represents devolution's party-political dimension: 'thin', 'shrewd', 'grubby', an adaptive and expedient British state strategy for the post-imperial Union.[32] The development of various strains of Home Rule thinking dating back at least to the nineteenth century, devolution became formalised as a recommendation of the Royal Commission on the Constitution, the Kilbrandon Commission, which had been established in 1969 following the election of the Scottish National Party MP Winifred Ewing in Hamilton in 1967.[33] This process has been stilted, and subject to the wrangling not just of the British state but of powerful interest groups within it, such as the Westminster political parties, and outside it, such as the Church of Scotland. One clear illustration of the 'grubbiness' of devolutionary history is the Labour-led introduction of the 'super-majority' amendment into the Scotland Act 1978, widely perceived as an effort to stymie Scotland's lukewarm endorsement of devolution in the subsequent 1979 referendum in the name of party-political advantage. Viewed from this angle, Scotland's literary culture follows electoral trends a step or two removed, and the compacts and compromises of professional politicians and state institutions are the main engine of devolutionary change.

The recognition of this 'machinic' quality is not concurrently a dismissal of the role of 'culture' in British political devolution.[34] Emphasising the state motor behind devolutionary movement does not itself mean that literary culture was not caught up with the process. However, the question raised by this division is not strictly whether politics or literature provides the motive power for devolution: what is at stake is the question of the boundaries of literary nationalism itself. The larger effect of foregrounding the 'grind' is to efface the instrumental logic that yokes Scotland's literary culture to the fated establishment of new national-political conditions. Alex Thomson has suggested that the 'metaphorical sublimation of political energy into literary production [. . .] belongs to the realm of the cultural manifesto rather than that of critical history'.[35] This is borne out in the national-political continuum of Scottish writing since 1979. At one end, Alasdair Gray's fiction lends itself naturally to the imagination of his own 'better nation'. In the middle, the stramash around whether the immiseration of Joy Stone in Janice Galloway's *The Trick is to Keep Breathing* (1989) really represents an 'absent Scotland' is an example of the way that literary works pointing in different social-political directions can be forcibly co-opted into national service.[36] The devolutionary inflections of outlying Scoto-British works like William Boyd's *A Good Man in Africa* (1981) or George MacDonald Fraser's *Flashman* franchise (1969–2005) – with their far more pronounced racial-colonial dimension – to a great extent remain unexplored.

Scotland's devolutionary history is also a postcolonial history, though evidently not in the sense of a 'formerly colonised nation'. Indeed, some critics have read devolution itself as a 'postcolonial process', either as a new configuration of the British constitution after Empire, or the 'end-game' for the British state form.[37] The crystallisation of Scotland's subordinate place within the Union triggered by the 1979 referendum, and reinforced by the Thatcher administration's use of Scotland as a policy testing ground, overlapped with the rapid expansion of postcolonial studies as a formation within cultural criticism, often dated to the publication of Edward Said's seminal *Orientalism* (1978).[38] The pioneering analysis of postcolonial thinkers across diverse fields of the discipline, and across diverse contexts in the postcolonial world, offered new tools for the analysis of relations within the imperial centre both for Scottish critics and for Scottish writers.[39] Scottish writing, meanwhile, provided an evidence base for a local contention that orthodox postcolonial studies had insufficiently recognised 'the internal, intranational distinctions, tensions and fissures in British culture and politics'.[40] At the level of cultural manifesto, the particular combination of postcolonial thinking and the determinism of 'literary nationalist' thought has had the tendency to reify 'Scottish Literature' as what Connell calls 'a coherent and *a priori* entity' with little interrogation of its own disciplinary formation or its cultural exclusions.[41] Here, a forthright engagement with black writing offers something to a more radical and less instrumental Scottish literature. Guyana-born Wilson Harris's *Black Marsden* (1972), prominently set in an Edinburgh familiar to him, would hardly fit the cultural politics of literary devolution, but nevertheless is indisputably part of a more expansive understanding of 'Scottish' writing.

Connell has described the way that *a priori* 'Scottish literature' underlines a form of racial particularity, citing Cairns Craig's use of Frantz Fanon to imply that Scotland is racially distinct from the 'dominant' – apparently colonising – culture of England.[42] Other critics have similarly mobilised Fanon as an illustrative comparison for Scottish culture. In *The Eclipse of Scottish Culture*, Craig Beveridge and Ronald Turnbull describe Fanon's 'inferiorisation' thesis and suggest that Scots were, under Union, nationally racialised as a 'natively brutish and vicious people' that required 'the civilising hand' of England.[43] Gavin Miller goes further, equating the linguistic dimensions of French colonial racism, and the Fanonian realisation of the materiality or 'fact' of blackness, to the chastisement of Scots-speaking schoolchildren in *1982, Janine*.[44] These are further examples of what Connell calls the 'dazzling confusion of textual and social forms of exclusion' that positions Scottish literature as a racially defined post-colonisation national culture.[45] These comparative examples offer broad similarities. However, implying that the Scots are part of Fanon's 'wretched of the earth', or that the language politics of contemporary Scotland are analogous to the racial politics of the United States, misses the profound form of social exclusion constituted by racism.

These critics are in good company. Maya Angelou, on visiting Stirling Castle, spoke about what she saw as the common struggle for freedom between African Americans in the Civil Rights movement and Scots like Robert Burns and William Wallace.[46] But this comparative analysis misses or minimises the way that the defining elements of an inferiorised Scottish culture are, viewed through different methodological or imaginative prisms, closer to the racialising operations of the imperial centre than the experience of racialised, colonised and enslaved peoples. Allardyce, the Scots-speaking plantation manager in Andrew O. Lindsay's fantasy of Robert Burns's emigration to the Caribbean, *Illustrious Exile* (2006), describes his fear of the slaves, with their 'gapin mooths, fu' o' teeth, and their thick pintles hingin' doon their thighs'.[47] The dehumanising of the slave, and the brutality of the plantation system, are all described in the

Scots closely associated with the reimagined narrator of the novel, a bona fide icon of Scottish literary culture. Furthermore, the Fanonian 'inferiorisation' paradigm, with its emphatically racial-colonial character, makes the black subject, their racialisation indivisible from that process of inferiorisation, into an exemplary 'other' to Scottish national culture. There may be relatively few black speakers of Scots, but the implication of the 'inferiorisation' comparison is that black experience lies 'out there', in the world beyond the parameters of Scottish literature and the nation. Scotland and its literary tradition are enmeshed with precisely that colonial history.

If conceptualising a black Scotland helps to break open some of the racial-ethnic assumptions underpinning Scottish literature, it must simultaneously remain alive to the opposite end of the spectrum, where, rather than being a discrete ethno-racial national culture, Scotland is defined by its hybridity. Alastair Niven's essay 'New Diversity, Hybridity and Scottishness' provides a helpful index and sensitive readings of racialised and migrant writers operating in Scotland to 2007, but it also offers these writers as evidence of the 'hybridity' that is 'the very nature of Scottish literature'.[48] Gavin Miller points to the collection *Beyond Scotland* (2004) as another example, where Scotland is recast as a 'complex, forward-looking, heterogeneous identity' rather than 'narrow and reductive in its nativism'.[49] Miller's article is a counter-attack against critics of a Scottish national tradition, reading a 'new essentialism' in claims of Scotland's fundamental heterogeneity. In a race-critical sense, this scepticism applies equally to the mode of celebratory, soft-focus multiculturalism implied by the 'transformative' and 'vibrant' influence of black and Asian writers on Scottish literature.[50] The fact that Scotland's Makar is a black woman is politically significant and contributes to a national literary timbre and orientation, but it is worth remembering that she is also appointed directly by the Scottish Government, and the autonomy of the role is curtailed by its public relations function for that government. The pose of pluralism has an instrumental purpose in British and Scottish politics alike.

Blackness and black writing in post-war Britain

Before proceeding any further with the implications of a black Scotland, it is important to establish what 'blackness' means in this specific conjuncture, or more accurately, its capacity for meaning: what Paul Gilroy calls its 'multi-accentuality'.[51] 'Black' does not refer to a biologically definite group, or a coherent and mappable social formation, but instead to a discursive product – a 'social fact' – that is both globally distributed and highly contingent on social-historical context. 'Black' did not come into being with the epoch of European colonialism – Dunbar's 'Blak' shows that the signifier was in use in the sixteenth century at least – but it was the need to legitimise the domination and enslavement of colonised populations that supercharged the definition and dissemination of racial taxonomies. Empire and slavery incepted a specific definition of blackness constructed, according to Achille Mbembe, as a limit 'constantly conjured and abjured', 'invented to signify exclusion, brutalization, and degradation'.[52] The afterlife of those colonial taxonomies involves their reinforcement, redefinition, negation or political appropriation, played out against the persistence of their structural inscription in economic inequality and 'societal' or structural racism. This is the field in which contemporary blackness is made and remade. Literature offers a specific angle into such a field, one responsive to, but set apart from, sociological taxonomies, encoding, in Mbembe's words, the 'luminous, fluid, and crystalline character' of blackness, a 'strange subject, slippery, serial, and plastic, always masked, firmly camped on both sides of the mirror'.[53] This metaphor of a two-sided mirror is appropriate for the paradoxes of contemporary blackness, occurring across multiple planes. Blackness is simultaneously a biological fallacy and an immutable social fact; it is an emancipatory political community 'inhabited by melancholia and mourning', in dialogue with the violence and exclusion fundamental to its historical creation; within it lies both the aspiration to be 'after race', and the need to foreground race as a crucial structuring principle in the modern world; it must form the basis of critique, and yet that critique always runs the risk of reinscribing exactly the taxonomic logic which it attempts to disempower.[54]

As I have suggested, the closest conceptual antecedent to black Scotland is 'black Britain' itself, though the domestic geographical co-ordinates of that Britain are almost entirely English. This formation was first named by Chris Mullard's *Black Britain* in 1973, and only partially overlaps with the articulations of blackness emergent from Fanon's francophone Caribbean or W. E. B. DuBois's United States of America.[55] Kobena Mercer defined the blackness of black Britain as a strategic rearticulation of racial categories, a 'symbolic unity' fashioned from 'signifiers of race difference' that represented solidarity among 'Asian, Caribbean and African peoples, originating from a variety of ethnic backgrounds and sharing common experiences of British racism' that encompassed the decades of Commonwealth migration following the end of the Second World War.[56] Such a formation was explicitly political, addressing itself to the British state, critical of imperialism and neo-imperialism, and avowedly anti-racist. But in 1994, when Mercer was writing, the moment of solidarity he described had largely already passed. Contemporaneously, Gilroy had pointed out that the 'cultural tide has turned decisively against ideas of racial kinship produced in the 1960s', which by the 1990s appeared 'naïve, outdated, and sentimental'.[57] Stuart Hall's famous 'New Ethnicities' lecture in 1988 had called for the 'end of the innocent notion of the essential black subject', via greater attention to its constructedness, assumptions and exclusions.[58] Subsequently, black Britain has retrenched back towards the 'core' Afro-Caribbean group that had dominated the original solidarity movement, drawing on a hegemonic global-political blackness defined by much starker racial demarcations inherited from the United States. This was rendered clearly in the angry reaction to the University of Kent's branding of Black History Month in 2016 with the faces of Zayn Malik and Sadiq Khan, which would have fitted the British racial-political zeitgeist three or four decades earlier, but which only served to illustrate the firm exclusivity of black and Asian racial taxonomies since the millennium.[59] The attenuation of black as a signifier of broad solidarity has thus transpired within the timeframe of devolution. Indeed, it is itself a form of 'devolution' that both breaks up a political power base and emphasises cultural particularity over more radical change – what A. Sivanandan called the transformation from 'political culture' to a 'cultural colour'.[60]

In parallel to the emergence of both state multicultural taxonomies and the development of a bounded, racially defined politics, the boundaries between black African or Afro-Caribbean and 'British Asian' categories have become more strictly policed in terms of critical and publishing paradigms.[61] It was a 'literary' event – the reaction to the publication of Salman Rushdie's *The Satanic Verses* in 1988–9 – which has been read as symbolising a point of divergence, the 'collapse' of black Britain, evidencing 'the heterogeneity of nonwhite experiences and values in Britain'.[62] Nevertheless, the currency of a unified 'black Britain' has lasted longer in the arts. Black British Literature as an academic discipline has retained a trace of that shared response to British racism and hegemonic whiteness, in part because of its historical scope. Taking the example of James Procter's anthology *Writing Black Britain 1948–1998*, 'black' writers in this equation might include V. S. Naipaul, Hanif Kureishi and Meera Syal as readily as George Lamming, Linton Kwesi Johnson and Buchi Emecheta.[63] Literary works are less liable to provide the clean divisions of ethnic loyalty that characterise both British state multiculturalism and the use of racial taxonomies for politically progressive, anti-racist purposes; they are a cultural terrain in which racial signification is offered for interrogation and rendered unstable. The history of post-war black Britain has been the gradual formalisation and 'centring' of the category of black writing, even as the signifier 'black' experienced its own devolutionary process, detaching from the master narrative of the 1960s to the 1980s and transforming into a more neutral, census-defined category of 'black, Asian and minority ethnic', an example of one of the 'generalizable (and ethni-cally indeterminate) signifiers of difference' conducive to state strategies of political multiculturalism.[64] By the turn of the millennium, with the publication of Zadie Smith's *White Teeth* (2000), 'black British literature' had become established as a genre and as an academic discipline; certainly contested, 'in no sense harmonious, unifiable or internally coherent', but ontologically secure.[65]

In the same period, then, the heterogeneous formations of Scottish writing and black British writing were openly engaging with the shifting priorities of the post-imperial British state, to manage a changing consti-tutional order and a new state politics of race. Both had significant impli-cations for 'Britishness' too, an imagined community in which the state has always played a central role. However, these two literary-historical accounts are seldom, if ever, invoked as part of the same cultural history. Despite the considerable scope of black Britain as a field of critical analysis, Britain's constitutional status and intranational differentiation is almost completely absent from its purview. Reflecting wider public discourse in which England and Britain are interchangeable national formations, many works of black British criticism invoke a nationally British context to dis-cuss England, or vice versa, a 'highly problematic gesture adopted by many academics who seek to generalize their studies of ethnic minority commu-nities in London and Manchester to represent experiences of all black and minority ethnic communities in Britain'.[66] Conversely, despite the post-millennium boom in 're-racialising' Scotland historically and contempo-raneously, the critical exposition of blackness as a theoretical concept and as a lived experience remains underdeveloped; Graeme Macdonald points out that in a devolutionary period 'characterised by significant immigrant arrival to Britain, a black and/or Asian presence in Scottish culture seems at best marginal, at worst invisible'.[67]

A fervour of culpability: Scotland's black history

Far from being peripheral to the racial projects of Empire, Scots have been central in developing those raciologies, which partly stemmed from the requirement to define and regulate Scotland within a complex picture of racial Union. Often, the racial 'others' against which an Anglo-Saxon Scotland could be defined came from within Scotland itself. In England during the Jacobite Uprisings, '[d]isloyal Scots were usually portrayed by government propaganda as lice-ridden cannibals with insatiable and dis-orderly sexual appetites' in keeping with stereotypes of colonised people.[68] These racialising practices were overwhelmingly focused on Highland

Scots. Inverting this racialisation, by proving Lowland Scots to be racially worthy of membership of the Union, became a crucial cultural and intellectual project, establishing a distinction between 'Celticist' and 'Anglo-Saxon' or 'Teutonic' strains. Scotland and England were never 'antithetical Celtic and Germanic nations', Colin Kidd argues; instead, '[p]ride in Celtic Scotland was more than counterbalanced by a Saxonist race identity', and 'the dominant narrative of Scottish nation-building was not Celticist, but Teutonist, and, as such, closely aligned with the prevailing myths of English nationhood'.[69] Scottish Enlightenment thinkers developed a consensus about race and 'social evolution' that aligned Lowland Scots racially with the English through whiteness, and maintained colonial subjects and Celts alike as a defining 'other'.[70] These thinkers included conventional 'racialists' and more radical 'polygenists'. David Hume, in the notorious footnote to 'Of National Characters', remarked that he was 'apt to suspect the negroes to be naturally inferior to the whites'.[71] In *Sketches of the History of Man* (1774), Henry Home, Lord Kames, postulated the idea of polygenism: that there was more than one species of human. He illustrated his thinking with reference to the insurmountable differences between the 'tall and well made' Abyssinians and the 'black colour of negroes, thick lips, flat nose, crisped woolly hair, and rank smell'.[72] Raciological thought was pursued further in nineteenth-century Edinburgh, in the work of physician authors such as Robert Knox and John Crawfurd. Knox held that the 'black races' could not 'become civilized', and that 'a black man [is] no more a white man than an ass is a horse or a zebra'; counter-intuitively, he was also against slavery, which he saw as breaching 'the inalienable right of man to a portion of the earth on which he was born'.[73] Beyond the colonial rationale of slavery and dispossession, Robert J. C. Young suggests that Knox and Crawfurd's racialised ethnography represented the Scottish invention of white Anglo-Saxonism, in order to legitimise the racial Union between England and Scotland.[74]

The philosophical and scientific development of race hierarchies in Scotland had correlations in the racial dimensions of Scottish literature at that time. Walter Scott, like the Victorian raciologists, was dedicated to settling Scotland within the Union. However, his work stressed the Highlands of Scotland as a colonial frontier that could be incorporated into the imperial project. In the *Waverley* novels, Highlanders were ethnicised as colonial subjects in need of imperial domination and civility, 'charming, angry, volatile and ultimately immature'.[75] Although Scott was not himself a polygenist, in *Rob Roy* (1818), the central character is racialised, 'a kind of anthropoid ape' that Ian Duncan suggests takes an aesthetic lead from James Burnett's polygenetic theory.[76] Rational Scots – the good white subjects of the British Union – were defined against the primitive energies of the Highlander like Rob Roy, earlier stages of the same trajectory of historical development. Celts, however, did not provide the only racialised counter-example to Union Scots. There were external racial others, such as the radical alterity of the Muslim Saladin, arrayed against the nobility of the Scottish knight Sir Kenneth in *The Talisman* (1825).[77] Reading the boundaries between Norman, Saxon and Jew in Walter Scott's *Ivanhoe* (1819), Cairns Craig suggests that Scott is 'one of the links that binds Hume to Knox in a tradition of intensifying racial discriminations'.[78] Scott wrote little about a black–white race hierarchy, but the symbolic divide between the white Union Scot and the black colonial 'other' was emphatically represented by other Scottish writers like John Buchan.[79] As well as being a writer of prodigious output, Buchan was a prominent Unionist, ardent imperialist and colonial administrator who was Governor General of Canada towards the end of his life. Buchan was a proponent of the 'white man's burden', who, as Bill Schwartz points out, 'sought to universalize the values he believed to be the especial preserve of the white man' through his novels.[80] *Prester John* (1910) is emblematic of this project, a novel featuring a colonial Scot, David Crawfurd, and in which 'black [is] pitted against white, barbarism against civilization', and the true 'evil' is the threat of miscegenation presented by the mixed-race status of the Portuguese mercenary Henriques to an imperial order premised on racial purity.[81]

These examples demonstrate the way that elements of Scottish literature, culture and national history have helped construct a racial commonality underlining the Union, a practice which has sometimes aligned with the raciological priorities of the larger British Empire. This racial Union remains extant in contemporary Britain, unable or unwilling to discard the armature of imperial mythology. Much of Scotland's black history has taken place abroad, in the global theatre of that imperial project, which has subsequently formed the basis of much of the postcolonial enquiry: the 'fervour for admonition and admission of Scottish colonial culpability' that Graeme Macdonald suggests is an element of an anti-imperial argument emergent from Scotland.[82] Much of this has been in disciplinary history, such as Tom Devine's work on imperial Scotland and slavery, or Douglas Hamilton's history of Scotland in the Caribbean.[83] But this has also been significantly a literary-cultural and critical development too. Irvine Welsh's *Marabou Stork Nightmares* (1995) writes back directly to *Prester John*. James Robertson's *Joseph Knight* (2003) restores the Caribbean slave-holding of Jacobite exiles into the 'torn, faded, incomplete map' of national memory made up of Scott's romances.[84] In the same mode as Robertson, a number of recent novels excavate, or dramatically reimagine, a history of Scots in the context of plantation slavery: Robert

Burns in Lindsay's *Illustrious Exile*; Richard Mason of *Jane Eyre* in Robbie Kydd's *The Quiet Stranger* (1991); John Gladstone in David Dabydeen's *Johnson's Dictionary* (2013). Likewise, these fictions have helped to drive a rapid expansion in critical attention to the Caribbean in the Scottish historical imagination, spearheaded by writers like Carla Sassi and Michael Morris.[85] In these accounts, the historical and contemporary valence of 'black' played a significant role in tracing a racial-imperial history and its legacy in present-day Scotland.

A robust focus on Scotland's imperial history is a vital precondition to establishing an effective anti-racist politics. However, that black history has not entirely been abroad, and not entirely within the historical period defined by formal Empire. Scotland also has a contemporary history of race and racism, which has existed in the shadow of the larger British formation. This is, of course, partly sociological. There is no doubt that black Britain is firmly grounded in Commonwealth migration to metropolitan England in the post-war period. Scotland, by contrast, has a smaller population with a genealogical connection to that phase of migration. In the 2011 census, 92 per cent of respondents in Scotland identified themselves as 'White: Scottish' or 'White: Other British'.[86] Britain's 'non-white' population grew from 30,000 immediately after the war to over three million by the end of the century, but only a fraction of those people arrived or were born in Scotland.[87] In the twenty-first century, census indicators of 'ethnic minority' point to differences of constituency as well as scale between Scotland and England; the former has proportionally a far larger Pakistani population and a smaller West Indian or African population than the latter.[88] Furthermore, the census flags up a further texturing of Scottish national distinctiveness from England. Evidence from 2011, parsed by the Centre on Dynamics of Ethnicity (CoDE), shows that in Scotland, 'more of each Black and Asian minority claimed a Scottish-only national identity than claimed an English identity in England', while 'fewer claimed a British-only national identity than in England'; as CoDE registers, the 'census results clearly suggest that Scottish national identity is currently more ethnically inclusive in Scotland than is English in England'.[89] The national orientation of Scotland's minoritised people already presents a challenge to their straightforward incorporation into 'British diversity'. Furthermore, these demographics have significant consequences for the sociological dimension of black expressive culture. Rather than being part of a sizeable minority with a pronounced demographic presence and equivalent literary scene, the context for black writing in Scotland is often marked by relative isolation, resulting in a greater orientation towards the 'critical mass' of black social, cultural and political formations elsewhere. Conversely, for a Scottish literary formation that has sometimes been positioned as a Deleuzian 'minority' within Britain, black writing – 'minor' along a different axis – forces a reconceptualisation of that formation's majoritarian characteristics.[90] Just as Scotland's ostensible 'minority' within Britain has not precluded the exercise of considerable cultural influence and critical reflection on the Union, the 'minority' of racialised people in contemporary Scotland, both numerically and in terms of cultural visibility, does not preclude their significance in Scottish or British national terms.

Niblett's suggestion that 'black Scottish identity' became more significant after the referendum is true, but black Scots had been published over a decade prior to 1997, and the political potential of blackness in terms of decolonisation processes and resistance to neo-imperial reorganisation had already left a mark on Scottish writing. After 1979, the black signifier started to have a belated, though still limited, purchase in Scottish literature. White writers like Alasdair Gray, James Kelman and Irvine Welsh adapted an anti-racist politics that had already been mobilised in black studies and black writing in England, the United States and other postcolonial nations: this was a response both to the visible racism of Scottish society, to British government policies of citizenship and migration, and to a much broader conversation around decolonisation taking place on a global scale. Meanwhile, black Scottish writers first gained visibility through playwriting and poetry in the middle of the 1980s, though their work emerged from, and was often directed towards, black life in London. Maud Sulter pioneered an explicitly politicised black poetics in collections such as *As a Black Woman* (1985) and *Zabat* (1989);[91] Jackie Kay's debut play *Chiaroscuro* (1985) directly addressed questions of inclusion and exclusion in black politics. Her debut poetry collection *The Adoption Papers* examined some of the racial assumptions of Scottish life in 1991.[92] The second referendum in 1997 provoked a new moment of national self-scrutiny in writing and publishing. Although the proposed devolved Parliament was passed at the ballot box, supposedly marking some kind of definitive break, the underlying pressure to re-naturalise Britain constitutionally and as a unified cultural formation actually intensified around devolution. Where poetry first explored the linguistic possibilities for representing blackness in a Scottish context, fiction writers picked up the baton and began interrogating the realities and potentialities of a black Scotland. A push towards 'marketing the margins' around the millennium in metropolitan England also manifested in Scotland: black writers like Luke Sutherland and Suhayl Saadi were published and marketed explicitly as part of a genre of Scottish multicultural writing; Jackie Kay's only novel, *Trumpet* (1998), also dates from this period.[93]

This is only the most available subsection of a much larger body of work that could be taxonomised as 'writing black Scotland'. I take such a category to imply the discursive production of blackness within a Scottish national-cultural frame, rather than a canon of 'black writing' determined by author. This critical paradigm includes the works of black writers either from, or directly attentive to, Scotland, but also examines the way that blackness has been represented in writing by white and Asian authors. Such a methodology attempts a delicate balancing act. On the one hand, it recognises the authenticity of black writers' diverse racial experiences. It provides a partial restorative function, which recentres and promotes black authorship against the racial exclusions of the publishing industry, the academy and wider society, foregrounding 'narratives that retell the histories of blackness', told from 'new vantage points [. . .] previously excluded from the public sphere'.[94] On the other hand, the consolidation of 'black writing' underlined by an implicit or explicit link to a racially defined author has not been without criticism. In the 1980s, both Salman Rushdie and Fred D'Aguiar pointed out that categories like 'black British' constituted a reductive, reifying taxonomy that made an unbreakable link between form and the racialisation of writers. Biographical criticism continues to exercise a tenacious grip on black British literary criticism, leading to what Sara Upstone describes as a 'shocking tendency to make reductive autobiographical readings of black British writings'.[95] Defining a critical field in this way is also commensurate with black British cultural studies as a larger disciplinary precedent, which would include a politics of representation, and the construction of blackness, in non-black-authored texts as part of its contestatory praxis. We could look to David Dabydeen's groundbreaking work in the field, *The Black Presence in English Literature*, as an example here.[96]

Meanwhile, returning methodologically to an explicitly national frame swims against the tidal pull of postmodern anti-nationalism, though this is in keeping with the unique dynamics of Scottish nationalism itself. Putting forward a Scottish national literature as a unit of analysis pushes against the prevailing grain of postcolonial thinking, where mobile identities, displacement and transnationalism are dominant paradigms. In black British terms, this dates back at least to Paul Gilroy's *The Black Atlantic* (1993), which was pivotal in changing the trajectory of the field. Gilroy suggests a transatlantic frame of reference for black cultural production, mapped onto the historical routes of the slave trade and migration. For Gilroy, the 'national paradigm' is outmoded: locked to a territorial integrity that is unsustainable after globalisation, and dedicated to the preservation of an impossible ethno-purism. This counter-national tendency retains considerable influence in contemporary accounts of black British literature. But even in his defence of a transnational black Britain, John

McLeod observes that '[n]ations are not so easily soluble, either imaginatively or materially'.[97] Responding to *The Black Atlantic*, Dave Gunning argues that, in effect, the abolition of the national removes black cultural politics 'from any location from which political change might be effected'; he points out that anti-racism is necessarily 'articulated within the political, cultural and juridical structures that make up the national ideological landscape at any given time'.[98] Nations are 'real', and provide the political, cultural and legal structures to which anti-racist politics must necessarily be addressed. It is significant that such 'structures' are nationally specific to different national formations within the UK itself: observations of national-institutional specificity, and the operations of states, have particular consequence in Britain, where the emphasis on a transnational paradigm in some ways complements the 'banality' of British nationalism, and more specifically the rendering of the Union itself as banal: seamless, natural, obscure and permanent.[99] Rather than effecting a kind of postmodern displacement of the nation, a national framework affords a renewal of critique in a Scottish and British context.

Writing Black Scotland thus attempts to balance a literary-national critique against the reinscription of a literary-national destiny, offering a retrospective examination of literature, and recent devolutionary history, that brings to light race, racism and racialisation in contemporary Scotland. Chapter 1 diagnoses the 'Britishness' of black Britain: in particular, the relationship between black British studies and continued efforts to renew unified Britain in both constitutional and imaginative terms via a mechanism of officially recognised identities, encompassing both political multiculturalism and devolution. Tracing the field from the early 1980s to 2017, the chapter argues that black British studies, and in particular literary studies, have neglected Britain's devolutionary fragmentation. Black writing has been posited as 'rejuvenating' Britishness, while Britain's sub-nations have been positioned as ethnically exclusive and dangerous in a way that feeds back into a state narrative of Britain's fundamental diversity. Drawing on the example of Scotland, the chapter suggests ways that post-British nationalism is better placed than Britain itself to accommodate an emancipatory and anti-racist politics. Chapter 2 focuses on a developing awareness of a black politics in the period following 1979 in Scottish writing, paralleled with the rise of black cultural criticism in Britain in the same period. Examining a range of writers from Alasdair Gray through Maud Sulter and Jackie Kay to Irvine Welsh, the chapter maps the contours of anti-racism, decolonisation, an explicit black politics, through a shifting engagement with the black signifier which changes locus gradually, from an international context to the prominent cultural production and activism of black England, and eventually to a more consistent focus on blackness in Scotland.

The later chapters of the book focus on works that actively represent black experience in Scotland. Chapters 3 and 4 are case studies that examine blackness in two Scottish novels published in the period following the Scottish devolution referendum of 1997: Jackie Kay's *Trumpet* (1998) and Luke Sutherland's *Jelly Roll* (1998). Both novels portray a national 'black Scotland' that owes a debt to black Atlantic precursors, emerging at a crucial devolutionary moment. This national discourse resituates transatlantic pivots of a black cultural politics – with a particular emphasis on jazz music – into a Scottish national context. Set in the ideological context of the aftermath, or evolution, of Thatcherism, *Trumpet* examines the relationship between blackness and the competing national claims of Scotland and Britain. The novel is threaded through with the unresolved question of a black radical politics configured as a lost past, a frustrated present and a possible future delinked from the status quo of Britain's racial and constitutional settlement. Conversely, *Jelly Roll* is focused unwaveringly on the lived experience of racism, on the white contours of Scotland's imagined community, and on its anti-racist mythologies. Engaging directly with the literary moment hyper-determined by the impact of *Trainspotting*, *Jelly Roll* presents, in grotesque terms, a radical demand for the Scottish literary imagination to make visible and to confront contemporary racism.

Chapter 5 reflects on the 'devolution' of blackness under political multiculturalism, reading Suhayl Saadi's *Psychoraag* (2004) as a case study of the multicultural novel in Scotland. The novel is 'multicultural' both in terms of its commodity status and as an aesthetic project that responds to a state politics of cultural management developed by New Labour and elaborated by the Scottish Executive after 1999. Infringing on the strict demarcation of racial taxonomies through its recurring examination of the black signifier and the category of 'Asianness', the novel makes use of two psychopathological tropes to interrupt the culturalist turn in British race discourse: a return to Frantz Fanon and the 'psycho-existential' condition of the racialised body; and a Foucauldian counter-rational 'madness' that subverts state-organised multicultural 'control systems'. Turning to 2020, my conclusion offers a guarded prognosis for a civic nationalism that goes beyond multicultural tolerance to address claims for racial justice. Over the past decade, representations of multicultural tolerance have remained vital in efforts to shore up a British national narrative, while deferring precisely those questions of racial justice and rights – for example, the contradiction between Windrush deportations, the 'hostile environment policy', and the celebrated, symbolic, and highly qualified, admission of Meghan Markle into the monarchic heart of the British nation. By way of addressing this, I advance some ideas about the implications of 'devolving' black Britain in an English national context.

A final note on the methodological challenges inherent in the scholarship of race. 'It is one of the penalties of toying with the race-notion,' writes Jacques Barzun, 'that even a strong mind trying to repudiate it will find himself making assumptions and passing judgements on the basis of the theory he disclaims'.[100] Any attempt to grapple with race and racism is in danger of recirculating and reinforcing the significations, if not the sentiment, of a racial hierarchy. The need for stable referents in the analysis of colonial discourse, biocentric racism and cultural absolutism, ethnocentrism, white supremacy and even anti-racism, means that racial taxonomies are reproduced even as they are critiqued. Neglecting race, however, plays into a post-racial narrative that denies the enduring material and discursive conditions of race and racism. As Howard Winant and Michael Omi explain in their influential work on race formation, 'opposing racism requires that we notice race, not ignore it, that we afford it the recognition it deserves and the subtlety it embodies'.[101] Race language is, in Gilroy's words, 'insufficient but [. . .] necessary in a world where racisms continue to proliferate and flourish'.[102] The resonance of 'black' and its connection to a longer history of both racism and race-activated politics means it is uniquely placed to register the 'political denial of race and racism through a mobilization of the language of culture', the prevailing racial context of the modern world, a 'semantic shift [which] has gradually led to an inability to openly engage with race, its roots in modern European political thought, and its pernicious and persistent consequences for individual lives'.[103] *Writing Black Scotland* tracks how Scottish literature encodes the historically and subjectively contingent articulations of blackness in a key period of devolution in both Scottish national and British ethno-cultural terms, forcing a reconceptualisation of Scottish nationhood that stands against the hushing of race and racism within a 'post-racial' Britishness. A consequence of this critical focus is to open new frontiers: in black British literary studies, identifying the post-imperial stresses in the edifice of Britishness; and in Scottish literary studies, bringing the critical resources and history of black studies to bear on devolutionary Scotland. Ultimately, *Writing Black Scotland* carries forward the project captured in Maud Sulter's collage photography, such as in the image of 'Twa Blak Wimmin' that comprises its cover: the ongoing effort to emplace black history and its echoes in contexts in which it has otherwise been silenced, diminished or forgotten.

Notes

1. Dunbar, William, 'Of Ane Blak-Moir' in Louise Olga Fradenburg, *City, Marriage, Tournament: Arts of Rule in Late Medieval Scotland* (Madison: University of Wisconsin Press, 1991), pp. 255–6.
2. Morris, Michael, *Scotland and the Caribbean c.1740–1833: Atlantic Archipelagos* (London: Routledge, 2015), pp. 34, 166.
3. Gilroy, Paul, *The Black Atlantic: Modernity and Double Consciousness* (London: Verso, 1993), p. 58.
4. Dunbar, Paul Laurence, *The Collected Poetry of Paul Laurence Dunbar*, ed. Joanne M. Braxton (Charlottesville: University of Virginia Press, 1993 [1913]); see 'IndyRef: Culture and Politics Five Years On', *Stirling Centre for Scottish Studies* (2019), https://stirlingcentrescottishstudies.wordpress.com/2019/09/24/indyref-culture-and-politics-five-years-on-summary/ (last accessed 1 March 2020).
5. Dimeo, Paul and Gerry P. T. Finn, 'Racism, National Identity and Scottish Football' in Ben Carrington and Ian McDonald (eds), *'Race', Sport and British Society* (London: Routledge, 2001), pp. 29–48: 39.
6. Baker, Houston A., Jr, Manthia Diawara and Ruth H. Lindeborg (eds), *Black British Cultural Studies* (Chicago: University of Chicago Press, 1996), p. 2.
7. Young, Robert J. C., *The Idea of English Ethnicity* (Oxford: Blackwell, 2007), p. 31; see Jenkinson, Jacqueline, 'The Glasgow Race Disturbances of 1919' in Kenneth Lunn (ed.), *Race and Labour in Twentieth-Century Britain* (London: Frank Cass, 1985), pp. 43–67.
8. Niblett, Michael, 'Scotland' in David Dabydeen, John Gilmore and Cecily Jones (eds), *Oxford Companion to Black British History* (Oxford: Oxford University Press, 2010), p. 433.
9. Davidson, Neil and Satnam Virdee, 'Understanding Racism in Scotland', in Neil Davidson et al. (eds), *No Problem Here: Understanding Racism in Scotland* (Edinburgh: Luath Press, 2018), pp. 9–12: 9.
10. Miles, Robert and Leslie Muirhead, 'Racism in Scotland: A Matter for Further Investigation?' in David McCrone (ed.), *Scottish Government Yearbook 1986* (Edinburgh: Unit for the Study of Government in Scotland, University of Edinburgh, 1986), pp. 108–36: 108.
11. For example, Jan Penrose and David Howard highlight that, at the end of the 1990s, Scotland recorded 7.3 per cent of racially motivated incidents while having only 2.1 per cent of the UK's people from 'minority backgrounds', and that Central Scotland recorded racist 'incidents' at a rate fifteen times higher than London; Penrose, Jan and David Howard, '*One Scotland, Many Cultures*: The Mutual Constitution of Antiracism and Place' in Claire Dwyer and Caroline Bressey (eds), *New Geographies of Race and Racism* (Farnham: Ashgate, 2008), pp. 95–111: 97.
12. Davidson and Virdee, 'Understanding Racism', p. 9; Meer, Nasar, 'What Do We Know about BAME Self-Reported Racial Discrimination in Scotland?' in Davidson et al. (eds), *No Problem Here*, pp. 114–27: 117; Haria, Jatin, 'Race, Ethnicity and Employment in Scotland' in Davidson et al. (eds), *No Problem Here*, pp. 199–211: 206; Young, Carol, 'Changing the Race Equality Paradigm in Scotland's Public Sector' in Davidson et al. (eds), *No Problem Here*, pp. 180–98: 181.
13. Connell, Liam, 'Modes of Marginality: Scottish Literature and the Uses of Postcolonial Theory', *Comparative Studies of South Asia, Africa and the Middle East* 23:1&2 (2003), pp. 41–53: 49–50.
14. See Owusu, Kwesi (ed.), *Black British Culture and Society* (London: Routledge, 2000), p. 6; Davidson and Virdee, 'Understanding Racism', p. 10.

15. Hall, Stuart, 'Minimal Selves' in Baker, Diawara and Lindeborg (eds), *Black British Cultural Studies*, pp. 114–19: 116.
16. Folorunso, Femi, Gail Low and Marion Wynne-Davies, 'In the Eyes of the Beholder: Diversity and Cultural Politics of Canon Reformation in Britain – Femi Folorunso in Conversation with Gail Low and Marion Wynne-Davies (9 December 2004)', in Low and Wynne-Davies (eds), *A Black British Canon?* (Basingstoke: Palgrave Macmillan, 2006), pp. 74–90: 84.
17. Folorunso et al., 'In the Eyes of the Beholder', pp. 84–5.
18. Nairn, Tom, *The Break-Up of Britain: Crisis and Neo-Nationalism* (London: Verso, 1977).
19. See Pitcher, Ben, *The Politics of Multiculturalism: Race and Racism in Contemporary Britain* (Basingstoke: Palgrave Macmillan, 2009), p. 44.
20. See Devine, Tom, 'The Break-Up of Britain? Scotland and the End of Empire', *Transactions of the Royal Historical Society* 16 (2006), pp. 163–80: 180.
21. Devine, 'The Break-Up', p. 179.
22. Penrose and Howard, '*One Scotland, Many Cultures*', p. 96, original emphasis.
23. For a refutation of the connection between Scottish nationalism and anti-English racism, see Nairn, Tom, *After Britain: New Labour and the Return of Scotland* (London: Granta, 2001), pp. 204–8.
24. McCrone, David, *The New Sociology of Scotland* (London: Sage, 2017), p. 100.
25. See Hague, Euan, Benito Giordano and Edward H. Sebesta, 'Whiteness, Multiculturalism and Nationalist Appropriation of Celtic Culture: The Case of the League of the South and the Lega Nord', *Cultural Geographies* 12 (2005), pp. 151–73: 153.
26. Schoene, Berthold, 'Going Cosmopolitan: Reconstituting "Scottishness" in Post-Devolution Criticism' in Schoene (ed.), *The Edinburgh Companion to Contemporary Scottish Literature* (Edinburgh: Edinburgh University Press, 2007), pp. 7–16: 10; McCrone, David, *Understanding Scotland: The Sociology of a Nation*, 2nd edn (London: Routledge, 2001).
27. See for example electoral gains in the last ten years for the Sweden Democrats, the Finns Party, the Danish People's Party, the PVV in the Netherlands and the Alternative for Germany Party ('European Election Database', *Norwegian Centre for Research Data*, www.nsd.uib.no/ (last accessed 1 November 2017)); Alana Lentin and Gavan Titley's *The Crises of Multiculturalism: Racism in a Neoliberal Age* (London: Zed Books, 2011) provides a broad analysis of developing racisms across contemporary Europe.
28. Hames, Scott, *The Literary Politics of Scottish Devolution: Voice, Class, Nation* (Edinburgh: Edinburgh University Press, 2019), p. xii.
29. Hames, *Literary Politics*, p. xii.
30. Craig, Cairns, *The Wealth of the Nation: Scotland, Culture and Independence* (Edinburgh: Edinburgh University Press, 2018), pp. 225–6.
31. Hames, *Literary Politics*, p. 23.
32. Hames, *Literary Politics*, p. xii.
33. Bogdanor, Vernon, *The New British Constitution* (London: Hart Publishing, 2009), p. 89.
34. Hames, *Literary Politics*, p. 79.
35. Alex Thomson, '"You Can't Get There from Here": Devolution and Scottish Literary History', *International Journal of Scottish Literature* 3 (2007), www.ijsl.stir.ac.uk/issue3/thomson.htm (last accessed 30 March 2020).
36. See Norquay, Glenda, 'Janice Galloway's Novels: Fraudulent Mooching' in Aileen Christiansen and Alison Lumsden (eds), *Contemporary Scottish Women Writers* (Edinburgh: Edinburgh University Press, 2000), pp. 131–43.
37. Gardiner, Michael, *The Cultural Roots of British Devolution* (Edinburgh: Edinburgh University Press, 2004), pp. ix–x.

38. Devine, 'The Break-Up', p. 166.
39. See, for example, Gardiner, Michael, Graeme Macdonald and Niall O'Gallagher (eds), *Scottish Literature and Postcolonial Literature: Comparative Texts and Critical Perspectives* (Edinburgh: Edinburgh University Press, 2011).
40. Macdonald, Graeme, 'Postcolonialism and Scottish Studies', *New Formations* 59 (2006), pp. 116–31: 116.
41. Connell, 'Modes of Marginality', p. 41.
42. Connell, 'Modes of Marginality', p. 43.
43. Beveridge, Craig and Ronald Turnbull, *The Eclipse of Scottish Culture* (Edinburgh: Polygon, 1989), p. 6.
44. Miller, Gavin, '"Persuade Without Convincing . . . Represent Without Reasoning": The Inferiorist Myth of Scots Language' in Eleanor Bell and Gavin Miller (eds), *Scotland in Theory: Reflections on Culture and Literature* (Amsterdam: Rodopi, 2004), pp. 197–209: 200–1.
45. Connell, 'Modes of Marginality', p. 42.
46. *Angelou on Burns*, dir. Elly M. Taylor (Taylored Productions, 1996).
47. Lindsay, Andrew O., *Illustrious Exile: Journal of my Sojourn in the West Indies by Robert Burns, Esq. Commenced on the First Day of July 1786* (Leeds: Peepal Tree Press, 2006), p. 213.
48. Niven, Alastair, 'New Diversity, Hybridity and Scottishness' in Ian Brown (ed.), *The Edinburgh History of Scottish Literature*, vol. 3: *Modern Transformations: New Identities (from 1918)* (Edinburgh, Edinburgh University Press, 2007), pp. 320–31: 331.
49. Miller, Gavin, 'How Not to "Question Scotland"', *Scottish Affairs* 52:1 (2005), pp. 1–14: 1.
50. Niven, 'New Diversity', p. 329.
51. Gilroy, Paul, *Small Acts: Thoughts on the Politics of Black Cultures* (London: Serpent's Tail, 1993), p. 112.
52. Mbembe, Achille, *A Critique of Black Reason*, trans. Laurent Dubois (Durham, NC: Duke University Press, 2017), p. 6.
53. Mbembe, *Critique of Black Reason*, p. 7.
54. Mbembe, *Critique of Black Reason*, p. 33; see also Gilroy, Paul, *Against Race: Imagining Political Culture Beyond the Color Line* (Cambridge, MA: Harvard University Press, 2001).
55. Mullard, Chris, *Black Britain* (London: Allen and Unwin, 1973); see Eldridge, Michael, 'The Rise and Fall of Black Britain', *Transition* 74 (1997), pp. 32–43: 36.
56. Mercer, Kobena, *Welcome to the Jungle: New Positions in Black Cultural Studies* (London: Routledge, 1994), p. 271.
57. Gilroy, *Small Acts*, p. 12.
58. Hall, Stuart, 'New Ethnicities' [1988] in James Procter (ed.), *Writing Black Britain 1948–1998: An Interdisciplinary Anthology* (Manchester: Manchester University Press, 2000), pp. 265–75: 267–8.
59. 'Black History Month Row over Zayn Malik Image', BBC News, www.bbc.co.uk/news/uk-england-37772968, 26 October 2016 (last accessed 1 October 2017).
60. Quoted in Shukra, Kalbir, *The Changing Pattern of Black Politics in Britain* (London: Pluto Press, 1998), p. 62.
61. See Ledent, Bénédicte, 'Black British Literature' in Dinah Birch (ed.), *The Oxford Companion to English Literature*, 7th Edition (Oxford: Oxford University Press, 2009), pp. 16–22.
62. Baker, Diawara and Lindeborg (eds), *Black British Cultural Studies*, p. 8.
63. Procter, James, *Writing Black Britain 1948–1998: An Interdisciplinary Anthology* (Manchester: Manchester University Press, 2000).
64. Pitcher, *Politics of Multiculturalism*, p. 29.
65. Procter, *Writing Black Britain*, p. 9.

66. Hopkins, Peter, 'Politics, Race and Nation: The Difference That Scotland Makes' in Claire Dwyer and Caroline Bressey (eds), *New Geographies of Race and Racism* (Farnham: Ashgate, 2008), pp. 113–24: 121.
67. Macdonald, Graeme, 'Scottish Extractions: "Race" and Racism in Devolutionary Fiction', *Orbis Litterarum* 65:2 (2010), pp. 79–107: 80.
68. Pittock, Murray G. H., *Celtic Identity and the British Image* (Manchester: Manchester University Press, 1999), p. 27.
69. Kidd, Colin, 'Race, Empire, and the Limits of Nineteenth-Century Scottish Nationhood', *The Historical Journal* 46:4 (2003), pp. 873–92: 876–7.
70. Young, Robert J. C., *Colonial Desire: Hybridity in Theory, Culture, and Race* (London: Routledge, 1995), p. 83.
71. Garrett, Aaron and Silvia Sebastiani, 'David Hume on Race' in Naomi Zack (ed.), *The Oxford Handbook to Philosophy and Race* (Oxford: Oxford University Press, 2017), pp. 31–43: 31; the original footnote from 1753 included 'negroes, and in general all the other species of men'; the posthumous edition from 1777 reduced this to only 'negroes [and] whites'.
72. Burnett, James, *Sketches of the History of Man*, ed. James Harris (Indianapolis: Liberty Fund, 2007 [1788]), pp. 23–4.
73. Knox, Robert, *The Races of Man* (London: Henry Renshaw, 1850), pp. 39, 162–3.
74. Young, *The Idea of English Ethnicity*, p. 31.
75. Pittock, *Celtic Identity*, p. 27.
76. Duncan, Ian, *Scott's Shadow: The Novel in Romantic Edinburgh* (Princeton: Princeton University Press, 2007), pp. 112–15.
77. Said, Edward, *Orientalism* (New York: Pantheon Books, 1978), pp. 101–2.
78. Craig, *Wealth of the Nation*, pp. 117, 136.
79. See Sassi, Carla, 'Sir Walter Scott and the Caribbean: Unravelling the Silences', *The Yearbook of English Studies* 47 (2017), pp. 224–40.
80. Schwartz, Bill, *The White Man's World* (Oxford: Oxford University Press, 2012), p. 213.
81. Schwartz, *White Man's World*, pp. 273–4.
82. Macdonald, 'Postcolonialism and Scottish Studies', p. 116.
83. Devine, Tom, *Scotland's Empire* (London: Penguin, 2012) and (ed.) *Recovering Scotland's Slavery Past: The Caribbean Connection* (Edinburgh: Edinburgh University Press, 2015); Hamilton, Douglas, *Scotland, the Caribbean and the Atlantic World 1750–1820* (Manchester: Manchester University Press, 2010); Mullen, Stephen, *It Wisnae Us: The Truth about Glasgow and Slavery* (Edinburgh: RIAS, 2009). These followed the more affirmative *The Scottish Empire* by Michael Fry (Edinburgh: Birlinn, 2002).
84. Robertson, James, *Joseph Knight* (London: Fourth Estate, 2003), p. 27.
85. Morris, *Scotland and the Caribbean*; Sassi, Carla, 'Acts of (Un)willed Amnesia: Dis/appearing Figurations of the Caribbean in Post-Union Scottish Literature', in Giovanna Covi, Joan Anim-Addo, Velma Pollard and Carla Sassi (eds), *Caribbean–Scottish Relations: Colonial and Contemporary Inscriptions in History, Language and Literature* (London: Mango Publishing, 2007), pp. 131–98.
86. Scotland's Census, 'Ethnicity, Identity, Language and Religion', www.scotlandscensus.gov.uk/ethnicity-identity-language-and-religion (last accessed 29 September 2019).
87. Hansen, Randall, *Citizenship and Immigration in Post-War Britain* (Oxford: Oxford University Press, 2000), p. 3.
88. Hopkins, 'Politics, Race and Nation', p. 116.
89. Centre on Dynamics of Ethnicity, 'Who Feels Scottish? National Identities and Ethnicity in Scotland', *The Dynamics of Diversity* (Manchester: Joseph Rowntree Foundation and Manchester University Press, 2014).
90. Deleuze, Gilles and Félix Guattari, *Kafka: Towards a Minor Literature*, trans. Dana

Polan (Minneapolis: University of Minnesota Press, 1986 [1975]); for an account of Scottish literature as 'minority', see Crawford, Robert, *Devolving English Literature*, 2nd edn (Oxford: Oxford University Press, 2000), p. 6.

91. Sulter, Maud, *As a Black Woman* (London: Akira Press, 1985); *Zabat: Poetics of a Family Tree* (Hebden Bridge: Urban Fox Press, 1989).

92. Kay, Jackie, *The Adoption Papers* (Tarset: Bloodaxe Books, 1991).

93. Kay, Jackie, *Trumpet* (London: Picador, 1998).

94. Baker, Diawara and Lindeborg (eds), *Black British Cultural Studies*, p. 6.

95. Rushdie, Salman, '"Commonwealth Literature" Does Not Exist' in *Imaginary Homelands* (London: Granta, 1992), pp. 61–70; D'Aguiar, Fred, 'Against Black British Literature' in Maggie Butcher (ed.), *Tibisiri: Caribbean Writers and Critics* (Sydney: Dangaroo Press, 1989), pp. 106–14; Upstone, Sara, *Rethinking Race and Ethnicity in Contemporary British Fiction* (London: Routledge, 2017), p. 19.

96. Dabydeen, David (ed.), *The Black Presence in English Literature* (Manchester: Manchester University Press, 1985).

97. McLeod, John, 'Fantasy Relationships: Black British Canons in a Transnational World' in Gail Low and Marion Wynne-Davies (eds), *A Black British Canon?* (Basingstoke: Palgrave Macmillan, 2006), pp. 93–104: 100.

98. Gunning, Dave, 'Anti-Racism, the Nation-State, and Contemporary Black British Literature', *Journal of Commonwealth Literature* 39:2 (2004), pp. 29–43: 34, 35.

99. See Billig, Michael, *Banal Nationalism* (London: Sage, 1995); Kidd, Colin, *Union and Unionisms: Political Thought in Scotland 1500–2000* (Cambridge: Cambridge University Press, 2008), pp. 23–31.

100. Barzun, Jacques, *Race: A Study in Modern Superstition* (London: Methuen, 1938), pp. 29–30.

101. Omi, Michael and Howard Winant, *Race Formation in the United States: From the 1960s to the 1990s* (New York: Routledge, 1994), p. 159.

102. Gilroy, *Small Acts*, p. 14.

103. Lentin and Titley, *Crises of Multiculturalism*, p. 68.

Chapter 1

The Britishness of Black Britain

In Ashley Dawson's *Mongrel Nation: Diasporic Culture and the Making of Postcolonial Britain*, Daniel Defoe's *The True-Born Englishman* (1701) features as a pointed example of a text opposed to the ethno-purist nationalism usually associated with Enoch Powell.[1] In the poem, Defoe describes the eponymous, metonymic English man as a 'het'rogeneous thing' issuing from a 'mixture of all kinds', and the English as a 'mongrel half-bred race' in which 'scarce one family is left alive / Which does not from some foreigner derive', anticipating the late twentieth-century boom in hybridity theory by the best part of three centuries.[2] *The True-Born Englishman* makes great show of its philosophical defence of migration and heterogeneity, and rejection of Anglo-Saxon supremacy. It seems to be fitting for a reading of postcolonial British syncretism, where the 'newness introduced to Britain by members of the Asian and African diaspora also offered important routes of escape for many from stultifying local traditions'.[3] Defoe's poem has done similar work signalling national heterogeneity elsewhere, not least in providing the epigraph to Benedict Anderson's *Imagined Communities*.[4] However, when read in the light of its political context, Defoe's quasi-pluralism is both more partial and more instrumental.[5] The incipient British Union is the backdrop behind the poem, and Defoe's invocation of Britain's fundamental heterogeneity has a distinctive purpose: to refute critics of the Dutch-born King William III and the Act of Settlement (1701), and to naturalise the Protestant claim on the British throne.[6] Rather than being primarily a philosophical defence of the vulnerable 'other' or an ideal of heterogeneity, the poem was composed as a nation-building intervention. Defoe attempted to address the fundamental weakness of Britain as a mobilising ideology in the eighteenth century, pursuing a 'formation of national consciousness' that entailed the 'eradication of existing "national aversions" and "immortal prejudices"'.[7] In its promotion of a heterogeneous Anglo-Britishness, *The True-Born Englishman* could be described as the first use of diversity in defence of the embryonic British Union.

Dawson's argument that Commonwealth migrants and their descendants '[enact] fresh ways of being British' is a twenty-first-century echo of Defoe's nation-making project, the 'het'rogenous' Union.[8] He is far from alone in making such a claim. In a period of constitutional uncertainty from 1979, when the prospect of independence for Scotland has presaged the end of an integral British Union in its historical form, black British literary criticism has pulled in the opposite direction, towards 'restoration'. In political discourse, Britain's racial diversity has increasingly been mobilised to evidence a new Britishness that aligns with the state's project of bolstering British unity – a form of multicultural governmentality. This governmentality is not simply a straightforward neoliberal multiculturalism that seeks to submerge difference into a levelled-off tableau of opportunities for consumption, or commodifies difference into 'exotic' products, although it has elements of both. It also pursues an adaptive stabilising of the British signifier itself in a moment of escalating threat. Dawson's argument is one example of the way that important literary-critical attempts to broaden and deepen the ethnic imagination of Britishness – themselves generally critical of state multiculturalism – have coincided with the Union needs of British multicultural governmentality. Enmeshed within the 'banality' of Unionism, black British literature as a discipline has taken Britain's constitutional continuity for granted and struggled to negotiate the ongoing evolution of the Union, the political charge of Britain's constituent nations, and the implications of post-Britishness, both in terms of England and Scotland.[9] This is what I describe as the 'Britishness of black Britain'.

Far from marking the apogee of British racist confidence, the American-style vision of continual racial conflict prophesised by Powell in his famous 1968 speech was actually a late, symbolic utterance of explicit imperial racism. Powellite rhetoric ran counter to the new needs of the British state: namely, to manage ideas of difference within a new post-imperial macro-narrative of nation.[10] Britain's devolutionary period has been defined by those changing needs. The question of precisely how to name the post-imperial nation was unclear through the 1980s, where an ethnicised Englishness often stood in for Britain in Thatcherite rhetoric, and devolution as a state policy was entirely marginalised. The tightening up of Britishness as the definitive national formation for the United Kingdom came after Thatcher, and owed something to a shift in black critical thought itself in the late 1980s and early 1990s, marked particularly in the changing orientation of thinkers like Stuart Hall and Paul Gilroy, towards an active contestation of British nationhood: 'putting the black in the Union Jack'. This anti-racist politics would then be taken up by New Labour's own redefinition as a 'One Nation' party. Ben Pitcher describes this narrative as an 'elaborated Britishness', pointing to the way that race had shifted from a 'thorn in the side of the political establishment' to become 'constitutive of its very identity'.[11] The logic of identity-validation within larger Britishness has not only applied to race, however. Seen from the perspective of the state, national devolution has also moved from a 'thorny issue' to part of a newly configured post-imperial Britishness.

This reconfigured Britishness has a clear literary-critical registration. The reception of Zadie Smith's *White Teeth* (2000) set the tone for a narrative of a 'revitalised' British writing benefiting from cultural 'transfusion', where heterogeneous elements – including Scottish ones – expanded the limited gene pool of Anglo-Britain's stagnant white homogeneity, in a call back to the biological antecedents of racialisation. It is also at this point that 'black British literature' comes into existence as a named canon of works, a literary history and an academic discipline. To establish the context for this correlation, I map out the role that a state politics of race and ethnicity has played in bulwarking a post-imperial narrative of Britishness, and its constitutional bedrock, against the threat posed by re-emergent sub-nationalisms, with Scotland to the fore. This politics has been responsive to, and has even included contributions from, some prominent black British thinkers. I then turn to the forms of 'Britishness' that are implied by black British literary criticism. My central argument here is that since the establishment of the Scottish Parliament, the new discipline of black British literature has often unexpectedly dovetailed with the requirements of that British state nationalism. Such criticism has sometimes included a gesture towards devolution, but always one couched in a state-centric understanding of regional delegation rather than as a developing national politics. Finally, using the example of Paul Gilroy's *After Empire* (2004), I suggest a post-British logic is already at work in black British studies that has yet to be fully articulated. *After Empire* proposes a civic localism that is scaled to national England, but which fails to make a decisive break from Britishness at a time when 'break-up' was more thinkable than it had been since the eighteenth century. The need to update black British literary studies with a renewed focus on the complexity of Britain's national formations has become especially acute in that thinkable moment, and could help to disentangle the ongoing racism of the state form from the purported egalitarianism of British public life. The way difference has been turned to managing that understanding of the recent history of black Britain, meanwhile, helps to establish the basis for reading black writing in

Scotland against the 'banal' reaffirmation of the Union through a politics of race.

Black Union Jack:
devolution and multicultural refurbishment

Tom Nairn, often alongside Perry Anderson, has argued that the British state is archaic, crisis-stricken, 'a basically indefensible and unadaptable relic' rather than a modern state-form. The post-imperial late twentieth century was the 'twilight of the British state', when its contradictions would lead to its inevitable, accelerating disintegration.[12] Nairn provides a detailed charge sheet of Britain's intrinsic weaknesses: sclerotic first-past-the-post voting and a two-party system; an autocratic Parliament dedicated to its own preservation via the recirculation of tradition and precedent rather than meaningful democracy or political action; an uncodified constitution presenting a sizeable obstacle to reform; an anachronistic and Disneyfied monarchy; the backwardness of an unelected head of state and upper chamber in Parliament; a regressive system of class distinctions; a failure of modern industrial planning leading to a slavish dependence on finance capitalism; and many more failings besides.[13] Evidently, the continuation of Britain in this form relied on the support of the national formations which had entered into the Union in the first place. Its weaknesses have thus been exacerbated by the end of the gravitational force of Empire, which had impelled the initial formation and coherence of Britain, and bound the 'home' nations together. In Nairn's account, Britain's projected break-up takes place along the national fault lines which predate the Union and the British Empire altogether, which remain extant up to the present day, and which reopen inexorably in the absence of Empire. That Britain has not yet broken up is testament to the adaptive efforts of the British state, which has always taken a proactive role in ameliorating constitutional conflicts, underwriting the 'imagined community' or national narrative of Britishness, and supporting 'continuous cultural effort not to *expose* its divisions'.[14]

Consequently, Britain has always operated according to a system of 'ethnicity management', 'a deliberately composite identity-mode, which [. . .] sought to subsume rather than to assimilate [and] relegated rather than exalted "ethnicity"'.[15] Ethnicity management begins with the very national formations that comprised Britain in 1707. Defoe's *The True-Born Englishman* provides an illustrative example of just that identity-mode in action. In a new form, ethnicity management also applies to the redefinition of Britishness after Empire. Counter-intuitively for a country that had overseen three centuries of racialised imperialism, two centuries of slave-trading, the slaughter at Morant Bay, the Jallianwala Bagh massacre, the Bengal famine, the crushing of the Mau Mau uprising, and decades of racism directed at black people in post-war Britain, the legislative conditions for a post-imperial Britishness were not explicitly defined according to ethnic or racial characteristics. As Ian Baucom has described, the 1948 Nationality Act 'identified Britishness as a mandatory but "unbound" seriality', so to be a British subject 'was to belong to a potentially unlimited collectivity', rather than an ethnically exclusive group place-bound by the United Kingdom.[16] It was only via later legislation that white anglophone advantages were concretised in citizenship and immigration law.[17] While the walls came down on extending British citizenship to non-white members of the Commonwealth, the question of what to do with citizens 'already here' has preoccupied that adaptive and state-driven national narrative ever since.

In the aftermath of the 'Rivers of Blood' moment in 1968, a 'double-facing' model of British nationalism emerged to replace imperial Britishness in the 1970s and 1980s. The Immigration Act 1971 introduced the principle of patriality, differentiating between those who had been born or had a parent born in Britain from all other Commonwealth citizens – a de facto racist mechanism which privileged white people. Edward Heath's immigration policies were cemented by Margaret Thatcher's election victory on the back of anxieties around the 'swarming' of Britain by migrants.[18] The delicate segmentation of Britain according to culture allowed for the continuation of a largely unspoken but resilient ethno-cultural white 'core', underlined by a 'commonsense nativism' around which cultural others could be demarcated and managed.[19] The unbroken continuity of Britain's 'white backbone' also had clear implications for the Union, especially in the need for an amplified discourse of Britishness in the period immediately following the 1979 Scottish devolution referendum. Indeed, the relative white homogeneity of Scotland compared to a more diverse England meant that appeals to British national values, a thin veneer on the surface of white exceptionalism under the New Right, reinforced the implication of a fundamental racial commonality at the heart of Union.

The phase of race relations and devolutionary politics which followed immediately after the publication of *The Break-Up of Britain* provide two respective examples of governmental ethnicity management at work. The first is the referendum on Scottish devolution held in 1979. As Scott Hames says, the trigger was pulled on the 'starting pistol' for devolution in 1967, with the explosive election of the first Scottish National Party (SNP) MP, Winifred Ewing, to represent the formerly safe Labour seat of Hamilton.[20] Ewing's election led to the setting-up of a Royal

Commission on the Constitution in 1968 to address the question of Britain's constitutional future. The outcome of the Commission was the 1973 Kilbrandon Report, which recommended devolution for Scotland and Wales, but also strongly emphasised its greater mission: reinforcing Britishness.[21] Subsequently, the 1979 referendum returned popular support for devolution by a narrow margin, 51.62 per cent to 48.38 per cent. However, an amendment introduced by Labour MP George Cunningham required the total number of 'yes' votes to represent 40 per cent of eligible voters in Scotland. The devolved Scottish Parliament was delayed by twenty years, and the tenuous and informal party alliance between the minority Labour government and the Scottish National Party dissolved, paving the way for the election of Margaret Thatcher. What had seemed like a symbolic moment in the constitutional realignment, if not the break-up, of Britain instead heralded a decade of muscular and chauvinist Anglo-British nationalism, a narrative of greatness restored to Great Britain, acted out in various theatres from the Malvinas to Orgreave and Northern Ireland.

The late 1970s and early 1980s were also a significant period in a British state politics of race. By the end of the 1970s, the racism of British public life was coming under sustained criticism and activist pressure. Urban policing and criminal justice in England that disproportionately targeted black men was only the most material manifestation of racism in a country where race was, in Hall's formulation, 'the prism through which the British people are called upon to live through, then to understand, and then to deal with, the growing crisis', the crisis of 'the blacks'.[22] The turn of the 1980s marked a succession of intellectual interventions addressing British state racism, including the influential *Policing the Crisis* (1978) and *The Empire Strikes Back* (1982).[23] Black political activism, and street-level outrage, crystallised in the aftermath of the New Cross fire in January 1981, where thirteen young black people were killed in a suspected racially motivated arson attack. Police inaction led to the formation of the New Cross Massacre Action Committee and the March 1981 Black People's Day of Action, and continued inaction and police persecution in London led to the outbreak of the Brixton uprising in April 1981.[24] While the black political moment of 1981 did not threaten a 'break-up' of Britain in the way that a Scottish nationalist politics did, it nevertheless obliged a state-level adjustment to Britain's redoubtable imperial logic of race and class, and to the template of Britishness itself. That adjustment was instigated by the Scarman Inquiry into the Brixton uprising. The outcome of that inquiry, the Scarman Report, was a significant step in the implementation of a new political multiculturalism, which offset the provision for continued racialised policing with a greater degree of representation in 'decision-making, access to resources and political influence' for groups designated by a state taxonomy of race or 'ethnicity'.[25]

What is clear from the outcome of the Kilbrandon Commission is that the devolution offering in 1979 was a political strategy designed to rein in Scottish nationalism: a compromise solution that would allow for Scottish national 'distinctiveness' to be expressed within a larger British constitutional settlement, and where the Parliament at Westminster would retain ultimate power. The multicultural strategies which Scarman spearheaded were strikingly similar: they were effectively a recommendation that ethnic 'distinctiveness' should be recognised within a larger British framework, allocated local political power and resources, and laundered in the name of 'celebrating difference', with consequences for an earlier iteration of black politics:

> Multiculturalism now meant taking black culture off the streets – where it had been politicised and turned into a rebellion against the state – and putting it in the council chamber, in the classroom and on television, where it could be institutionalised, managed and reified.[26]

Arun Kundnani describes this management as a move from a prior mode of defence to a proactive system of control, through a series of inoculating institutional settlements in the media, local government and education. Kilbrandon and Scarman both had as their critical objects political power bases that lay outwith the sphere of direct state influence and the accepted parameters of Britishness: Scottish independence and black activism. And both came to a similar managerial compact that rewarded the incorporation of those causes back into the fold of Britishness via limited concessions. While each had specific party-political dimensions, the need to be responsive to changing national conditions in Britain was certainly a challenge for the state as a whole. Taken together, Kilbrandon and Scarman are an indication of the way that the state-maintained 'imagined community' of Britishness was adapting to the demands of polities via a policy of flexible ethnicity management, even in a moment before multiculturalism became a central part of the political lexicon.

The interregnum marked by Thatcher's decline and fall provided an opportunity for the further opening-up of the ethnic dimension of Britishness. Stuart Hall's influential 1988 'New Ethnicities' lecture was a watershed moment in this regard.[27] Hall, 'black Britain's leading theorist of black Britain' according to Henry Louis Gates Jr, identified a critical expansion of the frame of blackness in Britain, moving beyond what he described as the struggle over the relations of representation, to prioritise a politics of representation.[28] This would involve elaborating 'a concern with the absence or marginality of the black experience [and] its simplification and its stereotyped character' in order to critique the role of 'culture and ideology, and the scenarios of representation – subjectivity, identity, politics', to give them 'a formative, not merely expressive, place in the constitution of [black] social and political life'.[29] This would necessitate the 'end of the innocent notion of the essential black subject', through the recognition of the constructedness of blackness, and its stratification.[30] Black political solidarity, Hall argues, had involved the strategic homogenisation and yoking together of diverse subject positions to achieve anti-racist ends. In the future, black cultural politics must be reflexive, and attend to difference. But Hall's lecture had also featured striking references that indicated a changing relationship between blackness and nationhood in Britain:

> We still have a great deal of work to do to *decouple* ethnicity, as it functions in the dominant discourse, from its equivalence with nationalism, imperialism, racism and the state, which are the points of attachment around which a distinctive British, or, more accurately, English ethnicity have been constructed.[31]

Echoing the title of Paul Gilroy's *There Ain't No Black in the Union Jack*, which had been published the previous year, Hall goes on to argue that '[f]ifteen years ago we didn't care, or at least I didn't care, whether there was any black in the Union Jack. Now not only do we care, we *must*'.[32] For Hall, with considerable justification, Englishness was the ethnocentric carrier for an imperial legacy of racism. The solution was to repurpose British nationhood as a fully non-ethnicised category of belonging, to put the black into the Union Jack.

Hence Britishness, emblematised in the Union flag, rather than Englishness, becomes the stage for claims of belonging and subjecthood, and an anti-racist and anti-fascist politics. Such political momentum pulls against an idea of 'break-up' in its conscious sidelining of an Englishness that Hall saw as resistant to 'radical appropriation'.[33] As a long-standing critic of the British state, Hall initially seems a strange figure to associate with the proactive refurbishment of Britishness. Hall shares much with Nairn: his evolving critique of Britain is political-constitutional, and recognises the state's deployment of race as a diversion from structural and democratic failures in Britain, most sharply from 1978, with his 'Racism and Reaction' and the publication of *Policing the Crisis*. Like Nairn, Hall saw Britain as a compromised technocracy, dedicated to preserving an outdated class system and an autocratic Parliament for which the preservation of political systems and institutions took precedence over actual political action. Hall's position vis-à-vis English versus British nationhood makes perfect sense within the context of Thatcher's politics of ethnic nationalism and the outspoken white supremacy of English nationalist organisations. The exclusivity of English nationhood within the English New Left had also been an influence; *The Empire Strikes Back* was in part 'conceived as a corrective to the narrowness of the English left whose version of the "national-popular" continues to deny the role of blacks and black struggles in the making and the remaking of the working class'.[34] Alluding to the same exclusivity, Hall identified himself as a 'colonial' who felt more comfortable in the 'socially anonymous' metropolitan south than in the badlands of England that lay outside of London, wherein lay 'non-metropolitan working-class life'.[35]

Nairn, doubtless with one eye on Hall, a long-time associate through the *Universities and Left Review* and the *New Left Review*, recognised a belief that 'one breathes more easily in a non-ethnic "Britain" than one would upon the narrower ground of England'.[36] But such a 'breathable atmosphere' relies on the continuation of Britishness, and comes at the cost of a constitutional definition for Britain's component national formations, particularly England:

> As long as that more restricted terrain [of Englishness] remains constitutionally undefined the newcomer is bound to sense that it could be defined in other ways: ethnically (or even racially), along the lines so emphatically prospected by Powellism in the 1960s.[37]

In this account, which has considerable purchase in British public discourse, English nationalism is a shadow-formation, a repository for racist imperial baggage and Powellite ethno-purist fantasies, inherited and repurposed by neo-fascist groups such as the National Front or Combat 18. However, positioning England in this way also serves the needs of the state itself. The prospect of an independent Scotland can still just about be naturalised in the British imaginary, perennially deferred, heard mostly as a clamour for recognition and limited self-governance in the mode of past late-colonial relationships. The prospect of a constitutionally defined England poses a serious problem for the late-Union state, which was made clear by absolute rejection of devolution for England in the Kilbrandon Report. An independent England, in a certain very specific sense the 'last colony of the British Empire', remains, for most, literally unimaginable.

Putting the black into the Union Jack was a powerful image that symbolised the rejection of ethnocentrism, but also reflected how an idea of black Britain might work to support Britishness in the devolutionary period. Even though this renegotiation of Britishness came most clearly at the expense of a new Englishness, it also provided plaster for the cracks that were reopening as a result of a renewed call for devolved government in Scotland. The Campaign for a Scottish Assembly, a broad-based movement formed in the aftermath of the 1979 referendum, issued its Claim of Right for Scotland in 1988, the same year as Hall's 'New Ethnicities' lecture. The Claim of Right, which included many Scottish MPs and MEPs as signatories, affirmed the 'sovereign right of the Scottish people to determine the form of Government best suited to their needs', a reminder of the consensual nature of the Act of Union which helped pave the way for the 1997 referendum. Predictably for a Conservative administration that had sought to avoid the issue of devolution completely after 1979, the then Secretary of State for Scotland, Malcolm Rifkind, confirmed that the government were 'deeply committed to the unity of the United Kingdom', and did not 'believe that Scotland would benefit from an additional layer of government'.[38] By the start of the 1990s, therefore, the political challenges that the government had attempted to address via the 1979 referendum and the Scarman recommendations had resulted in two related outcomes as far as a unitary Britishness was concerned. A. Sivanandan had predicted in 1976 that governmental strategies of containment for black radicalism would 'solve its "black problem"' by having 'diverted revolutionary aspiration into nationalist achievement, reduced militancy to rhetoric, put protest to profit'.[39] That prediction was largely being borne out. An earlier radical black politics had been co-opted into reliance on the state through the strategies of integration implemented after Scarman, and a black cultural politics had moved towards the redefinition of Britishness.[40] Meanwhile, the question of Scottish sovereignty was being reopened, but the emerging form of devolution was largely amenable to the continued existence of the Union state itself.

New Labour: elaborated Britishness and the future of Britain

The need to resolve both devolution and black Britons' claims to nationhood was recognised by Tony Blair and New Labour, and was core to the narrative of reinvented and reinvigorated Britishness they offered. The need for proactivity in developing an inclusive Britishness was acute for Blair's administration, in their mantra of regeneration and forward movement, their acquisition of the 'One Nation' party identity from the Conservatives, and as a bulwark against any further concessions to Scottish nationalism after the promised devolution referendum of 1997. The guiding philosophy of Blairism, based on Giddens's doctrine of the 'Third Way', was a move to contest the social-democratic political centre ground, and downplay the party's historical emphasis on class conflict and public ownership. But the promised reformative zeal of New Labour was illusory, especially in constitutional terms, where their radical rhetoric masked a 'shameless fall-back upon the changeless verities of common sense, empiricism, and British traditionalism'.[41] This reheated 'One Nation' narrative worked to reposition Britishness away from a staid imperial remnant towards Cool Britannia, a nostalgic vision of Britain's popular culture, and a 'patriotism for the future'.

The coincidence of the millennial reinvention of black Britain and the management of unruly sub-British nationalisms is to be found in what Ben Pitcher calls New Labour's 'elaborated Britishness', which combined devolutionary concessions to Scotland, Wales and Northern Ireland with an official discourse of multiculturalism.[42] The process of elaboration involved appropriating markers of difference, such as 'black', as symbols of a reforged and revitalised Britishness, at ease with a new multicultural identity. New Labour's reorientation was defined

> not simply by an ostensible change of attitude towards Britain's minority communities, but [. . .] moreover involved concerted attempts to *redescribe the nature of British society in light of their symbolic admission to the national community*.[43]

Political multiculturalism in Britain was thus expedient for the state beyond, or in synergy with, its smoothing of relations within a neoliberal economic order – what Slavoj Žižek would call the cultural logic of multinational capitalism.[44] It had a specific application in the context of the post-imperial reinvention of the British Union: black Britons provided an illustration of a new 'national community'. Fulfilling the objective of the Kilbrandon Commission over two decades earlier, Scottish devolution now provided a component, as another elective 'identity' category, in the master category of elaborated Britishness.

The clearest illustration of this British identity management, addressed both to black people and to the Scottish national question, is found in the Runnymede Trust's Commission on the Future of Multi-Ethnic Britain, and its published output *The Future of Multi-Ethnic Britain* (2000), commonly called the 'Parekh Report'.[45] Primary among its objectives was to '[make] Britain a confident and vibrant multicultural society at ease with its rich diversity'.[46] This reformist spirit precluded any kind of dramatic constitutional recommendations. Although the report rhetorically asks at an early stage 'does "Britishness" have a future?', the possibility that it does not is not seriously considered.[47] Although the Parekh Report was rooted in Britain's history of race relations discourse, it extended its definition of 'multi-ethnic' to include the national formations of Scotland, Wales and England, a manoeuvre which reproduced the tendency of the Kilbrandon Commission to see national formations as 'identities' in need of recognition. National difference is framed as a series of structuring questions within a section entitled 'Rethinking the National Story':

> How are the histories of England, Scotland and Wales understood by their people? What do the separate countries stand for, and what does Britain stand for? Of what may citizens be justly proud? How has the imagined nation stood the test of time? What should be preserved, what jettisoned, what revised or reworked? How can everyone have a recognised place within the larger picture?[48]

Indicatively, Scotland's 'national story' is introduced via *Braveheart* – Highland romance, kilted anachronism and the staunch anti-Englishness of the perennial national underdog – rather than through an autonomous national culture, a millennium-old state, the Scottish Enlightenment, or a willing imperial partnership within the constitutionally defined Union.[49]

The moderate reformism of the Parekh Report is suggestive of the way that discourses of multiculturalism marshal and regulate political unevenness for the benefit of Britain. The appeal for a 'recognised place within the larger picture' summarises the implicit national logic of the report, which is to subsume an anti-racist politics and demands for national sovereignty together into a 'revised' and 'reworked' Britishness based on recognition of claims of cultural difference. Despite the fundamental category distinction between Britain's racialised minorities and Scotland as a national formation, they are represented within the report as isomorphic ethnic categories available for reconciliation within an elaborated Britishness. The findings of the Commission – itself only a body *close* to the state – were decried and mostly ignored by the New Labour government of the day because of its finding that British national identity remained largely white and ethnically exclusionary, which did not fit with a Blairite narrative of a Britain that had moved on from its racist past.[50] In one respect the Parekh Report marked a dramatic shift from the racial common sense of earlier decades; this was one of the reasons its thin recommendations found little purchase in a New Labour political landscape, defined by a rhetoric of change masking a politics of continuity. In other respects, rather than marking a definitive national break, Britain's multicultural turn signalled by *The Future of Multi-Ethnic Britain* was simply another evolution of British ethnicity management.

New Labour's brand of multiculturalism undoubtedly adjusted the implied white-ethnic dimension of Anglo-Britishness under Thatcherism towards a stronger narrative of British pluralism. But as with so many New Labour positions and policies, an emphasis on public relations masked what was significantly a continuation of Thatcher's nationalist mobilisation of essential culture, and the continued usefulness of racialised others as political scapegoats; New Labour's turn to multiculturalism and the symbolic elevation of British diversity was 'perfectly compatible with anti-immigrant populism'.[51] As a group of Britain's notable sociologists of race, led by Les Back, wrote at the midpoint of the New Labour regime, '[d]espite New Labour's gestures towards cultural diversity and inclusion, its body politic beats to the rhythm of a white heart', caught between a 'melancholic desire for an imperial past' and 'liberal models of social inclusion' within a globalised economy organised on national grounds.[52] For Ben Pitcher, this 'white heart' could be indexed in '[d]raconian asylum and immigration legislation, a racialized security agenda, and an aggressive discourse of assimilation' targeted at non-white populations and Muslims in particular.[53] Anti-migrant rhetoric depicting Britain as a 'tolerant' society which had become exhausted through the absorption of too much cultural difference – the very idea of 'swamping' that had seen Powell defenestrated but Thatcher exalted – was rebooted by David Blunkett in 2002 to justify a call to educate the children of asylum seekers in 'accommodation centres'. In this respect, New Labour multicultural governmentality was a case of *plus ça change, plus c'est la même chose*: largely an evolution of the same hierarchal resolution of a white 'core' ethnicity with the management of its ethnic 'others'.

What is often missed in calling out the hypocrisy and cynicism of New Labour's politics of race is its usefulness as a rhetoric deployed as a stock defence of the Union, where the ostensibly tolerant and multicultural character of Britain is implicitly juxtaposed against the purportedly ethnocentric character of Scottish or English nationalism. Speaking in 2000, Blair attempted to secure devolution as a settled British constitutional arrangement, suggesting that Scottish nationalism '[dictated] a retreat from an inclusive British identity', premised on diversity, to one premised on quasi-racial purity, 'rooted in nineteenth-century conceptions of territory and blood'; Blair's reference to 'successive waves of invasion and immigration and trading partnerships', that provide the discrepant basis for a plural Britishness, echo directly the same invocation of heterogeneity in *The True-Born Englishman*.[54] Implying Scottish nationalism followed a Victorian-era ethno-purism was a strategy adopted by the 'Better Together' campaign during the referendum on Scottish independence, augmented by the constant drip-feed of stories of 'anti-English racism'; this was one reason why Alistair Darling, the leader of 'Better Together' and one of the signatories of the Claim of Right for Scotland, equivocated on the suggestion that SNP nationalism had a 'blood and soil' character, language recognisable as referring to the racial mythologies of National Socialism.[55] In a similar vein, Sadiq Khan told the 2017 Scottish Labour conference that in the light of divisions introduced by contemporary 'national populism' such as Brexit or Donald Trump, 'there's no difference between those who try to divide us on the basis of whether we're English or Scottish, and those who try to divide us on the basis of our background, race or religion'.[56] While Khan only implies that Scottish nationalism is 'no different' to apartheid, while immediately distancing himself from the suggestion that 'nationalists are somehow racist or bigoted', his words nevertheless model the way that race has moved from a formation antagonistic to the British state in the late 1970s to a mobile symbol of 'a more United Kingdom', aligned with the state's priorities in light of constitutional pressures on the Union. The state's multicultural governmentality is not only about the management of difference, but has direct implications for national-constitutional integrity in the devolutionary period. The question of black Britain, therefore, is imbricated with the larger fortunes of the British Union.

Blackness as elaboration: black British literature

Even if Tony Blair never formally referenced the epochal *White Teeth*, the promotion and critical reception of Zadie Smith's novel positioned it as 'the definitive representation of twentieth century British multiculturalism'; it even contained a couple of Scottish characters to round out the cast.[57] While the literary features of the novel retained sharp edges, it came to symbolise the completed transition from Powellism to modern multiculturalism: the making new of post-imperial Britain. Meanwhile, the academic study of black British literature, which had begun with David Dabydeen's pioneering work in the 1980s, rapidly proceeded into disciplinarity and institutionalisation at more or less the same time as the New Labour project of 'elaborated Britishness'. Presaged by collections such as A. Robert Lee's *Other Britain, Other British* (1995), James Procter's *Writing Black Britain 1948–1998: An Interdisciplinary Anthology* (2000) is a seminal point for a developing discipline. Procter's anthology was closely followed by many other works, some of the more salient being Susheila Nasta's *Home Truths: Fictions of the South Asian Diaspora in Britain* (2001), C. L. Innes's *A History of Black and Asian Writing in Britain* (2002), Alison Donnell's *Companion to Contemporary Black British Culture* (2002), Procter's *Dwelling Places: Postwar Black British Writing* (2003), Mark Stein's *Black British Literature: Novels of Transformation* (2004), R. Victoria Arana and Lauri Ramey's collection *Black British Writing* (2004), Kadija Sesay's *Write Black, Write British: From Postcolonial to Black British Literature* (2005) and Gail Low and Marion Wynne-Davies's *A Black British Canon?* (2006). Retrospectives from the major university presses are also a good barometer of disciplinary security. Dabydeen, Gilmore and Jones's *Oxford Companion to Black British History* (2007) has a significant literary element; *The Cambridge Companion to Black and Asian British Writing 1945–2010*, edited by Deirdre Osborne, was published in 2016, and was followed shortly afterwards by *The Cambridge History of Black and Asian British Writing*, edited by Susheila Nasta and Mark Stein. Taken together, these works represent an expansion of the recognition of black writers, 'recovering and establishing a cultural history of black Britain', and providing a wide-reaching and critical engagement with post-war racism.[58]

However, in these accounts, 'British' remains a loose organising principle rather than a developed theorisation, in keeping with Dave Gunning's observation that in black British criticism '[t]he British nation's ability to act as a determinant of literary and cultural meanings is deferred. [. . .] "British" is invoked while being concurrently denied any explanatory power'.[59] For a start, the majority of the field is geographically, socially, culturally and politically focused on England, with an associated blurring of national boundaries between England and Britain. The idea of a 'deferred explanatory power' resonates clearly with ideas coming out of Scotland on the 'banality' of the Union, and the 'naturalisation' of Britain as a seamless and unbroken continuity based on a set of pre-existent and 'natural' values.[60] What emerges from black British literary criticism, coinciding with the re-establishing of Scotland's Parliament in 1999, is the call for a redefined Britain that acts as a stabilising force despite, or more accurately all the more effectively *because of*, a concomitant critique of its exclusions. This often takes the form of a celebration of a new model of confident Britishness characterised by reinvention, plurality and unity. Alison Donnell, for example, says that black literary history provides a 'wonderful and compelling narration of Britain's "collective autobiography"'.[61] While Donnell recognises the entropic disintegration of the category 'black-British-artist', it is the global scale of transnationalism that threatens its integrity rather than any prospect of fragmentation from within. In the context of devolutionary Britain, the political implications of a compelling and novel collective narrative for Britishness are clear.

The national restoration performed in these readings of black British writing is more than an excavation of a 'diverse' record of the British past. It also provides a syncretic cultural transformation, a form of genetic transfusion, the life-giving properties of which ensure the continued health and evolution of British culture necessary in the present and for the future. In this respect, black British literary studies share a cultural nationalist orientation with much Scottish literary criticism, in which literary culture itself is put to work reforging the imagined community and cultural integrity of the nation. Mark Stein's *Black British Literature* provides an illustration of this inadvertent bulwarking. Stein's perceptive account of Britain's 'novels of transformation' recognises the instrumental function of celebrating black and Asian writing, which acts as a form of multi-cultural laundering for the state. However, the 'core' integrity of Britain remains undisturbed. For Stein, black writing performs an operation on Britishness, and vice versa, through a process of syncresis in which '"[B]lackness" redefines "Britishness" and "Britishness" redefines "blackness"'.[62] He registers that the 'British' element of black British is not settled, offering instead an interpretation that blackness provides a 'check' to Britishness: '[t]he category black British literature does not tend to reify nationalist categorization since the second adjective is kept in check by the first'.[63] This observation holds true in the context of an ethnically exclusive Britishness, where black writers open an imaginative space in an otherwise exclusionary literary culture. It has the opposite effect in the context of an elaborated Britishness, where the 'black' modifier offers instead a legitimation of the progressive orientation of modern Britain. As established by Blair's 'Britain' speech, the invocation of a racially inclusive pluralism is no guarantee against this different kind of nationalist reification. Forward momentum is ensured by the description of black British writing as a quasi-biological restorative influence, where black British writers are a 'significant part of a newly invigorated British culture'.[64] The claim of 'invigoration' implies a welcome biological disturbance in the moribund gene pool of British culture; far from unique to Stein, this chimes with the moment of Cool Britannia, and of a British national 'confidence' that had taken on fresh impetus and necessity in the aftermath of the election and referendums of 1997 respectively. In this regard, it resembles a new iteration of an older model of 'British culture', the infusion of 'Celtic genius' familiar from Matthew Arnold, in which the 'ethnies' of Scotland, Ireland and Wales provide the invigoration of 'English spirit' or 'English genius' via an intrinsic 'energy' and 'lively Celtic wit'.[65]

Similarly, R. Victoria Arana and Lauri Ramey's collection *Black British Writing* (2004) attends to the 'reinvention' of Britain made possible by the introduction of diverse new influences. A celebratory tone of adaptable and repurposed Britishness is initially signalled by the Union flag emblazoned on the cover of the paperback edition. The introduction identifies a twenty-first-century black British movement that emphasises the strong placedness of a new generation of contemporary black writers, '[b]orn in England, Scotland or Wales, often to racially mixed families, they do not write about their *staying power* because they are not the ones who migrated. Britain, they affirm, *is* their country'.[66] Contained within this nominal gesture towards Britain's constituent national formations is a subtextual restatement of Britain's fundamental unity, naming them only to bring each back under the umbrella of Britain as the definitive country of black writers. The literary moment Arana and Ramey described is a heady, conflictual mix of avant-garde and popular, democratic and profitable, activist and British-institutional.[67] This final point is germane, because state support for 'black'-coded cultural products – the injunction to 'just get something black made' – was a manifestation of multicultural governmentality, a New Labour strategy that sought to instrumentalise cultural production for the purposes of social inclusion.[68] Illustratively, Arana conjoins a putative avant-garde black cultural dynamism to a political moment of 'Reinventing Britain', a phrase intended as a decisive break from ethno-purist mythologies of the past, but one which inadvertently invokes a state-sponsored institutional rejuvenation of the British national-cultural brand. In 1997, 'Reinventing Britain' had already been adopted as a buzz-phrase by the British Council, and, as Robert Crawford has pointed out, had strikingly failed to register the national challenge from Scotland (or Wales, Ireland and England) within that 'reinvention'.[69] Arana has elsewhere downplayed the constitutional in British cultural-nationalist terms in favour of imaginative national 'reinvention': 'to re-invent Britain will require, all are agreed, more than a series of constitutional reforms: it will take [. . .] brilliant and accessible works of the creative imagination'.[70] Echoing the 'cultural manifesto' that claims devolution as a literary achievement, Arana calls for a black British equivalent, instrumentalised in the re-engineering of Britishness via a 'vibrant' cultural nationalism rather than through the dry orchestration of constitutional change.

A Blairite language of British reinvention, with its explicit connection to state priorities, endures in contemporary scholarship which has placed the literary imagination of black writers, and the literary treatment of race, at the centre of refurbishing Britishness. The most significant recent contribution to the literature of race in Britain has been Sara Upstone's *Rethinking Race and Identity in Contemporary British Fiction*. Upstone's worthwhile objective is to examine the literary imagination of 'a future British society less dominated by racial prejudice', and the ways in which contemporary writers have imagined the movement towards a 'post-racial' future.[71] Instructively, she locates that literary-critical project in a field of 'new' Britishness: 'staking literature's claim for a role in defining the precise nature of the "new Britishness" discourse which has come to define twenty-first century debates about the future of multi-racial Britain'.[72] This 'new Britishness' is notable for its proximity to the 'elaborated Britishness' of the New Labour moment, right down to the near word-for-word reproduction of the official title of the Parekh Report, *The Future of Multi-Ethnic Britain*. Upstone's book is structured around a literary genre of 'utopian realism', broken down into distinct elements, read as projecting radical new social and aesthetic alternatives to the cemented racial divisions of contemporary Britain. However, utopian realism is also strongly associated with the political philosophy of New Labour, specifically in the 'Third Way' rhetoric of Anthony Giddens, Blair's intellectual mentor.[73] Giddens first mooted the idea of utopian realism as the reinvigoration of centre-left social democracy in *The Consequences of Modernity*, an idea which would prove instrumental for the multicultural tone of New Labour.[74] Indeed, Upstone points to Phoebe Griffith and Mark Leonard's *Reclaiming Britishness* (2002) as a signature text in resolving this 'multi-racial' future. Leonard was a pre-eminent architect of 'Cool Britannia', a New Labour 'wunderkind' charged with the rebranding of Britain in the late 1990s. His United Colours of Britain subordinated ethnic difference into a 'brand Britain' narrative of choice, and provided a central plank in New Labour's portfolio of neoliberal multicultural policies and discursive tools. The nationally reformative *Reclaiming Britishness* deals in the language of state nationalism, invoking 'shared British values' and 'the battle for Britishness'.[75] *Rethinking Race* itself has some echoes of the nation-building multicultural celebration of Griffith and Leonard: Monica Ali's *Brick Lane* '[speaks] to the possibility of a positively multicultural Britain'; literary depictions of '[migrant] encounters' have 'positively shaped a new collective British identity'; the success of novels like *Small Island* and *Anita and Me* 'speaks to a Britishness beyond race: that stories of Britain's history, stories of multicultural communities, are now universal stories'.[76] It is not surprising that reading via the political precepts of Griffith and Leonard would end up here, with the erasure of difference into a British multicultural universality perfectly suited for the revivification of the Union in a 'Britishness beyond race' and a process of levelling off necessary for what Žižek calls the 'universal anonymity of Capital' lurking behind the screen of observed multicultural difference.[77].

To return to Dave Gunning's original observation, in this analytic mode Britishness is 'denied any explanatory power'; it is imagined as a historically resilient ethnocentric nationalism upon which literature operates in an ameliorative manner, to forge a 'new Britishness' suitable for the pluralist post-imperial moment. Cultural critics like Hall and Gilroy recoiled at the cynicism and emptiness of New Labour's politics of race, but the long-term ambition of the government's 'elaborated Britishness' with respect to reinforcing the Union has never really been repudiated except as a kind of nationalistic miscalibration, one that either impedes proper transnational thinking or is simply the wrong *kind* of Britishness. *Rethinking Race* indicates the way that the institutionalisation of black writing has evolved in a partially symbiotic relationship with a revivified Britishness during a period in which the constitutional integrity of Britain has been called into question, and has been refurbished by a redrawn and 'elaborated' category of Britishness characterised by strong state-level intervention. Hence, the point is not that cultural theorists of race in Britain have been willing servants of state-level British nationalism or neoliberal multiculturalism, but instead that black British criticism has often struggled to grapple with the consequences of Britain's 'other' national formations; in short, to achieve something that Paul Gilroy himself demands, 'the detailed unfolding of cultural formations', here in the form of tangible national culture that pulls against a 'restored' Britishness.[78]

There is a different problem with attempts to 'devolve' black Britain, which are more cognisant of the biases of contemporary 'Britishness', moving away from the centralising narrative that takes metropolitan England as Britain, and pointing out Scotland's distinctiveness. Procter's *Dwelling Places* emphasises scope, attending to works across the post-war period, across literary genres and across the geography of Britain. This last point is important, as one of the critical ambitions of Procter's work is to map the literature of uncharted black experience outside the frame of reference that has historically predominated, localised in the two largest metropolises in England. To this effect, the very first subheading of *Dwelling Places* is 'Devolving Black Britain'. This is a particular kind of devolution: one that addresses the imagination of Britain as a 'homogeneous unified flatland' in favour of a broader geographical base, with more attention to local specificities.[79] Procter's analysis engages directly with Scotland through Jackie Kay, where he argues that the 'tension [. . .] between the black Scottish speaker and the English south' lays bare 'internal, regional and *national* differences' and 'dissent towards the hegemonic centre [i.e. London]'.[80] Indicatively, Scotland is bunched together with Blackpool and Manchester in a chapter marked as 'the North'. So, while national distinctiveness is named, it is hard to differentiate between national Scotland and the sense of Scotland as simply a large region within Britain and a Parekhian 'identity' within Britishness. Similarly, Corinne Fowler's 'A Tale of Two Novels' offers a 'devolved approach to black British writing' via an examination of the fortunes of two novels, coded 'black British' and published almost simultaneously in 2000: Zadie Smith's *White Teeth* and Joe Pemberton's *Forever and Ever Amen*.[81] Here, place provides an important differentiation between the mass-market appeal of Smith, situated within 'young and vibrant life in the capital', and the critical diagnosis of northern provincialism that quickly adhered to Pemberton's work.[82] Fowler's article argues that literary commissioning and marketing in Britain is centred on representations of precisely the metropolitan centre of gravity that Procter had already identified, and aims 'to contradict the dominant reading of London as the nucleus of multi-racial Britain'.[83]

Procter and Fowler's devolution of black British writing provides nuanced and decentralised critique of an abstract or placeless 'Britishness'. However, there is a problem inherent in framing this as a process of devolution: it conflates regional specificity within Britishness – looking harder at neglected areas of Britain – with the political-constitutional category of devolution, in which geographies are only one element and the scope is constitutional and, most pressingly, national. This disjunction maps on to the perspectival differences Michael Gardiner outlines between devolution viewed from the British state and from Britain's constituent nations:

> [T]hose in devolved areas tend to see the [devolutionary] changes occurring as national and bring longstanding and comprehensive national cultures to this viewpoint, whereas the state government goes to great lengths to convince the English public that the process is regional and that there is no national worry.[84]

The latter description echoes both the ambition of the Kilbrandon Commission and New Labour policy, to reinforce Britain via a process of regional recalibration that attends to Scottish demands for greater autonomy without upsetting the English too much, or opening up uncomfortable constitutional questions for the British state. Ultimately, Fowler's objective is to achieve a 'fuller range of British writing', which reveals the way that two critical priorities pull against one another, one that expands and details Britishness, the other that thinks through, if not anticipates, its fragmentation.[85] Devolution within this subsection of black British literary criticism is close to the British state's interpretation: a kind of regional management, an extension of local government, that presents no threat to the constitutional status quo of Britain as would, say, an independent Scotland ending the Union.

Graham Huggan describes the way that the desire 'that other voices be heard, that non-mainstream views be included and celebrated [. . .] can easily lend itself to various forms of exploitation and manipulation'.[86] Black British criticism lies within this problematic. The drive to diversify the cultural landscape, to expand the critical lens and national-cultural enfranchisement, and to struggle against white domination, runs the risk of playing into the elaboration of a frictionless and 'natural' Britishness that staves off a post-imperial constitutional reckoning and, in the preservation of an ethno-cultural Englishness, actually maintains racism.[87] Jacob Ross's introduction to *Closure*, a collection of black British short stories, provides a good example of exactly this conflict:

"Black Britishness" is what it is – a lived reality that is like air or breath or blood: important, but hardly at the forefront of one's consciousness except in moments of confrontation or self-assertion, and even then, it is not always recognised as such.[88]

The 'unconscious' quality of black Britishness Ross describes subtly acknowledges a history of anti-racism and the progressive egalitarianism that has brought about such a state of normalisation. That black Britishness is something which can even be 'background' to lived experience is the result of hard-won political struggles that have exposed and opposed racism in Britain. The critical refusal inherent in the expression '[it] is what it is' sublimates some of the exhaustion of racial representation, both as subjects of that representation and as artists called upon to be representatives. This constitutes a victory, in moving past the point when the right to nationhood was still acutely in the balance for black people in Britain. But the total naturalisation of the quality of 'being black British', equated to a respiratory or a circulatory system, situates the category of the national in a space beyond politics. The abstraction of Britishness plays into a state-national project in which a multicultural governmentality redefines Britain, to return to Ben Pitcher, via 'symbolic admission' into the national community.[89] The category of black Britishness must remain contingent, just like all 'Britishnesses', not least because it might be suddenly withdrawn as a result of Nairn's long-predicted 'break-up'.

Two World Wars, no World Cups: Paul Gilroy and *After Empire*

As part of his ongoing project to foreground and examine black expressive culture, often in the context of national Anglo-Britain, Paul Gilroy has come even closer to thinking through the implications of 'non-Britishness' – the national claims of Britain's constituent nations, and even the possibility of post-British national culture. In 'Art of Darkness', as early as 1990, Gilroy establishes a strong set of post-British credentials, as he articulates something of the complex relationship between an umbrella British national category and constituent nations:

To be British is, in any case, to contract into a category of administrative convenience rather than an ethnic identity. [...] The term 'English', which is often mistakenly substituted for it, acts as a partial and manifestly inadequate cultural counterpart. The disjuncture between the two terms is a continual reminder not just of English dominance over Scots, Welsh, and Irish people, but also that a British state can exist comfortably without the benefit of a unified British culture. The idea of an authentic cultural content of our national life is therefore constructed through an appeal to Englishness rather than Britishness. It is around this concept that the difficult tasks of creating a more pluralistic sense of national identity and a new conception of national culture revolve.[90]

This passage is revealing. Gilroy recognises the 'Anglo-British conflation' as a kind of mistaken substitution. The suggestion of English 'dominance' over the Scots, Welsh and Irish people only serves to manifest that conflation in a different form, through an erroneous isomorphism. England is dominant in terms of size, but *imperial* domination is a British trait; Scotland and Wales are colonial partners; swathes of England are more aptly described as 'oppressed' geographies than, say, parts of Scoto-British Edinburgh; Ireland has been dominated by the British Empire, not restricted to England but prominently including Scotland and Wales, which was satirised in *Trainspotting*'s 'Bang to Rites'.[91] It is also a marker of the moment of *Small Acts* that authentic 'national life' is constructed through Englishness rather than Britishness, a state discourse which was already shifting after Thatcher as Britishness took centre stage as a 'unifying culture'.

In *Small Acts*, Gilroy saw black culture as a vernacular English culture: 'part of a wider cultural struggle to affiliate with England and, in so doing, to change what it means to be English'.[92] This contestation of Englishness was at odds with the direction signalled by Stuart Hall in 'New Ethnicities', and foreshadows Gilroy's ongoing texturing of black cultural production against the backdrop of conflicting nationalisms within Britain. The difference between a refurbished Britishness and post-British nationhood crystallises in *After Empire*, one of the most important works to address the racial dimension of nationalism in Britain under New Labour. The book's central thesis has been influential: that race, and in particular blackness, signifies a melancholia representing an imperial past, that incurs associated feelings of shame and loss. Immigrants and their descendants are

> unwanted and feared precisely because they are the unwitting bearers of the imperial and colonial past [. . .] who, trapped inside our perverse local logic of race, nation, and ethnic absolutism not only *represent* the vanished empire but also refer consciousness to the unacknowledged pain of its loss and the unsettling shame of its bloody management.[93]

This is a phenomenon contingent on the inherent visibility of blackness, the visual trigger for affective responses, that forms a complete sign with blackness as a cultural formation that has often centred the commemoration and contestation of Empire's 'bloody management'. Britain '[concedes] that it does not like blacks and wants to get rid of them', sentiments which prove psychically difficult to square with the repeated invocations of fairness, tolerance and equality that are the common currency of 'British values'.[94] Melancholia results. Gilroy links this post-imperial melancholy directly to British national decline in language that would not be out of place in Nairn's excoriations: Britain suffers from a 'perennial crisis of national identity' where anti-migrant populism reveals a national 'guilt-ridden loathing and depression'; an 'increasingly brittle and empty national identity' where 'intermittent racial tragedies [. . .] punctuate the boredom of chronic national decline with a functional anguish'; nostalgic fantasies of the World Wars are the 'gritty presence' inside the 'glittery but battered package of Britain's perennially suspended modernization'.[95] These pathologies are registered in culture, and for Gilroy it is popular culture that most clearly encodes 'the country's relentless meltdown'.[96] *Changing Rooms* and *Ground Force* represent displaced agency, where home improvement acts as a surrogate for the 'untouchable, immutable, and resistant' aspects of British social and political life: social class, Parliamentarianism, monarchy. Ricky Gervais's *The Office* presents 'the small-minded Englishness of lonely, damaged men [. . .] who think they have the full measure of the country's transformation but have utterly failed to grasp what it requires of them'.[97]

Gilroy recognises Britain as a fragmenting national formation experiencing gradual break-up, within which Scotland particularly is clamouring for greater political representation, if not full independence.[98] This has been sealed in the outcomes of devolved government, where 'Scotland and Wales are evidently having a better time than the English' in terms of social benefits such as student grants and welfare for senior citizens.[99] Gilroy presents a picture in which an incoherent, outdated and nostalgic Britishness is set to be undone by constitutional pressures from within, and to be replaced by a cosmopolitan England – smaller-scale, with a new and critical outlook on colonialism, characterised by a social democratic 'convivial cosmopolitanism' and 'the rebirth of English tolerance and generosity'.[100] He starts to build post-British momentum, also evidenced by readings of popular culture: Mike Skinner of The Streets is the icon of a new Englishness, vernacular, operating on a 'less-than-imperial scale' – even a modern poet who 'refigures an English pastoral consciousness' and imagines a 'postcolonial Englishness'.[101] Meanwhile, he argues for a renegotiation of the idea of England, no longer 'a synonym for Britain' and now necessarily reduced to 'fit the diminished ideological space between political devolution based on alternative ethnicity and economic regionalization'.[102] Gilroy's 'devolution' is specifically ethnic and regional, but not constitutional, and hence not mutually exclusive to the continuation of Britain in its current form.

This is a crucial limitation of *After Empire*. Gilroy shows how the relationship between racism and the entwined national formations of Britishness and Englishness is difficult to disentangle. A good example is in his analysis of the tribalism, martial nostalgia and confused national mourning encoded in the football chant 'Two World Wars and One World Cup', a 'true-Brit' anthem echoing 'around many British sports venues'.[103] The chant has a 'perlocutionary power' which 'can effectively *produce* the artificially whitened, comprehensively rehomogenized national community to which ultranationalist discourse casually refers'.[104] What is missing is an elaboration of the contradiction at the heart of this chant, which has a direct bearing on the 'national community' that is Gilroy's critical object. England is not generally cited as the 'victor' in either World War; the 'blitz spirit' is used as a powerful and unifying symbol of precisely the British national achievement which Gilroy criticises extensively throughout *After Empire*. Conversely, international association football occupies a space beyond Britishness. Neither Scotland, Wales nor Northern Ireland have ever distinguished themselves in their pursuit of the World Cup; the World Cup final of 1966 is incontrovertibly an English national achievement, and can never be deployed as a symbol of British unity. The chant, with the perlocutionary generation of atavistic white homogeneity that Gilroy diagnoses, directly registers the contradiction between a macronarrative of Britishness and the thwarted realisation of England. Indeed, it is suggestive of a form of sublimated Englishness – corroborating Nairn's argument that it is the constitutional suppression of England that allows racism to flourish under the St George's Cross, rather than any intrinsic quality of English nationhood itself.[105]

Despite astutely demarcating the parameters of an English cosmopolitanism and localism that strongly implies post-Britishness, Gilroy alternates between British and English national frames, and at the end of the book returns to the sanctuary offered by a continuing Britain. His call for a 'restored and healthier Britain' indicates the resting point for *After Empire*: no claim for the 'restoration' of Britain is without political counterweight in devolutionary terms.[106] The idea of a 'restoration' has a specific tone of constitutional regulation and stability associated with the return of immutable class privilege – monarchy – and which reverberates loudly in a constitutional-political moment defined by the re-establishment of the Scottish Parliament and the growing influence of the Scottish National Party. Falling back on the security of elaborated Britishness is partly a consequence of a larger problem with nationalism in *After Empire*, which attempts to balance the need for a new national imaginary in England with Gilroy's core project of an anti-nationalist, planetary humanism, resulting in an amalgam with limited political purchase. Laura Chrisman has suggested that *After Empire*, like the earlier *Against Race*, is absent of 'all positive evaluations of contemporary black political culture'; she argues that in his repurposing of Fanon for a cosmopolitics, Gilroy dematerialises and disembodies an explicitly black critical thought, and 'transplants Fanon's pro-nationalist sentiments into their opposite: his own anti-nationalist soil'.[107] In this light, the 'restoration' of Britishness makes sense, where a black politics is absorbed into the new ethnic order of Britishness under New Labour. To invert Hall's judgement on English nationalism, it turns out that Britishness is also highly 'resistant to radical appropriation'.

Post-Britishness

'What would we find,' asks John McLeod, 'if we were to read black British writing for its critique of England rather than its rewriting of Britain?'.[108] This is the final step which *After Empire* struggles to take: the potential of a post-British England, and what it might become in a progressive sense. Historically and contemporaneously, most writers coded as black British live in England, vote in English local elections, obey English laws, studied in an English primary, secondary and tertiary education system, are exposed daily to stories of English national sporting greatness or ignominy, have no devolved parliamentary representation or national literature of England, and live relationally with many other English people in the same situation. This is unquestionably a 'British' context too, and the entanglement between English and British nationhood is hardly limited only to black Britain. But such an entanglement is extremely significant 'after Empire', in a post-imperial context in which race, to return to Ben Pitcher's argument, has moved from an antagonistic relationship with the state towards being a crucial prop to its legitimacy and stability. The prize of an ethnically inclusive British national constituency, viewed from another angle, plays into the priorities of the Union state in its post-imperial crisis of definition. The question of a modern, civic Englishness is necessarily suppressed by Britishness, and it is this possibility that is opened up by refocusing attention on the 'blackness' of Britain's sub-nationalisms, England and Scotland alike.

Just as the prospect of an independent Scotland 'forces the English to consider more deeply than ever who they might be', Scottish writing in the devolutionary period has proved hard to square with state-led attempts at British cultural unity, in much the same way that the stubborn national characteristics of Scottish writing have interrupted any attempt to produce a unified and national 'British literature' after Empire.[109] Here, the reintroduction of an idea of 'black Scotland' takes on new significance. I have suggested that black British literature and culture more broadly have been proactively read for reformative impulses that operate on a fairly static concept of Britain as an ethnocentric formation. To approach the question of blackness from a nationally Scottish perspective, therefore, disrupts the smooth operation of this 'black British' disciplinarity. Likewise, it makes impossible the taxonomic assumptions of New Labour and the Parekh Report, in which 'black' and 'Scottish' are conceptually distinct ethnicities within the umbrella category of British. It is to the question of blackness in Scotland that I now turn.

Notes

1. See Dawson, Ashley, *Mongrel Nation: Diasporic Culture and the Making of Postcolonial Britain* (Ann Arbor: University of Michigan Press, 2007), p. 6.
2. Defoe, Daniel, *The True-Born Englishman*, in *The Earlier Life and the Chief Earlier Works of Daniel Defoe*, ed. Henry Morley (London: Routledge, 1889), pp. 175–218: 194.
3. Dawson, *Mongrel Nation*, p. 7.
4. See Anderson, Benedict, *Imagined Communities: Reflections on the Origin and Spread of Nationalism* (London: Verso, 1991 [1983]); see also Stein, Mark, *Black British Literature: Novels of Transformation* (Columbus: Ohio State University Press, 2004), p. xiii.
5. As Ashley Marshall has observed, Defoe's own 'categorical condemnation of Catholicism' echoes throughout his satirical work, and the specific 'struggle between Protestantism and Catholicism' underlies *The True-Born Englishman*; see 'Defoe as Satirist', *Huntingdon Library Quarterly* 70:4 (2007), pp. 553–76: 557.
6. Richetti, John, *The Life of Daniel Defoe* (Oxford: Blackwell, 2006), pp. 12, 61.
7. Kidd, Colin, 'Protestantism, Constitutionalism and British Identity under the Later Stuarts', in Brendan Bradshaw and Peter Roberts (eds), *British Consciousness and Identity: The Making of Britain 1533–1707* (Cambridge: Cambridge University Press, 1998), pp. 321–42: 322, 338.
8. Dawson, *Mongrel Nation*, p. 7.
9. Kidd, *Union and Unionisms*, pp. 23–31.
10. See Barker, Martin, *The New Racism: Conservatives and the Ideology of the Tribe* (London: Junction Books, 1981).
11. Pitcher, *Politics of Multiculturalism*, p. 44.
12. Nairn, *Break-Up*, p. 75.
13. See Nairn, 'The Twilight of the British State' in *Break-Up*, pp. 11–91 and Nairn, Tom, *The Enchanted Glass: Britain and its Monarchy* (London: Vintage, 1994).
14. Gardiner, *Cultural Roots*, p. 11, original emphasis.
15. Nairn, *After Britain*, p. 250.
16. Baucom, Ian, *Out of Place: Englishness, Empire and the Locations of Identity* (Princeton: Princeton University Press, 1999), p. 10.
17. Primarily the 1962 and 1968 Commonwealth Immigrants Acts, the 1971 Immigration Act and the 1981 British Nationality Act; see Baucom, *Out of Place*, pp. 8, 12–13, 24.
18. Barker, *The New Racism*, p. 23.
19. Bourne, Jenny, '"May We Bring Harmony"? Thatcher's Legacy on "Race"', *Race and Class* 55:1 (2013), pp. 87–91: 90.

20. Hames, *Literary Politics*, pp. 81–2.
21. Hames, Scott, 'Narrating Devolution: Politics and/as Scottish Fiction', *C21 Literature* 5:2 (2017), pp. 1–25: 13–14.
22. Hall, Stuart, 'Racism and Reaction', *Five Views of Multi-Racial Britain* (London: Commission for Racial Equality, 1978), pp. 23–35: 30.
23. Hall, Stuart et al., *Policing the Crisis: 'Mugging', the State, and Law and Order* (London: Macmillan, 1978); Centre for Contemporary Cultural Studies, *The Empire Strikes Back: Race and Racism in 70s Britain* (London: Routledge, 1982).
24. See Sivanandan, A., 'Resistance to Rebellion: Asian and Afro-Caribbean Struggles in Britain', *Race and Class* 23:2–3 (1981), pp. 111–52: 147–8.
25. Shukra, *Changing Pattern*, pp. 53–5.
26. Kundnani, Arun, 'The Rise and Fall of British Multiculturalism' in Gavan Titley (ed.), *Resituating Culture* (Strasbourg: Council of Europe, 2004), pp. 105–12: 106.
27. Hall, 'New Ethnicities'.
28. Quoted in Alexander, Claire (ed.), *Stuart Hall and 'Race'* (London: Routledge, 2011), p. 458.
29. Hall, 'New Ethnicities', pp. 266, 267
30. Hall, 'New Ethnicities', pp. 267, 268.
31. Hall, 'New Ethnicities', p. 272, original emphasis.
32. Hall, 'New Ethnicities', p. 273, original emphasis.
33. Later in his career, Hall would recognise Englishness as a necessary negotiation: 'I do think Englishness is something we need to talk about, but it's a contested terrain that is structured powerfully against a contemporary radical appropriation'; quoted in Jonathan Derbyshire, 'Stuart Hall: We Need to Talk about Englishness', *The New Statesman*, 23 August 2012 (last accessed 3 April 2018), n. pag.
34. Centre for Contemporary Cultural Studies, *The Empire Strikes Back*, p. 7.
35. Hall, Stuart, 'Life and Times of the First New Left', *New Left Review* 61:1 (2010), pp. 177–96: 185.
36. Nairn, *After Britain*, p. 40.
37. Nairn, *After Britain*, p. 40.
38. HC Deb (21 December 1988), vol. 144 col. 428, https://api.parliament.uk/historic-hansard/sittings/1988/dec/21 (last accessed 18 August 2019).
39. Sivanandan, A., 'Race, Class and the State: The Black Experience in Britain', *Race and Class* 17:4 (1976), pp. 347–68: 347.
40. Shukra, *Changing Pattern*, p. 110.
41. Nairn, *After Britain*, pp. 20–2.
42. Pitcher, *Politics of Multiculturalism*, p. 44.
43. Pitcher, *Politics of Multiculturalism*, pp. 33–4, emphasis added.
44. Žižek, Slavoj, 'Multiculturalism, or, the Cultural Logic of Multinational Capitalism', *New Left Review* 225:1 (1997), pp. 28–51.
45. Parekh, Bhikhu (ed.), *The Future of Multi-Ethnic Britain: Report of the Commission on the Future of Multi-Ethnic Britain* (London: Profile Books, 2002 [2000]).
46. Parekh, *Future of Multi-Ethnic Britain*, p. viii.
47. Parekh, *Future of Multi-Ethnic Britain*, p. xv.
48. Parekh, *Future of Multi-Ethnic Britain*, p. 15.
49. Parekh, *Future of Multi-Ethnic Britain*, p. 16.
50. Pitcher, *Politics of Multiculturalism*, p. 40.
51. Kundnani, 'Rise and Fall', p. 107.
52. Back, Les et al., 'New Labour's White Heart: Politics, Multiculturalism and the Return of Assimilation', *Political Quarterly* 73:4 (2002), pp. 445–54: 453, 447.
53. Pitcher, *Politics of Multiculturalism*, pp. 27, 32.
54. 'Tony Blair's Britain Speech', *The Guardian*, 28 March 2000, www.theguardian.com/uk/2000/mar/28/britishidentity.tonyblair (last accessed 1 September 2019).
55. 'Scottish Independence: Salmond in Darling Interview Apology Call', BBC News

(2014) www.bbc.co.uk/news/uk-scotland-scotland-politics-27793285 (last accessed 1 September 2019).

56. 'Sadiq Khan: Scottish Labour's Best Days Still Lie Ahead with Kezia at the Helm', *Labour List* (2017), http://labourlist.org/2017/02/sadiq-khan-scottish-labours-best-days-still-lie-ahead/ (last accessed 1 September 2019).

57. Head, Dominic, 'Multiculturalism of the Millennium: Zadie Smith's *White Teeth*' in Richard J. Lane, Rod Mengham and Phillip Tew, *Contemporary British Fiction* (Cambridge: Polity Press, 2002), pp. 106–19: 106.

58. Procter, *Writing Black Britain*, p. 4.

59. Gunning, 'Anti-Racism', p. 31.

60. See Kidd, *Unions and Unionism*; Gardiner, Michael, *The Return of England in English Literature* (Basingstoke: Palgrave Macmillan, 2012), p. 3.

61. Donnell, Alison, 'In Praise of a Black British Canon and the Possibilities of Representing the Nation "Otherwise"' in Low and Wynne-Davies, *A Black British Canon?*, pp. 189–204: 192.

62. Stein, *Black British Literature*, pp. 183, 8.

63. Stein, *Black British Literature*, p. 17.

64. Stein, *Black British Literature*, p. 20.

65. Arnold, Matthew, *On the Study of Celtic Literature* (London: Smith, Elder and Co., 1864), p. 96.

66. Arana, R. Victoria and Lauri Ramey, *Black British Writing* (Basingstoke: Palgrave Macmillan, 2004), p. 3, original emphasis.

67. Arana and Ramey, *Black British Writing*, p. 2.

68. Nwonka, Clive James and Sarita Malik, 'Cultural Discourses and Practices of Institutionalised Diversity in the UK Film Sector: "Just Get Something Black Made"', *The Sociological Review* 66:6 (2018), pp. 1111–27.

69. Crawford, *Devolving English Literature*, p. 309.

70. Arana, R. Victoria, 'Aesthetics as Deliberate Design: Giving Form to Tigritude and Nommo' in Arana (ed.), *Black British Aesthetics Today* (Newcastle upon Tyne: Cambridge Scholars Publishing, 2007), pp. 1–13: 3.

71. Upstone, *Rethinking Race*, p. 4.

72. Upstone, *Rethinking Race*, p. 5.

73. See Nairn, *After Britain*, p. 54.

74. Anthony Giddens, *The Consequences of Modernity* (Cambridge: Polity, 1990).

75. Griffith, Phoebe and Mark Leonard (eds), *Reclaiming Britishness* (London: The Foreign Policy Centre, 2002), p. xi.

76. Upstone, *Rethinking Race*, pp. 142, 21, 23.

77. Žižek, 'Multiculturalism', p. 44.

78. Gilroy, Paul, *After Empire: Melancholia or Convivial Culture?* (Abingdon: Routledge, 2004), p. 161.

79. Procter, James, *Dwelling Places: Postwar Black British Writing* (Manchester: Manchester University Press, 2003), p. 1.

80. Procter, *Dwelling Places*, pp. 190–1, emphasis added.

81. Fowler, Corinne, 'A Tale of Two Novels: Developing a Devolved Approach to Black British Writing', *Journal of Commonwealth Literature* 43:3 (2008), pp. 75–94.

82. Hilary Mantel, quoted in Fowler, 'A Tale of Two Novels', p. 81.

83. Fowler, 'A Tale of Two Novels', p. 82; these ideas were developed further in Pearce, Lynne, Corinne Fowler and Robert Crawshaw (eds), *Postcolonial Manchester: Diaspora Space and the Devolution of Literary Culture* (Manchester: Manchester University Press, 2013).

84. Gardiner, *Cultural Roots*, p. ix.

85. Fowler, 'A Tale of Two Novels', p. 90.

86. Huggan, Graham, *The Postcolonial Exotic: Marketing the Margins* (London: Routledge, 2001), p. 154.

87. See Gardiner, *Cultural Roots*, p. 165.
88. Ross, Jacob (ed.), *Closure: Contemporary Black British Short Stories* (Leeds: Peepal Tree Press, 2015), p. 11.
89. Pitcher, *Politics of Multiculturalism*, pp. 33–4.
90. Gilroy, *Small Acts*, p. 75.
91. Welsh, Irvine, *Trainspotting* (London: Vintage, 2004 [1993]), p. 210.
92. Gilroy, *Small Acts*, p. 76.
93. Gilroy, *After Empire*, p. 110.
94. Gilroy, *After Empire*, p. 114.
95. Gilroy, *After Empire*, pp. 97–8, 116, 119.
96. Gilroy, *After Empire*, p. 124.
97. Gilroy, *After Empire*, p. 152.
98. Gilroy, *After Empire*, p. 98.
99. Gilroy, *After Empire*, p. 130.
100. Gilroy, *After Empire*, p. 166.
101. Gilroy, *After Empire*, pp. 104–5.
102. Gilroy, *After Empire*, p. 130; Gilroy had already expressed an identical sentiment in the new introduction to *There Ain't No Black in the Union Jack* ((London: Routledge, 2002 [1987]), p. xxv.
103. Gilroy, *After Empire*, p. 117.
104. Gilroy, *After Empire*, pp. 119–20.
105. Nairn, *After Britain*, p. 40.
106. Gilroy, *After Empire*, p. 166.
107. Chrisman, Laura, 'The Vanishing Body of Frantz Fanon in Paul Gilroy's *Against Race* and *After Empire*', *The Black Scholar* 41:4 (2011), pp. 18–30: 19.
108. McLeod, John, 'Black British Writing and Post-British England', in Claire Westall and Michael Gardiner (eds), *Literature of an Independent England: Revisions of England, Englishness and English Literature* (Basingstoke: Palgrave Macmillan, 2013), pp. 175–87: 177.
109. Kumar, Krishnan, *The Making of English National Identity* (Cambridge: Cambridge University Press, 2003), p. 248.

Chapter 2

'You Got a White Voice': Blackness in Devolutionary Scotland

Prabhu Guptara's concise entry for Wilson Harris's *Black Marsden* (1972), in his annotated bibliography of black British literature, describes it as simply 'Harris's first novel about blacks in Britain'.[1] While technically correct, the implication of this description minimises two of its important characteristics. The first is that 'Britain' does not do justice to the specificity of *Black Marsden*'s substantially Scottish setting, nor to its relationship to a Scottish literary tradition. Harris, an émigré author from Guyana, stated that the 'strange subjectivity of the Scottish imagination' is one with which he felt 'at home'.[2] Scots in the Caribbean had already featured in his first novel *Palace of the Peacock* in the figure of Cameron, by implication a descendant of Jacobite exiles, whose 'great-grandfather had been a dour Scot, and his great-grandmother an African slave and mistress'.[3] *Black Marsden*, in intertextual relation with a range of influential Scottish works, similarly engages this 'shared subjectivity' by invoking an explicit tradition, signalled by epigraphs from Hugh MacDiarmid, James Hogg and Kurt Wittig, and as Alan Riach observes, the plot shares many elements with Hogg's *The Private Memoirs and Confessions of a Justified Sinner* (1824).[4] *Black Marsden*'s detailed Edinburgh cityscape represents, as the novel's final sentence describes, 'one of the oldest cities in Europe', situated within a vision of worldly connectedness, a 'dawning thread of complex consciousness' that stretches from 'the shores of Scotland [. . .] around the globe'.[5] The novel's transnational imagination provides a unique bridge between Scotland and the Caribbean Artists Movement (CAM) in the 1960s and 1970s in London, a group that was the first to bear the designation of 'black British writing'.[6]

Second, the novel is completely distinct from even the quasi-naturalistic narratives of West Indian migration implied by Guptara's reference to writing 'about blacks in Britain', such as those of Sam Selvon, George Lamming or other CAM writers. Harris's writing is characterised by a 'complex texture of imaginative possibilities', an 'anti-realism' that totally reorganises temporal, spatial and narrative logics.[7] Commensurately, *Black Marsden*'s representation of race is defined by uncertain transposition. The character Knife is repeatedly re-racialised and re-epidermalised in the novel, transforming from a poor black Jamaican man, his face 'all pitted [. . .] a graveyard [. . .] a beehive', into a white man of aristocratic bearing, 'elegant' and 'expressionless'. Later, when Knife guides the protagonist Clive Goodrich through the post-colonial state of Namless, he is 'brown and more talkative than the others but he belonged to the same family as black Jamaican Knife and Marsden's white purgatorial Knife'.[8] The disconnection between Knife's contradictory raced characteristics and the consistent identification of him as a single character points to the provisional and constructed nature of race categories, a hyperbolic illustration of the way people can self-identify, or be racialised, differently in different contexts. This slippage is also part of the novel's playful deployment of race signifiers for other purposes. The novel is half-structured around an Edinburgh festival play, a 'tabula rasa' comedy, implying a space both white – the wax tablet – and black – the blank slate – into which esoteric elements enter via the ministrations and machinations of Doctor 'Black' Marsden himself. Marsden's blackness is not the same as Knife's. Indeed, his name seems ironic, emphasising that untrustworthy labelling process. The 'black' quality of Marsden is Faustian: he is closer to the esotericism, and the charisma, of Mephistopheles, Mikhail Bulgakov's Woland, or, as the epigraphs suggest, to James Hogg's Gil-Martin. 'Black' and 'white' are recurring, mysterious and entwined elements of the novel's aesthetic techniques: palimpsestic, the 'hidden blackboard in yesteryear's snow', and dialectic, the 'beautiful white' of the left hand and the 'beautiful black' of the right hand in Goodrich's idle dreams of a 'Comedy of Freedom'.[9] These motifs have their own historical resonance. Like other works emerging from CAM writers, *Black Marsden* hints at the tension between a named black politics – British Black Power was at its height at the end of the 1960s and early 1970s – and a literary imagination that necessarily resisted instrumentalisation.[10]

Race mutability and the Scottish national dimension come together in the moment when Mrs Glenwearie, Goodrich's Edinburgh housekeeper, unexpectedly reveals her past as an amateur actor, in which she was called upon to play both Grace Darling and Haile Selassie.[11] This is an absurd entanglement of Rastafarian messiah and white English heroine, with the intimation of blackface caricature, conjoined within a character who can recite 'Tam O'Shanter' from memory, and whose name directly connotes a tired-out formulation of touristic Scotland. Such confusion is coherent with the provocative juxtapositions, the protean, performative racial dimensions and the oblique intimations of racism of Harris's novel. It also signals a tangled field of cultural connection between black expressive culture and Scotland that remained mostly unimagined and untapped until a shift in the early 1980s. Black resistance to state racism, carried forward by street-level organisation and activism, and spearheaded culturally by figures like Linton Kwesi Johnson, became one of the defining counterweights to British state power, producing 'a body of transparently political writings, focused on local dimensions of injustice, and grounded in the experience of being black in Britain'.[12] At that moment, much Scottish literature and the political dimension of much black writing shared significant objectives, namely to challenge the ideological assumptions of Thatcherism; the unjust exercise of state power, and British institutional authority; the resolute cultural supremacy of Standard English, and the class system it represented; and the imperial yearning at the centre of British nationhood. Scottish writers in the period following 1979, for a variety of different reasons, tapped into the cultural-political zeitgeist of black experience, largely that of metropolitan England, but also through the transnational links of the black Atlantic to the Caribbean, the United States and Africa. The early works of black Scottish writers such as Maud Sulter and Jackie Kay, published in England, were energised by a politically conscious blackness, a lens through which to address black lived experience in a homogeneous white Scotland. Meanwhile, white writers including Alasdair Gray, James Kelman and Irvine Welsh mobilised blackness as part of a larger Scottish anti-colonial literary politics, and an interrogation of race and racism.

Aggregating these works is a project that extends David Dabydeen's *The Black Presence in English Literature* (1985), a collection which aimed to resituate and critique the literary representation of blackness, for the specific context of Scottish writing in the devolutionary period. Literary developments were actually catching up with Scottish academic research in black studies, in which Dabydeen, one of the pioneers of black British literary studies in the 1980s, played no small part. Much of the excavation of black history in Britain that would later form the basis of Dabydeen's co-edited *Oxford Companion to Black British History* (2007) had some basis in the department of English Literature at the University of Edinburgh, where the study of black writing was flourishing under the stewardship of Paul Edwards. Edwards was a Reader and later Professor of English and African Literature, from the 1970s until his death in 1992, and had an eclectic interest in African literature and 'the presence in Britain of people of African origin',[13] editing a modern edition of *The Life of Olaudah Equiano* (1969) and, with James Walvin, *Black Personalities in the Era of the Slave Trade* (1983).[14] He was a long-time collaborator with Dabydeen and contributed the only chapter on black writing, 'Black Writers of the Eighteenth and Nineteenth Centuries', to *The Black Presence in English Literature*.[15] Together, they went on to co-edit the Early Black Writers series published by Edinburgh University Press, five books from the early 1990s that focused on Ignatius Sancho, William Wells Brown, Robert Wedderburn, on black writing from 1760–1890, and letters from black settlers in Africa in the 1790s.[16] In addition to Wedderburn, the Early Black Writers scene at Edinburgh explored the lives of eighteenth- and nineteenth-century black people with a relationship to Scotland, such as James Ward, Anna Lashley-Tull and Tause Soga.[17] Furthermore, Edwards's 'salon' and extended academic network included significant black writers such as Harris, Kole Omotoso, Chinua Achebe and Caryl Phillips, for whom he reportedly offered comments on a preliminary draft of *Cambridge*.[18] Elsewhere in the Scottish higher education system, both Sam Selvon and Omotoso held positions as writers-in-residence at the Universities of Dundee (1975–7) and Stirling (1989–90) respectively. Even while Scotland remained marginal as a critical object in black British cultural studies, Scottish universities were providing an environment for the examination of black history and literatures.

'More red than black': Gray's *Lanark*

Like the 'black' in *Black Marsden*, the racial politics and subversive aesthetics of Alasdair Gray's *Lanark* (1981) bring the questions of race and racism to the fore in Scottish writing.[19] One of the most significant works of prose fiction in post-war Scotland, *Lanark* is both recollective and initiatory. Composed in various incarnations over three decades, the novel is regarded as a milestone, a 'state of the nation' text that pushed the boundaries of the novel form in ways that would be taken up by other writers. Those decades were also crucial in a larger timeline of decolonisation and black politics. Blackness in *Lanark* brings into relief the racial landscape of a post-Empire Scotland, and pre-empts some later comparisons between the marginal positions of Scots and the colonised world's racialised people. Painting an ambitious Old Testament mural inside a church in Cowlairs, the protagonist Duncan Thaw depicts Adam as black, in contrast to a 'pearly pink' Eve. Guilelessly, Thaw argues to a journalist from the *Evening News* that such a gesture is one of aesthetic and social unity, echoing Rubens's use of lines to show 'oneness' and colours to emphasise 'difference', to demonstrate that 'love makes different people feel like one'.[20] The Cowlairs minister's attempt at mitigation, that Adam is 'actually more red than black' as per the Hebrew translation of his name, disavows the wide-spread representation of Adam as a white paragon familiar in European art, but also manages to make the prospect of the artistic representation of Adam as a black man somehow ahistorical and unimaginable.[21] It becomes clear that the imagination of Adam as black constitutes a threatening radicalism in Scotland. The salacious tabloid story that results from the interview combines the 'Negro Adam', and the intimation of miscegenation, with a series of scandalising insinuations about Thaw himself: lustful, an atheist and a Marxist exposed as greedy for money. In this Scottish moral economy, breaching the unspoken sanctity of white Christianity seems to stand for a looming modernity, in which all progressive orientations are pathologised as individual moral deviance.

This 'making visible' of white assumptions forms a subtle part of the novel's broader social commentary. Thaw's black Adam is not the only example of a disruptive and generative black presence in the novel. The intertextual confessions in the 'Index of Plagiarisms' points to the way that the work of the Nigerian writer Amos Tutuola informs Lanark's own fantastical journeys. Tutuola has exerted some influence over contemporary Scottish writers, and his *The Palm Wine Drinkard and His Dead Palm-Wine Tapster in the Deads' Town* (1952) provides *Lanark* with the narrative model of a quest among 'dead or supernatural beings living in the same plane as the earthly'.[22] It is instructive that a storytelling mode that owes something to Tutuola's transliteration of Yoruba oral culture should provide the folkloric and linguistic resistance to bodies of 'official learning' and experiential regulation. Lanark's own 'Deads' Town' journey, which passes through the mouth opened up in the earth of the Necropolis and ends up in the mysterious Institute, has a racial politics encoded within it. The Institute embodies an Enlightenment history with its own raciological dimensions. Much Enlightenment rationalism had promulgated a racist worldview as part of a larger 'hierarchy of man'; Henry Louis Gates Jr has pointed squarely to David Hume as central to the *longue durée* of contemporary racism, providing the 'sanction of Enlightenment philosophical reasonings' to the myth of racial origin, which would echo on in the work of Immanuel Kant.[23] This is registered obliquely in *Lanark*'s treatment of 'official' or state-sanctioned learning, personified in figures such as Monboddo, the head of the governmental Council, and Professor Ozenfant, an arch-rationalist responsible for the scientific and medical Institute itself. Monboddo is explicitly linked in the 'Index of Plagiarisms' to the historical evolutionary thinker James Burnett, Lord Monboddo, who the Index notes has survived into posterity due to 'animadversions against his theory of human descent', and is one of a 'dynasty of scientific Caesars', and part of a genealogy of evolutionary thought both biological and linguistic.[24] The Institute demonstrates the material outcomes of the rationalism of Monboddo and Ozenfant in its hidden underbelly: a system of monstrous eugenicism and utilitarian cannibalism in which 'unfit' people are recycled for food or consumed for energy in the 'sinks' or 'pits' underground, a consumption of the human in the name of productivity with a strong correlation to slavery and other forms of racialised exploitation.

Lanark presents competing visions, between an anti-imperial transnational network suggested by the influence of Tutuola, and a neo-imperial continuity represented by the novel's figures of authority. During the novel's Epilogue and 'Climax' chapter, when both the reflexive experimentation and political analogy of the novel are at their sharpest, the novel's 'author-god' Nastler recommends that Lanark seek out 'a black man called Multan' who 'might be useful' in Lanark's quest to find a route out of the novel's 'overall plan'.[25] The meeting with Nastler takes place while Lanark, in his capacity as the Provost of Greater Unthank, attends the metropolitan Provan Assembly, an indeterminate delegate-based governance structure that is simultaneously reminiscent of institutional Edinburgh, Westminster, the then European Economic Community and the United Nations. Lanark, urban-industrial Scotland's putative representative, experiences a series of ignominies as his limited social and political literacy is continually exposed by the smooth operators of other interest groups, both national and corporate. Read alongside Lanark's eventual meeting with Multan of Zimbabwe, Nastler's emphasis on Multan's 'usefulness' hints at the prospect of radical potential through the association of African states, the 'black bloc'. This moment has clear historical roots in black anti-colonial nationalism: the 'black bloc' is suggestive of the Pan-African Congress, corroborated by Multan's articulate description of the neo-colonial exploitation of Africa. The composition of *Lanark* took place against the immediate backdrop of the Rhodesian Bush War (1964–79), or the Zimbabwe War of Liberation. Aside from the naming of Zimbabwe itself, there is a link to African liberation figures such as Robert Mugabe in the style of Multan's military garb and retinue, his reformative and independent post-imperial politics, and the very geopolitical marginality that seems to offer common cause to Lanark. Alignment with Multan's black collectivist politics offers a chance to disrupt the *telos* implied by the author-dictator's 'plan', to break definitively from an imperial project, and to intervene in the fated decline of Lanark's Unthank, or the post-industrial West of Scotland.

In Lanark's prospective meeting with Multan, *Lanark* anticipates later readings of Scotland as a proto-Fanonian national 'wretched', familiar from Beveridge and Turnbull's *The Eclipse of Scottish Culture*.[26] However, the novel introduces the possibility only to disavow it. When Lanark finally does meet Multan, the potential strategic alliance, as promised by Nastler, is proffered. Both post-industrial Unthank and post-independence Zimbabwe are deteriorating under an incipient neo-colonial and neoliberal economic regime, emblematised in *Lanark* by predatory corporations such as Algolagnics and Volstat, in thrall to the novel's abstracted 'creature' of capitalism, 'a conspiracy which owns and manipulates everything for profit'.[27] However, Lanark is rendered speechless at the precise moment when Multan offers common cause, and meaningful discourse seems possible:

> Multan said: 'Why you go on standing there if you got nothing to say?'
> 'I started this conversation and I don't know how to end it.'[28]

Despite the effects of a reorganisation of capital and production in the respective environments of Zimbabwe and Unthank, Lanark's silence indicates an inability to conceive of a shared resolution. One indictment here is against a lack of political confidence to achieve literally the revolutionary 'ends' of such an allegiance. Furthermore, this failure to act on the common trials of working-class Scotland and the African post-colony within a globalised world system is at some level a failure of discourse and of the imagination, of a conversation started but unfinishable. In the light of the nationally representative quality of the Assembly, Lanark's profound communicative difficulties in his encounter with Multan seem to suggest the insurmountable political disjunction between Scotland and the 'black bloc'. The moment pre-empts what Liam Connell calls the 'prevalent formula' in Scottish literary studies which designates Scotland as an English colony; *Lanark*'s counter-example of an actual postcolonial history makes clear that no such conflation is possible.[29]

The national aspirations of Lanark cannot be squared with the anti-colonial nationalism proposed in *The Wretched of the Earth*. Reading Lanark as an artist-representative, his unworldliness and lack of cosmopolitan *élan* might suggest an apt metaphor for an 'inferiorised' and introspective national culture. However, the postcolonial encounter with Multan, coded in racial terms, brings with it implications beyond a general parochialism or loss of confidence in Scottish politics and culture. It is significant that Lanark's whiteness becomes denaturalised, named and rendered visible, in his capacity as political representative at the international Provan Assembly. The dialogue compounds the sense of incongruity between disjoined polities. In the context of national profiles that are also racial, whiteness as a characteristic of the imagined Scottish nation is made manifest: the Scotland encoded in the character of Lanark remains a stubbornly white space. The disjunction between Unthank and Zimbabwe is not simply one of economics, geography or geopolitical power. It is also a racialised barrier that materialises at the level of language and imagination. Multan realises that Lanark requires an interlocutor:

> 'Let me help you off the hook, man. Come here, Omphale.'
> A tall elegant black woman approached. Multan said, 'Omphale, this delegate needs to talk to a white woman.'
> 'But I'm black. As black as you are,' said the woman in a clear, hooting voice.
> 'Sure, but you got a white voice,' said Multan, moving away.[30]

Unthank's representative is white; he cannot 'speak' to the black figure. Omphale, her name derived from the Greek for 'navel' or 'axis', is introduced as a prospective bridging presence between the linguistic and cultural positions of white Lanark and black Multan. Following Fanon's 'The Black Man and Language' from *Black Skin, White Masks*, it is instructive that Omphale's voice is the characteristic that reveals her whiteness. As Fanon argues, '[t]o speak means being able to use a certain syntax and possessing the morphology of such and such a language, but it means above all assuming a culture and bearing the weight of a civilization'.[31] Her voice is tantamount to donning the 'white mask' demanded of black people in order to 'assume the culture' – imperial, white – of Lanark.[32] Conversely, Multan's political blackness refuses to 'speak white'. This is amplified by the transliteration of his voice as sociolinguistically and idiomatically distinctive, a kind of televisual African-American which stands in for the decolonising ambitions of an international movement of black power, grounded in the United States and manifested around the world. Multan's speech also serves to emphasise Lanark's own Standard English, which adapts to the corporate and euphemistic idiom of Provan the longer he stays: 'I don't usually think in words like these but they seem appropriate here'.[33] Looping back to Liam Connell, the whiteness of Lanark's language is a dramatic reversal of the Cairns Craig argument about the 'colour of [Scotland's] vowels'.[34] Rather than offering a racialised differentiation from a rapacious and colonising England, the speaking voice of Scotland's literary-political representative instead secures the shared racial character of the whole of the British enterprise.

The race consciousness of *Lanark* is developed in Gray's later works in ways that continue to chisel away at Scotland's imperial past and present. The hyper-Scottified 'Jock McLeish' in *1982, Janine* constructs elaborate fantasies of restraint, imprisonment, surveillance and degradation, the psychosexual sublimation of a world understood as a giant 'security installation'.[35] One of the activities of McLeish's 'Forensic Research Punishment and Sexual Gratification Syndicate' is to import black women to Europe and America from South Africa, 'a fresh cargo of *black molasses*' destined for, among other places, Glenrothes via the Methil docks.[36] Black women are exoticised as objects of sexual slavery: Glenrothes, McLeish muses, 'does need the extra colour, the extra sweetness of some black molasses'.[37] The passage connotes an ideological sympathy between McLeish's authoritarian Benthamite outlook, heavily intimated to be part of his conservatism, and apartheid-era South Africa, a model 'security society' demarcated by racial zoning, stratified and fortified by pass laws, state surveillance and gated communities. But this reference is also a subtle moment of analepsis secured by the uncommon word 'molasses'. Later in the novel, McLeish reminisces about his youth as part of a group of artists who commandeer a disused property in Edinburgh in order to put on a play. The building is august but derelict, and the doors bear 'names indicating forgotten functions: *molasses room, sugar room, candy room, accounts*'.[38] The dusty, stone rooms are part of a forgotten economic history, rooted in the imperial sugar trade and plantation slavery, that underpins so much of Scotland's contemporary wealth, and which is still registered architecturally and in the onomastics of places like Jamaica Street and Tobago Street. McLeish's fantasies of sexual slavery are analogous to Scotland's actual history of slavery.

Gray was breaking ground in terms of Scotland's colonial culpability ahead of later, and more recognised, examples, and the boom in critical material on slavery that followed devolution. There is a similar attention to Scotland's 'fragmented and incoherent' imperial past in a 'profound amnesia' shared with Bella Baxter from Gray's *Poor Things* (1992).[39] In 'The Missionaries', Bella is introduced to the racial hierarchy of the world via the oratory of Dr Hooker, who reiterates the missionary burden of the 'Anglo-Saxon race' to which the chapter title refers; without the 'superior virtues' of whiteness, 'Black people eat each other'.[40] The lectures from Hooker and Astley on the racial-economic structure of the world are reminiscent of the 'official learning' foregrounded in *Lanark*. Rather than the abstracted moral and pedagogical duty that Dr Hooker describes, the realities of the 'white man's burden' are evidenced in a traumatising scene in Alexandria. The material basis of race difference is rendered economically and topographically, as white tourists throw coins to crowds of sick and destitute people from the raised platform of a hotel veranda.[41] The effect on Bella of this incomprehensible hierarchy, personified in a half-blind girl carrying a blind baby, is the cue for the novel's total abandonment of orthography: a span of six pages of indistinct, gouged and tear-stained handwriting.[42] Bella, a figure later appropriated as an icon of the prospective 'better nation' of an independent Scotland, stands for an intellectual curiosity unbowed by ideological prejudice, but also for a childlike condition of ignorance.[43] Her psychic shock at the violence of a racially hierarchised world echoes Lanark's experiences at Provan – both experience an epiphanic encounter with racialised difference – and denaturalises the whiteness of Scotland's nationally representative figures within a larger imagination of imperial history.

Ebonite in ethereal Scotland

Lanark's nationally representative Provan imagines Scotland at the beginning of the 1980s as inheriting a white raciological past, and still enmeshed within a post-imperial racial epistemology: a white country entering into a compact with a neo-imperial world order, premised on white solidarity. Little surprise, therefore, that Scotland's black writers working in the aftermath of *Lanark*'s publication were drawn to a diasporic, anti-racist black solidarity developing in England, while reflecting on the disconnection between that formation and life in Scotland. Metropolitan England provided the environment, opportunities and venues for black writers. Both Maud Sulter and Jackie Kay, active from the early 1980s, broke through initially in the context of a black arts movement in London. Sulter's first collection, *As a Black Woman*, was published by the radical black press Akira in 1985. The emphatically political quality of the collection is evident from the first, eponymous poem, 'As a Blackwoman', which details a history of reproductive control and racist violence imposed on black mothers, and argues that 'As a blackwoman / every act is a personal act / every act is a political act'.[44] What follows in Sulter's poetry adheres closely to that maxim, taking in a range of black political concerns including pan-Africanism, black feminism, the National Front, the gentrification of black Brixton, police racism, apartheid violence in South Africa and transracial adoption.

Sulter's aesthetics are firmly committed to what Stuart Hall calls 'the counter-position of "positive" black imagery', to oppose the pervasive racist stereotypes that were manifested acutely through Enoch Powell and remained active throughout the 1970s and into the 1980s, but her poetry also set down a marker against the monochromatic social and cultural context of Scotland.[45] Adapting and assembling a black feminist poetics for her own specific context from diverse transnational sources, Sulter's poetics are an example of 'sarkaesthetics', representations of the 'body experienced from a third-person perspective, through the external senses', which Paul C. Taylor describes as a key mediation between the social orientations he names as 'negrophobia' and 'negrophilia'.[46] A persistent thread through *As a Black Woman* and Sulter's subsequent *Zabat: Poetics of a Family Tree* is the celebration of blackness through the body: 'I want to rejoice / in the blackness / of the skin'; 'I want to sing / of Africa / in the touch'.[47] There is a hint of Afrofuturism in Sulter's invention of 'Ebonite', a material inspired by the strength and beauty of black bodies, both 'Solid as a / rock / of / ages / past' and possessing an erotic 'silkness'.[48] These lines owe much to the earlier 'Black is Beautiful' moment from the United States in the 1960s, a counter-aesthetic which had focused on 'revaloriz-ing' the black body.[49] The consequent belatedness of Sulter's sarkaesthet-ics points less to their derivative or anachronistic quality, and more to an attempt to introduce a counter-position into a Scottish context defined by loneliness. Illustratively, in 'Scots Triptych', blackness is 'a bond / before speech / or encounter' for two lovers exploring the east coast, gesturing towards its radical alterity in Scottish terms.[50]

Zabat continues the juxtaposition of an Afrocentric diasporic con-sciousness with both an alienating white Scotland and an oppressive British state. In 'A Poem of Love', 'Africa beckons us with her bittersweet call', a call away from Scotland as a 'retrograde beast' or 'surrogate home' that commodifies and consumes the 'communal soul'.[51] While the poem concludes with the assertion that 'We are african [*sic*] people and we are going home', this homecoming connotes a state of mind rather than a spatial return; with the development of a black consciousness arranged in opposition and resistance to a 'white ethereal cultural void', the persona argues that the 'entire world can be our rightful home'.[52] In 'Riot', that resistance is encoded poetically through engagement with the street-level violence of the Metropolitan Police in London, which links intertextually to the work of Linton Kwesi Johnson, probably the pre-eminent black poet in Britain in the early 1980s. The poem's persona is 'violated / by the power and anger / of this state which denies me', describing Britain as 'Babylon', the Rastafarian land of exile and a recurring Johnsonian trope.[53] The motif of blood in 'Riot', which also recurs in Johnson's poems from the 1970s such as 'Five Nights of Bleeding' or 'Song of Blood', with its 'drums poundin blood gushin down',[54] marks another commonality, articulating the consequences of police violence and a rhythmical circula-tory system that is, like Johnson's reggae bass-lined dub poetry, embodied in the heart, the communal experience of performance, and the poetics itself: 'blood pumps / rhythmically / in motion / and time / with my / heartbeat'.[55]

For a politically conscious black poet from Scotland, working in the mid-1980s, the questions posed by a writer like Johnson hold more sig-nificance than the devolutionary 'crisis' that purportedly animates other Scottish writing. Sulter's work evidences a different kind of Scottish poetic project. One is to describe Scotland as precisely a kind of 'white ethereal cultural void'. 'The Privilege of the Fairskinned' offers a juxtaposition of racism in England and Scotland; in the former, 'light skin gets you this / light skin gets you that', while in Scotland, 'Up there / If you're the only black / in the neighbourhood / it makes no difference // Nigger Darkie Paki / all means the same to them'.[56] The invited comparison is between a context of racial gradation and contestation versus one where non-white minority is so absolute that models of British political blackness remain in play by default, a distinction that would be confirmed and extended later in Suhayl Saadi's *Psychoraag*. In 'Historical Objects', Sulter's critique of colonialism in Africa focuses intently on Scotland's role in Empire via the epistemological power of the titular 'objects'.[57] Benedict Anderson argues that in the foundation, legitimation and adaptation of national narratives, 'museums, and the museumizing imagination, are both profoundly political', and they are acutely significant in the commemoration and contestation of colonial legacies.[58] The poem describes a black African and diasporic history through an assembly of imperially appropriated objects held in Europe, where the colonial project of collecting and narrating artefacts as part of the generation of new and instrumental knowledge, the postcolonial idea of 'epistemic violence', is connected directly to the missionary enterprise of David Livingstone that links Tanzania and Scotland. The contemporary inscription of that imperial history is a society structured according to the principles of a plantation hierarchy – a 'planation';[59] the injunction of the poem is that Scotland's imperial past must be forsworn because 'Civilisation can never / be written in the blood and bones of slavery'.[60]

Even a homogeneous, 'ethereally' white Scotland, still bound up with its unexamined imperial past, has a national distinctiveness that is apparent in Sulter's vernacular poetry. In 'Flight', the persona flees 'To the frozen North', to 'Another country', a country given clear definition by a dialectal shift away from standard English: 'Well a hid tae get away couldn'y staun the pressure / n a couldn'y face the reality o bein sae loved'.[61] Meanwhile, in 'Thirteen Stanzas', a black woman reminisces about life in Scotland in her youth, the 'shoapin centre', a 'roll n sausage', and 'heroin runnin'.[62] Commemorating a friendship with a white working-class woman who has undergone a hysterectomy, the poem offers a vision of a transracial feminism:

> rememberance · of yir fair self · of a friendship between
>   women · white working
> class woman · black working class girl · a cross · the divide
>   of race · we were
> women in struggle · women in struggle · women in
>   struggle · united[63]

While pan-Africanism and a black cultural politics in England provide Sulter with expressive models and a history of a different kind of struggle, poems like 'Flight' and 'Thirteen Stanzas' still encode the distinctive language politics that differentiate Scottish writing; they also constitute a claim on a literary language that had hitherto been the special preserve of white Scottish writers. Simply by experimenting with a vernacular Scots that represents black experience, Sulter's poetics are an eloquent refutation of any idea that the textual forms of exclusion diagnosed as characteristic of Scottish literature, and Scots language, can be compared to the totalising forms of social exclusion that define blackness under colonial and neo-colonial racism.[64]

In the context of a devolutionary Scotland whose implicit racial coding was primarily white, without being explicitly ethno-purist, black life was something that appeared to be happening 'elsewhere': either in a 'fantasy Africa', a heavily mediatised black America, or on the streets of the large English cities. This exteriority is visible in the writing of Jackie Kay, who would go on to become Scotland's Makar, but whose first significant work, the two-act play *Chiaroscuro*, was created and set in England.[65] The play provides an index of some of the exclusions that had defined what Hall called 'the essential black subject' at the crux of the 'New Ethnicities' argument, the political formation conceived of as predominantly male, heterosexual and Afro-Caribbean.[66] Kay's characters are positioned at symbolic and disruptive points on the spectra of black life. Yomi, a Nigerian Christian woman, represents a pole of sexual and racial orthodoxy; for her, non-heteronormative relationships are unnatural and blackness is simple, absolute and biocentric, 'in the blood'. Counterposed against Yomi are Beth and Opal, two lesbian women in a relationship, for whom blackness and mixed-racedness are ongoing social and political negotiations. The play is illuminated by moments of explicit political observation, such as Opal's exchange with one of her white patients: 'I just told her that I didn't like the word coloured, and she asked me what I'd call myself then. I told her black. She laughed and said "But you're a half-caste["]'.[67] The implication of the 'half-caste' label, and Yomi's exclusion of both Beth and Opal from blackness, approach mixed-racedness from different sides of a black–white binary, with the same underlying logic: a biocentric understanding of race that emphasises purity rather than the contingency of discursive race formation, or Opal's political self-identification and the authenticity of her lived experience. The quartet of characters in *Chiaroscuro* is completed by Aisha, implied to be the daughter of South Asian migrants whose grandmother was 'born in the Himalayas' and who, similarly excluded from a black political constituency, expresses dismay that Afro-Caribbean women tell her she has 'no right' to call herself black.[68] At the heart of the play is the examination of blackness as a political category and as a lived experience, and a concomitant rejection of colour gradation and biocentrism, particularly for black women.

While *Chiaroscuro* is marked by close attention to the assumptions and exclusions that feature in Kay's later work, clear national differentiation for Scotland is not one of them – excepting, perhaps, the moment when Aisha describes one of her primary fears as 'never [fitting] in back home [. . .] or worse they'd call me English'.[69] The characters themselves have transnational affiliations; references suggest the play is set in London, near Haringey, though the staging instructions are for a clear stage and predominantly 'pale grey' backdrop, neutralising its placedness.[70] The absence of any Scottish national specificity makes sense in the context of the play's genesis. It was commissioned by and workshopped with the Theatre of Black Women, a London-based black feminist collective, and was first performed in 1985 at the Gay Sweatshop × 10 Festival, before being presented later at the Soho Poly Theatre in London.[71] Like Sulter's poetry, the play flags up the way that black writing in Britain in the 1980s cohered around a 'scene' centred on English metropolitan life, a context that governed the early formation and reception of black Scottish writing.

Scotland features much more prominently in Kay's first poetry collection, *The Adoption Papers*, although the collection itself, like Sulter's work, was supported primarily by venues outside of Scotland, published by Bloodaxe, performed on BBC Radio 3, and with individual poems published in mainly American and English periodicals.[72] The first section, 'The Adoption Papers' themselves, dramatises a transracial adoption in Central Belt Scotland, marked by place-bound references and Scots: 'Ma mammy bot me oot a shop / Ma mammy says I was a luvly baby'.[73] The adoption is facilitated by a chance remark that 'we don't mind the colour', which suddenly offers parenthood to the would-be mother, suggestive of the way that, as John McLeod has delineated, the history of transracial adoption in post-war Britain can be read as a history of racial discrimination.[74] For social workers, the 'genetic culture' of racialised infants presented 'an immediate threat to the domestic environs of middle class England', while anti-racist practice coincidentally reinforced race 'matching' on the basis that only black parents could equip black children with the cultural literacy to negotiate racism.[75] Adoption is thus a site of stark racial definition historically, but, in its reorganisation of parent–child assumptions, brings about a quality of profound relationality across racial categories, 'putting into crisis [. . .] those "consanguinous" discourses which construct notions of racial and cultural sameness through metaphors of "common blood"'.[76] This crisis of consanguinity manifests in 'The Adoption Papers', as the adoptee expresses a profound natal connection to Scotland, 'the land I

come from / the soil in my blood', yet recognises the contradictory quality of consanguinous belonging, 'the blood, the tie, the passing-down /
generations', juxtaposed against her parents of a different 'tree'.[77]

The privileging of the elective over the biogenetic in transracial adoption has clear parallels to the civic–ethnic division in Scottish national
terms. The adoptee's meditation on 'soil in the blood' is twofold. It articulates the difficulty in disentangling a meaningful shared past – an *ethnos*
– from the myth of consanguinity and its racial correlates. These concerns
are pressing for Kay, informed by an upbringing in close proximity to the
anti-racist and pro-devolutionary Communist Party of Great Britain, for
whom her father was an organiser and parliamentary candidate.[78] It is also
a protestation of national belonging in the face of both racial assumptions
and the prevailing whiteness of Scotland which surface in the collection.
In 'Chapter 7: Black Bottom', the adoptee is racially abused at school by
students and teachers alike. Where Harris's Mrs Glenwearie can play Haile
Selassie in the church play, the adoptee is excluded from the school play
of *The Prime of Miss Jean Brodie* on the basis of a racial common sense,
and with it, excluded symbolically from the Scottish literary imagination
populated by white characters.[79] Instead, her sympathies are elicited by the
American Black Power movement in the figure of Angela Davis; black role
models are thin on the ground in Scotland, especially those with a meaningful politics of resistance attached. In 'Photo in the Locket', correspondence between one black woman in Africa and another in Scotland provides
a series of comparisons that paint a picture of the unrelenting mono-
chrome of the latter setting, synaesthetically reinforced by the pervasive
cold: 'My mother is white. My father is white. / My lover is white. At night
we lie / Like spoons breathing the same cold air'.[80] Indicatively, when the
two correspondents are united, the African woman notes that 'it's better
for her now down here / in London',[81] returning to the common thread
running through both Sulter and Kay's work: that London affords a sense
of black community and solidarity largely absent in Scotland at the time.

Kelman, optical race and the all-seeing state

Sulter and Kay were not the only Scottish writers focused on the racist injus-
tices of the British state on the streets of London. James Kelman's polemical
essays reveal an acute awareness of the realities of racism and race politics in
Britain. In his 1992 essay collection *Some Recent Attacks*, Kelman pointedly
observes that racism is a structural feature of British imperialism; that ethnicity applies only to people who are not white; that by the end of the 1980s
'30,000 racial attacks occur annually' in Britain; and that institutions of the

British state are designed to victimise black people.[82] Racism is not simply an English problem, either: he singles out for special attention the racially aggravated murder of the Somalian refugee Ahmed Shekh in Edinburgh in 1989, a topic to which he would return in *'And the Judges Said': Essays* (2002), where he makes clear that racism is a unilateral violence done to black people by white people, purposefully and reiteratively including Scotland in his frame of reference.[83] Such an anti-racism did, however, retain some class-based caveats, such as where Kelman argues that 'a great many black people' have 'no conception of [. . .] the everyday brutalities the British state perpetuates on [. . .] its so-called white brothers and sisters'.[84] This committed anti-racism finds some expression in Kelman's Glasgow novels, where his protagonists have moments of anti-racist consciousness: both Pat Doyle in *A Disaffection* and Sammy Samuels in *How Late It Was, How Late* signal their disapproval of racist sentiments and racist language.[85] Meanwhile, Kelman's developing interest in race and racism, and in particular whiteness and the representational challenges inherent in a white writer imagining black characters, is evidenced by a more direct engagement in his later novels, such as *You Have to Be Careful in the Land of the Free* (2004), *Mo Said She Was Quirky* (2012) and *Dirt Road* (2016).

Kelman has acknowledged an early influence from black American writers such as Richard Wright, Eldridge Cleaver, Ralph Ellison and James Baldwin, writers whose anti-racist political activation chimes with his own 'politics of commitment'. Like Gray, Kelman cites Amos Tutuola as an influence, one of a set of African writers, including Alex La Guma, Okot p'Bitek and Ayi Kwei Armah, whom he defined as resistant to cultural assimilation, an 'ultimate surrender' into a value system manifested in what Kelman calls a 'standard prose form'.[86] The rejection of this prose form, an English literature that carries the ideological weight and cultural values of imperial Britishness via an omniscient and 'neutral' third-person narrative, is one way in which the linguistic and orthographical challenges of his writing share a position with writers such as Tutuola. This commonality is also to be found in Sam Selvon, with whom Kelman claimed a shared perspective on literary language, and in the Caribbean Artists Movement:

> [CAM] recognised one fundamental issue, that for the artists of a marginalised culture there is little or no assessment of their creative output. Genuine criticism will not exist within a context defined by the dominant culture. Even where such creative output is noticed by the dominant culture it remains subject to it, judged by its criteria of what is 'good'.[87]

At the earlier point of *Some Recent Attacks*, this 'marginalisation' is a national phenomenon close to the 'inferiorisation' thesis of a racialised Scotland: for 'the ruling elite of Great Britain', 'so-called Scottish culture

[. . .] is inferior, just as *ipso facto* the Scottish people are also inferior'.[88] This position has been textured somewhat by *'And the Judges Said'*, insofar as the 'marginal' and 'dominant' cultures are less defined by a national 'people', in part because the very existence of CAM in England forces the recognition of the way that cultural dominance exerted in Britain is less a question of sub-national relationships and more a question of state-led cultural hierarchies, and class and racial stratification.

Consonance between black expression and Kelman's narrative form has already been noted, for example in Uwe Zagratzki's reading of a common 'rhetoric of situativity', 'immediacy and actionality' across blues singers and *How Late It Was, How Late*.[89] But such a consonance also exists in more local terms, in a shared cultural framework oriented towards a critique of Britain and class- and race-based domination. This is rooted in Kelman's first-hand witnessing of black lives in Britain's capital, where he worked alongside West Indian labourers on the Barbican site during the 1960s, and later collaborated with the Race Today Collective in London. Kelman had a long-standing friendship with John La Rose of New Beacon Books, who gave him reading recommendations, and with whom he twice collaborated to hold the International Book Fair of Radical Black and Third World Books.[90] The similarities between the protagonist of *The Busconductor Hines* and the West Indian writer Donald Hinds, a contemporary of Sam Selvon who, like Kelman, worked as a bus conductor, is fortuitous. It is also, as Kelman himself puts it, exactly the kind of literature that John La Rose might have recommended to him.[91] The coincidence between Hines and Hinds is more than homophonic. In 'Busman's Blues', Hinds presents a semi-autobiographical narrative of a newly arrived Jamaican bus conductor in London, whose juniority, frenetic working environment, sociability and independence of mind have some overlap with Rob Hines.[92] Hinds' short story transgresses 'standard prose form' not only through its transliteration of a London English, but also in its sharing something of the narrative mode of *The Busconductor Hines*, the effacement of differentiation between thought and speech that occurs in moments of narrative reverie:

> 'Yes, you will be all right.'
> 'Thanks,' she said.
> My privilege, I said voicelessly.
> I don't know, I thought she said, or maybe it was telepathic.
> I am dying to say that I've seen you before. But that is a bit hackneyed.
> Yes, it would be. Try something else.[93]

The shared features of *Hines* and Hinds introduces the possibility of some common aesthetic response across CAM and Kelman's typographical project to the ideological imperatives – largely British-imperial, class-based and white – of 'standard prose form'.

Moreover, the orientation of Kelman's fiction in the late 1980s and early 1990s towards state violence has an oblique but perceptible connection to black experience, specifically in the treatment of black men by the Metropolitan Police. Part of the evidence base for such a claim comes through in his non-fiction writing: detailed analysis of the racism of British police recurs through his essays, impelled by his long participation in the campaign for justice in the case of the murder of Stephen Lawrence. This critique of the British state is influenced by his experiences of anti-racist activism, and by the forms of cultural solidarity it opened up to him. In his fiction, the Scottish police are not represented as per the rebarbative Jim Taggart, the rule-flexing and mob-fraternising John Rebus or the effete middle-class officers of *Rab C. Nesbitt*. They are a faceless body of threat, a militarised occupying force – 'sodjers' in the parlance of *How Late It Was, How Late* – representative of state power. The increasing visibility of militarised police power in Britain, dramatically illustrated by scenes like the Orgreave picket during the Miners' Strike in 1984, had been a day-to-day reality for black men in London for much longer, and it is the latter experience that is suggested by crucial moments in Kelman's work. The closing scene of *A Disaffection* foregrounds the protagonist Pat Doyle's visibility in the eyes of the police, who he notices 'observing him openly and frankly', 'watching him now in a serious and suspicious manner'.[94] Foreshadowing the disparities between seeing and not-seeing inherent to the panopticist state in the later *How Late It Was*, Doyle feels acutely the power imbalance in being seen by state operatives, but unable to 'see' back. To look at the police is a 'sign of guilt, of criminality, of his being suspicious, a suspicious being'; unlike Sammy Samuels, the blind protagonist of *How Late It Was* whose final act is to vanish 'out of sight' into a taxi, Doyle specifically cannot find the refuge of a taxi.[95] The combination of Doyle's emphatic visibility and the reiteration of a lexis of suspicion echoes the so-called 'SUS' or 'suspected person' laws, the reawakening of Victorian-era acts regulating vagrancy that enabled stop-and-search policies disproportionately targeted at young black men in London. That inescapable visibility relies on visible difference that, while not being without class dimensions, has historically been most obviously phenotypical: it is the black man on the streets of London who cannot 'blend in', upon whom suspicion falls and upon whom the egregious violence of the state is commonly visited.

The acknowledgement in Kelman's essays of this violence provides further evidence for the sublimation of raced experience into his work. In *Some Recent Attacks* he points to black deaths in police custody – among others, of Amasase (Omasase) Lumumba, Joy Gardner, Ibrahima Sey, Brian Douglas and Wayne Douglas – in each case drawing attention to the police 'recording mode', to the descriptive language used of the killing, of the investigation and of the inevitable exoneration.[96] Lumumba, for example, died while 'being restrained by prison officers, allegedly attempting to break free'.[97] This language forms the basis of the 'impartial' state discourse deployed in *How Late It Was, How Late*, where white Scottish Sammy Samuels finds himself enmeshed in the same 'recording' language to describe the attack which causes him to lose his sight: 'They were using physical restraints. [. . .] Aye well that's all I'm saying miss it was restraints, they were doing restraints and I wound up blind'.[98] 'Restraints' is an obscuring euphemism, part of the discursive toolbox of state agencies, laid bare by the sharp disjunction between 'doing restraints' and the injuries Sammy suffers. The constant tapping of the administrator's keyboard accompanying Sammy's testimony reinscribes the recording function of such language, assembling a body of evidence that shapes the world textually according to the priorities of the state form. Kelman's account of Lumumba's death provides a direct precedent for this euphemistic enshrouding, where the reasonableness of police action is guaranteed by 'restraint' even in the aftermath of the death of the detainee.

Both *A Disaffection* and *How Late It Was, How Late* represent a police force, the actions of which bear a great deal of resemblance to the practices of racialised policing on the streets of London as much as to documented actions in other contemporaneous 'public' theatres such as the Miners' Strike or the Troubles. In *Playing in the Dark*, Toni Morrison questions why 'black people ignite critical moments of discovery or change or emphasis in literature not written by them'.[99] Her answer is tied to the particular condition of race in the United States, but the question might well be applied to a writer like Kelman. There is a vexed question of representation here, where black experience provides, if not a wholesale model, some adaptable raw materials put to use in Kelman's state-critical project that, in his own terms in *Some Recent Attacks*, is connected to the state's brutality towards its own 'white brothers and sisters' in Scotland. The violence directed at black people by the state provides an illustrative model of its unjust exercise of power more broadly: in the play of 'visibility' which characterises power differentials between individual citizens and an omniscient state personified in the police force, the visual character of race, the 'extra-discursive referent' in Gilroy's terms, is an amplifying feature.[100] An alternative interpretation is available. Rather than an act of experiential appropriation, the sensory deficits of Kelman's novels are suggestive of empathy and political solidarity; Sammy's blindness means he can no longer 'see' race, while his vulnerability, like Pat Doyle's, is cast explicitly as the police's superior ability to see him, in an attempt to work through the visual violation of racialised policing.

Welsh, denigration and the 'resignification of class'

Morrison's query about the 'critical ignition' provided by black people for white writers might also be usefully applied to Irvine Welsh, whose early novels track the uneven period between Thatcherism and the Scottish Parliament, and in which blackness is a consistent textual presence. Where black experience in Britain is rendered obliquely in Kelman's Glasgow novels, Welsh's fiction provides a much more explicit representation of race and racism in Scotland. That this is in part a response to the racial politics of Unionism and Thatcherism is clear in both *Trainspotting* and *Marabou Stork Nightmares*, but Welsh's first post-referendum novel, *Filth* (1998), makes clear that devolution provides no immediate solution to racism in Scotland, acknowledging instead the deep continuities in post-imperial melancholia that remain even after 1997. *Trainspotting*'s indictment of the racism of the late 1970s and 1980s is most explicitly found in the vignette 'Na Na and Other Nazis'. Dode, the cousin of Daniel 'Spud' Murphy, is the son of an itinerant West Indian sailor; his symbolic detachment from any patrilineal ancestry helps to naturalise him within the Edinburgh world of the novel, reinforced by his introduction, 'slumped in a chair, sippin a can ay Tennent's Lager'.[101] That this section is imagined as nationally constitutive is made clear by Spud's commentary, that 'some cats say that racism's an English thing and we're aw Jock Tamson's bairns up here [. . .] it's likesay pure shite man'; the abolition of the 'Scottish myth' of egalitarianism is clear in Spud's didactic gesture towards an emphatically Scottish racism.[102] However, despite Spud's words to the contrary, this identification of racism is markedly a Unionist, if not English, formation in 'Na Na and Other Nazis'. When Dode is subjected to racist abuse, it is within the context of a pan-British demography defined by staunch Unionism, a collection of Scottish, English and Belfast accents in a pub dominated by Orange Order marchers: 'One guy's goat a Skrewdriver T-shirt oan, another's likesay wearin an *Ulster is British* toap'.[103] The initial racist provocation of the vignette, 'Oi! Wot you fucking looking at nigger!', perpetrates nothing so much as an outsourcing of Edinburgh racism to an English skinhead stereotype.[104] The dialectal implication of 'Wot' aligns racist abuse with a South English voice, and even the exclamation 'Oi!' homophonically invokes a genre of punk music largely English-based and associated with Anglo-Saxon white supremacism, including Skrewdriver, the most notorious of the English neo-fascist skinhead bands. The master sign of the English skinhead is confirmed with the borrowed chants of 'You black bastard!' and 'Aint no black in the Union Jack' directed at Dode.

'Na Na and Other Nazis' concedes the absurdity of the 'Jock Tamson's bairns' mythology and the immanence of racist thought in Scotland, but also moves the language and frame of reference back to a recognisable Anglo-British scene. In this, *Trainspotting* observes that the psychopathological condition of post-colonial melancholy articulated by Gilroy, triggered by the visibility of the black figure as a latent reminder of the 'painful loss of Empire', is as much a problem in Scotland as in England, most easily mobilised as part of a nostalgic and confrontational Unionism. This finds a more explicit registration in Welsh's second novel, *Marabou Stork Nightmares*, which situates Scotland within a narrative of past imperial glories and modern 'settler neo-colonialism'. The *Bildungsroman* of the narrator, Roy Strang, is part-situated in the context of social deprivation in housing-scheme Edinburgh and the relative prosperity of expatriate life in white South Africa. As with *Trainspotting*'s white supremacists, the novel's racist Scots are marked out as Unionists, outspoken proponents of Empire clinging to a vision of imperial grandeur in a neo-imperial present. Roy's father John Strang's fierce loyalty towards Margaret Thatcher, the 'best fuckin leader Britain's hud', is apostasy for most strains of Scottish nationalist thought, and contributes to a holistic picture of Scottish Conservatism hardwired to the Union's imperial project, where '[t]he Scots built the empire n these daft English cunts couldnae run it withoot us'.[105] John's missionary zeal emphasises the so-called 'Scottish Empire', the central role of Scots in the British imperial enterprise, and, much like Michael Fry's account of Scottish history, is tinged with a note of regret for lost imperial adventure.[106] The stereotype of the imperial Scot is amplified even further by John's brother Gordon, an 'unreconstructed pro-apartheid white supremacist' and expatriate reaping a neo-colonial harvest in Johannesburg, whose political position is that Thatcher 'sold Rhodesia down the fucking river'.[107] Beyond even his brother's Conservative loyalties, Gordon represents post-colonial nostalgia at its most explicit and vitriolic, in which the 'reduced circumstances' of imperial Britain constitute a betrayal of the 'white man's world' by Thatcher's eventual settlement with Robert Mugabe in Zimbabwe.

Roy's childhood experiences form the raw stuff of a later dreamworld which manifests phantasmically the melancholic colonial fantasies of the contemporary Union. His vivid comatose dreams take the form of an elaborate imperial adventure constructed in his unconscious imagination in much the same mode as John Orr's 'bridge world' in Iain Banks's *The Bridge* (1986), fantasies which amplify the apartheid racial separation and domination of his sojourn in 'Sooth Efrikay'. The parodic colonial adventure framed in *Marabou Stork Nightmares* reworks elements of John Buchan's *Prester John,* and lacerates Buchan's conception of Britishness as a racially defined hierarchy of moral value. The 'larking' tone of Strang's safari hunt for the marabou stork, described as 'THE GAME', and his idiosyncratic travelling companionship with Sandy Jamieson, a former professional football player, dovetails with a British narrative of colonial recuperation that, as Gilroy explains, 'projects empire as essentially a form of sport'.[108] The exaggerated wholesomeness of the dialogue and the righteous quest to kill the stork are punctured by the material realities of apartheid racism, in the extreme poverty and prostitution of black children who offer sex acts 'for rand'.[109]

The brute historicity of the offer of sex for money, contrasted with the hyper-fictional adventure narrative, suggests the invasion of the dreamworld by suppressed memories of Roy's own time in South Africa. The moment of surfacing from the immersive colonial adventure accentuates some of the national politics at work in the novel. As Roy oscillates on the verge of waking from his coma, his internal monologue screams out, 'SCOTLAND. NO. THIS IS SUPPOSED TO BE AFRICA OR SOMEWHERE OR EVEN INSIDE MY HEAD WHICH IS NOT A COUNTRY'.[110] The moment is doubly suggestive. First, it points towards the abrupt end of a colonial fantasy configured as a return to consciousness, a 'remembering' that stands in opposition to postcolonial amnesia where 'the control breaks down and the memories come back', and where the comfortable separation between Africa and Scotland deteriorates.[111] Second, the threat of Scotland's sudden upper-case resurfacing as a *country*, which is involuntary and precipitous in the manner of waking from a dream, links the scission from an imperial past to the realisation of an autonomous future. The creation of Scotland-as-country, then, is dependent on 'waking up' both to the colonial past and its contemporary registration, but also to the nostalgic longing for a return to imperial hierarchies of paternal dominance acted out in Roy's safari adventures.

Roy's reflections on his experiences of apartheid South Africa form the basis of one of the novel's most contested passages, in which he links the 'ghettoisation' of peripheral housing estates in post-industrial Scotland with the official apartheid policy of racial segregation:

> Edinburgh to me represented serfdom. I realised that it was exactly the same situation as Johannesburg; the only difference was that the Kaffirs were white and called schemies or draftpaks. Back in Edinburgh, we would be Kaffirs; condemned to live out our lives in townships like Muirhouse or So-Wester-Hailes-To or Niddrie, self-contained camps with fuck all in them, miles fae the toon. Brought in tae dae the crap jobs that nae other

cunt wanted tae dae, then hassled by the polis if we hung around at night in groups. Edinburgh had the same politics as Johannesburg: it had the same politics as any city.[112]

This is a much more explicit 'denigration' – literally a 'turning black' – of the white Scottish working class than anything in Kelman. There is considerable ambiguity in Roy's provocative mobilisation of black suffering in the South African townships, the 'Kaffirs' in Afrikaaner racism, as an illustration of class division in Scotland. The observation of similarity between dispossessed black South Africans and white Scottish 'schemies' can be read as an orthodox historical materialist identification of race as effecting a division of the working class, which prevents the development of class consciousness. Meanwhile, the putative commonality between Muirhouse and Soweto is a recognition of the 'pay-off' of white supremacy, a function of class oppression that secures loyalty to a dominant class through race as a shared characteristic: the 'most wretched members' of the 'white race', 'exalted' in comparison to racialised groups, in return 'give their support to the system that degrades them'.[113] Instructively, Roy's observation that 'Edinburgh had the same politics as Johannesburg' was promptly borne out in Scotland by Edinburgh's failure to accommodate asylum seekers, and the practice of housing them in peripheral housing estates like Sighthill, out of sight and out of mind.[114] Oppositely, for Gavin Miller, the equivalence between white Niddrie and black Soweto is 'little more than a conscience-salving claim that he [Roy] is as much a victim as the woman he has raped', a reading perfectly consistent with the trajectory of Roy's character development and the larger moral force of *Marabou Stork Nightmares*.[115] Roy's consolation has a national dimension too: Carole Jones argues that the section is part of a broader trend in Scottish writing, which constitutes a 'white appropriation of black suffering', a claim or even colonisation of the 'moral authority' of blackness that is reinscribed by the lynching of Roy at the end of the novel.[116] While Jones doesn't point to *The Eclipse of Scottish Culture*, there is a clear link between this passage and the comparative analysis of Scottish writing and Fanon in Beveridge and Turnbull. Read in these terms, Roy's endorsement of shared denigration actually suggests an inversion of the thesis; the novel bears witness to the radical disjunction between the privileges afforded to white Scots in South Africa and the degradation of black lives under new postimperial conditions.

Welsh returns to, and redoubles, Roy's claim of shared denigration with black South Africans in his third novel, *Filth*. It makes sense that both *Trainspotting* and *Marabou Stork Nightmares* pivot around racism directly resulting from Scotland's relationship with a British past and present. The explicit Unionist cast of the novels' white supremacy reflects the way that a Thatcherite appeal to national unity traded on an implied racial commonality between England and Scotland, defined against the 'swamping' migrants of the Commonwealth whose exclusion from citizenship had been sealed by the Nationality Act of 1981. *Filth* must be read slightly differently: published in 1998, after the 1997 referendum that endorsed a Scottish Parliament, it tracks a moment of transition towards devolved governance. However, this incipient parliamentary Scotland is simultaneously bound to shallow myth-making and to the deep continuities of British imperial white supremacy. That *Filth* is nationally representative is comically emphasised by the name of the central narrator Bruce Robertson, literally a 'son of Robert the Bruce'. Adherence to the mythologised Scottish past he represents is not exclusive of either Unionism or sectarianism: Robertson is a prominent member of the 'craft' or Freemasons, a supporter of Heart of Midlothian F. C., and an outspoken anti-Catholic.[117]

Channelling Kelman's critique of state agencies animated by the racist violence of the police, Robertson also carries the ideological charge of the repressive 1980s British state, which views all 'uncontrollable elements' as a mass that must be controlled through the 'legitimate' violence of the police: 'I hate them all, that section of the working class who won't do as they are told: criminals, spastics, niggers, strikers, thugs, I don't fucking well care, it all adds up to one thing: something to smash'.[118] In the novel, after Gus Bain observes that 'Scotland's a white man's country. Always has been, always will be', Robertson reminisces about visiting the cinema with his estranged wife and daughter: 'I took Carole and wee Stacey tae see that Braveheart. How many pakis or spades did ye see in the colours fightin for Scotland? Same wi Rob Roy, same wi The Bruce'.[119] Robertson's racially defined defence of 'our blood, our soil, our history' directly adapts the language of Nazi ideology, and ups the ante considerably on Spud's rejection of the Scottish myth in *Trainspotting*.[120] Policing is an especially effective illustration of the way that the technical changes promised by devolution do not necessarily achieve a more fundamental uncoupling from the deep continuities of Britain. Robertson represents a profound culture of racism that remains undisturbed by the administrative correction of devolved powers of 'law and order'.

Filth is structured as a parodic murder mystery. It becomes apparent relatively early that Robertson's alter ego, also named Carole, is the murderer. The victim, a black man named Efan Wurie, exists as an absence at the heart of the novel and within Scotland on the cusp of devolution. The dehumanising violence with which Robertson kills Wurie at the outset is partly a straightforward signal of the racist violence of Scotland, which takes on prophetic weight in the light of the death of Sheku Bayoh in police custody in 2015.[121] But the obliterative quality of Wurie's murder also perpetrates the erasure of the black subject. As if in a poorly tended police file, narrative details that would texture Wurie's life are missing: he may or may not be the son of a Ghanaian diplomat; he may or may not have been targeted by racist violence in the past; his reasons for being in Scotland are unclear. In the discourse of the investigating officers, he is replaced as a subject by a litany of racist abuse terms, a vocabulary which Robertson has expanded while working in other police forces in England and Australia; these terms are so various and recurring as to become the text's primary aesthetic registration of race. The significance of the black minority in Scotland is a thorn in the side of the police, where 'silverys [a term of racist abuse] are about naught-point-one per cent of the popula-tion' yet have 'far too much to say for themself'.[122] Even the rationale for his murder displaces Wurie as a singular subjectivity. Robertson, moti-vated by sexual jealousy at the purported infidelity of his wife with an unknown black man, roves around Edinburgh looking for an appropriate victim; alighting on Wurie, he says 'Fuck it, any one will dae. We wanted to hurt'.[123] Such racial logic bears a striking resemblance to actor Liam Neeson's infamous confession that he had searched for random black men to provoke and kill in revenge for a crime committed by an unknown man.[124] This is less an uncanny echo than it is an indictment of a specific manifestation of racism in which black people are treated as possessing a quality of fungibility, a logic of interchangeable 'otherness' that goes back to the commodification and objectification of slavery.

Wurie's 'absent centrality' is suggestive of the way the actual black subject is rendered into an abstraction between the novel's two alternative modes of race politics. Arranged against Robertson's racist Thatcherite authoritarianism is the development of an anti-discrimination discourse that was already building momentum in Britain. Racism in the police force had come under particular scrutiny after the murder of Stephen Lawrence in Greenwich in 1992, an event of national significance that undoubtedly influenced the composition of *Filth* itself. Lawrence's murder led to the establishing of the Macpherson Inquiry in 1997, culminating in the publication of the Macpherson Report in 1999, which found that the Metropolitan Police were institutionally racist. In *Filth*, Wurie's murder is deemed 'racially sensitive' and obliges Robertson and others to attend 'Racism Awareness Training' meetings; Robertson utilises the pretence of 'community relations', which takes the form of liaising with the fictional Lothian Forum on Racial Equality, in order to avoid his workplace respon-sibilities.[125] This institutional racial sensitivity is exposed as a performa-tive sham when Toal, the Chief Inspector in charge of the investigation and apparent champion of modern policing, confides in Robertson that '[a] wog's a fuckin wog, eh'.[126] Arun Kundnani's observation that New Labour multiculturalism was perfectly consonant with anti-immigrant populism is apposite here: the performance of race sensitivity is not mutually exclusive with the continuation of racism in the institutional life of a state still mobilising imperial nostalgia and racialised scapegoats for political purposes. Devolution, meanwhile, offers no easy solution, since in *Filth* it is not only the state itself but local government, the 'New Labour wankers up the City Chambers', who are pushing an agenda of 'equal opps'.[127]

Filth emphasises the fundamental class-based rationale behind this 'equal opps' discourse via a ventriloquising didacticism similar to Roy Strang's speech on townships and peripheral housing estates. Articulating his successful path to promotion to Detective Inspector, consequently outranking and rendering obsolete the 'old-fashioned' racism of Bruce Robertson, Ray Lennox outlines his epiphany on multicultural 'correctness':

> Your behaviour has to be non-racist and non-sexist. You ken the score; all this equal opps stuff started when mass unemployment took its toll. You couldn't have upwardly mobile schemies taking jobs from the sons and daughters of the rich! So you bring in a handful of overprivileged coons as a Trojan horse sop to equal opps, while making sure you keep the good salaried jobs for the educated bourgeoisie. You start to introduce minimum qualifications, make a uni degree essential where it had never been needed in the past. That way you weed out the people that cannae bullshit your script. Of course, fuck all changes. In London coons just get to be truncheoned by a member of their own race once in a blue moon.[128]

The main observation on actual racism here is that it continues unabated, that the structural elements that preserve racism are untouched by multicultural sensitivity, that 'fuck all changes'. The scorn of 'uni degree' literacy is underscored by the parodic monologue of 'Self' and 'Other', recognisable as central features of postcolonial criticism, that Robertson's parasitical worm addresses to its host. The continued use of scandalising racist terms serves to maintain a tenuous link to Lennox's characterisation, hitherto seemingly incapable of this level of detailed political insight, while returning to the novel's linguistic puncturing of the doctrine of racial sensitivity – not as a defence of racism, but as a counterweight to the social policing of expression characteristic of the weaponisation of correctness within British class struggle.

This observation of the operation of class as structure in Britain is markedly different to the 'resignification of class' that Gavin Miller argues is characteristic of Welsh's critique of 'identity politics'.[129] For Miller, both *Filth* and *Marabou Stork Nightmares* satirise an idea of historical memory and 'moral inheritance' possessed by characters who have definitively broken from their working-class past: the black thread running through Robertson's life – coal mining and picking, the forcible ingestion of coal, and eventually, the black police uniform during the Miners' Strike – is representative of the forced manifestation of his hereditary 'filth'. Miller's account does not extend 'identity politics' to blackness. However, the divisions between these coding practices – 'black' as moral darkness, 'black' as the dispossession of the working class emblematised in mining and 'black' as race – are fuzzy in the novel. Blackness is mobilised, in much the same fashion as in *Marabou Stork Nightmares*, as a 'denigration' of workers during the Miners' Strike. This is both literal, in coal-caked white faces, and morally figurative, in the state narrative of miners as the 'enemy within'. However, race is entangled with this process of denigration, as Robertson's early, vituperative response to coal indicates:

> That filthy, dirty coal and the minging cunts that dig it. You dig it baby? You dig that coal brother?
> I don't fuckin well dig it or dig the filthy cunts that do.[130]

The idiomatic 'dig', 'baby' and 'brother' simultaneously evoke Robertson's anti-black racism and the hauntological incursions of his own abusive upbringing, and his 'betrayal' of the miners and his family, all precipitated by the sight of coal. There is more to Robertson's race hatred than his interpellation into a culture of institutional racism via his service in various police forces. But *Filth* has little to say about actual black lives or black politics; the novel's representation of racist language and violence is on some level an allegory of an experience of class in 1980s Britain, especially considering the strategic exclusion of Efan Wurie, the cosmopolitan son of an African diplomat, from that working class, and his symbolic obliteration in the text itself. Coal may provide the fuel for *Filth*'s interrogation of class politics in late twentieth-century Scotland, but in Toni Morrison's terms, the 'critical ignition' is provided by racialised blackness in the figure of Wurie. It is hard to divine whether the hijacking of black experience as a class metaphor is an acknowledgement of race as a strategy of class stratification, as in *Marabou Stork Nightmares*, or an indictment of the crass victimhood of Scots personified in Strang and Robertson. The two are not mutually exclusive, but both rely on the deployment of an abstracted blackness to achieve their ends.

The doors ajar: before and after 1998

One exceptional quality of *Black Marsden* in 1972 lay in the way it reflected on the instability of racial taxonomies, on their discursive dimensions and aesthetic slipperiness, in a framework adaptive of a Scottish literary tradi-tion that also gestured towards Scotland's imperial past and racial present. In 1998, *Filth* also situates an examination of the black signifier within a Scottish national context, though in a form clearly distinct from Harris's radical imagination. The absence of Efan Wurie as a fleshed-out and rooted subject – in terms of his textual elision, his cosmopolitan mobility and his symbolic obliteration – is emblematic of a larger dynamic of conspicuous absence in Scottish writing that lies between the publication of the two novels. In each of the examples I have described here, black existence is figured as something more vividly realised, more tangibly collective, politi-cal and social, outside of Scotland. That does not negate the significance of blackness for these Scottish writers; on the contrary, it demonstrates a need to interrogate the way black politics challenges both the adaptive modern British state form and the stubborn mythologies and imperial continuities of national Scotland.

It is significant that *Filth*, composed and published in the period imme-diately preceding the opening of the new Scottish Parliament, tempers the expectation of a new national order with the contemplation of a national past. Robertson's nominative significance, combined with his extreme racist violence and linguistic outrages, is indicative of a sublimated national racism. The novel does not depict a triumphant moment of new-found political confidence; indeed, it looks back to the social and political strug-gles of the 1980s, to the tenacity of imperial nostalgia, sectarianism and class struggle in Scotland, and envisages devolved government as a new stage of Union negotiation. In this respect, it shares something with what might be tentatively described as Scotland's black expressive culture. Sulter and Kay's work in the 1980s had been charged by and responsive to those social and political struggles, in mainly extraterritorial contexts – England, America and Africa. In the light of the cultural change seemingly promised by devolution, that orientation shifted subtly towards an interrogation of Scotland itself, facilitated by publishing priorities that accompanied the rising stock of Scotland nationally. Looking forward from that point, and even acknowledging the politically conservative quality of Scottish devolution, new imaginative conditions underwritten by new publishing opportunities in the narrative of a 'new Scotland' meant that the early anti-colonial and race-critical writing of a black Scotland in the post-1979 period could be taken forward.

Notes

1. Guptara, Prabhu, *Black British Literature: An Annotated Bibliography* (Hebden Bridge: Dangaroo Press, 1986), p. 90.
2. Harris, Wilson and Alan Riach, 'Wilson Harris Interview by Alan Riach', in Wilson Harris, *The Radical Imagination: Lectures and Talks*, ed. Alan Riach and Mark Williams (Liège: L3. Liège Lang & Lit, 1992), p. 63; Harris was also married to a Scottish writer, Margaret Burns.
3. Harris, Wilson, *Palace of the Peacock*, in *The Guyana Quartet* (London: Faber and Faber, 1985 [1960]), pp. 15–117: 39.
4. Riach, Alan, *Representing Scotland in Literature, Popular Culture and Iconography* (Basingstoke: Palgrave Macmillan, 2005), p. 114.
5. Harris, Wilson, *Black Marsden* (London: Faber and Faber, 1972), pp. 111, 60.
6. See Eldridge, 'Rise and Fall', p. 35.
7. Gilkes, Michael, *The Literate Imagination: Essays on the Novels of Wilson Harris* (London: Macmillan, 1989), p. 1.
8. Harris, *Black Marsden*, pp. 27–8, 70.
9. Harris, *Black Marsden*, p. 24.
10. See Shukra, *Changing Pattern*, pp. 31–3.
11. Harris, *Black Marsden*, p. 51.
12. Donnell, Alison, 'Nation and Contestation: Black British Writing', *Wasafiri* 17:36 (2002), pp. 11–17: 14.
13. Calder, Angus, *Revolving Culture: Notes from the Scottish Republic* (London: I. B. Tauris, 1994), pp. 186–9.
14. Killingray, David, 'Review: Black Writers in Britain 1760–1890', *Journal of African History* 35:1 (1994), p. 172; Rewt, Polly T., 'Introduction: The African Diaspora and its Origins', *Research in African Literatures* 29:4 (1998), pp. 3–13: 3.
15. Edwards, Paul, 'Black Writers of the Eighteenth and Nineteenth Centuries' in Dabydeen (ed.), *The Black Presence in English Literature*, pp. 50–67.
16. Rewt, 'Introduction', p. 11.
17. Rewt, 'Introduction', p. 5.
18. Rewt, 'Introduction', p. 3.
19. Alan Riach has read Gray and Harris comparatively as presenting a 'violence of anti-realism' that reaffirms the 'whole theatre' of Scottish nationhood, 'a history of partiality and incompleteness, attachment to imperialism and difference from it'; Riach, Alan, 'Other Than Realism: Magic and Violence in Modern Scottish Fiction and the Recent Work of Wilson Harris', *International Journal of Scottish Literature* 4 (2008), n. pag.
20. Gray, Alasdair, *Lanark: A Life in Four Books* (Edinburgh: Canongate, 2002 [1981]), pp. 325–6.
21. Gray, *Lanark*, p. 325.
22. See Lambert, Iain, 'This is Not Sarcasm Believe Me Yours Sincerely: James Kelman, Ken Saro-Wiwa and Amos Tutuola' in Gardiner, Macdonald and O'Gallagher (eds), *Scottish Literature and Postcolonial Literature*, pp. 198–209: 199–201; Gray, *Lanark*, p. 497.
23. Gates, Henry Louis, Jr, *Figures in Black: Words, Signs and the 'Racial' Self* (Oxford: Oxford University Press, 1989), pp. 17–18; the question of race in Scotland's 'darkening Enlightenment' has also been taken up by Cairns Craig in *Wealth of the Nation*, pp. 104–8.
24. Gray, *Lanark*, p. 494.
25. Gray, *Lanark*, pp. 498–9.
26. Beveridge and Turnbull, *Eclipse of Scottish Culture*, pp. 5–8; Fanon, Frantz, *The Wretched of the Earth* (New York: Grove Press, 2004 [1961]).

27. Gray, *Lanark*, p. 410.
28. Gray, *Lanark*, p. 505.
29. Connell, 'Modes of Marginality', p. 42.
30. Gray, *Lanark*, p. 505.
31. Fanon, Frantz, *Black Skin, White Masks*, trans. Charles Lam Markmann (London: Pluto Press, 2008 [1952]), p. 8.
32. 'Voice' retains a differentiating power that equates articulacy and poise with whiteness, illustrated sharply by David Starkey's observation that a 'successful black man' like MP David Lammy could be thought of as white by '[turning] the screen off so that you are listening to him on radio'; 'David Starkey Claims "the Whites Have Become Black"', *The Guardian*, 13 August 2011, www.theguardian.com/uk/2011/-aug/13/david-starkey-claims-whites-black (last accessed 25 July 2019).
33. Gray, *Lanark*, p. 506.
34. Connell, 'Modes of Marginality', p. 43.
35. Alasdair Gray, *1982, Janine* (Edinburgh: Canongate, 2003 [1984]), p. 59.
36. Gray, *1982, Janine*, p. 113, original emphasis.
37. Gray, *1982, Janine*, p. 114.
38. Gray, *1982, Janine*, p. 224.
39. Craig, Cairns, *The Modern Scottish Novel: Narrative and the National Imagination* (Edinburgh: Edinburgh University Press, 1999), p. 239; Gray, Alasdair, *Poor Things* (New York: Harcourt, 1992).
40. Gray, *Poor Things*, p. 139.
41. Gray, *Poor Things*, pp. 173–4.
42. Gray, *Poor Things*, pp. 145–50.
43. Specifically in the title of the online magazine *Bella Caledonia*, formed in 2007, https://bellacaledonia.org.uk/about-us/ (last accessed 30 March 2020).
44. Sulter, *As a Black Woman*, pp. 9–10.
45. Hall, 'New Ethnicities', p. 266.
46. Taylor, Paul C., *Black is Beautiful: A Philosophy of Black Aesthetics* (Chichester: Wiley-Blackwell, 2016), pp. 108–9.
47. Sulter, *As a Black Woman*, p. 11; *Zabat: Poetics of a Family Tree* (Hebden Bridge: Urban Fox Press, 1989).
48. Sulter, *As a Black Woman*, p. 39; *Zabat*, p. 23.
49. Taylor, *Black is Beautiful*, p. 16.
50. Sulter, *As a Black Woman*, pp. 15–18.
51. Sulter, *Zabat*, p. 21.
52. Sulter, *Zabat*, p. 22.
53. Sulter, *Zabat*, pp. 35–6.
54. Johnson, Linton Kwesi, *Mi Revalueshanary Fren: Selected Poems* (London: Penguin, 2002), pp. 6–8, 20.
55. Sulter, *Zabat*, p. 36.
56. Sulter, *As a Black Woman*, p. 23.
57. Sulter, *Zabat*, pp. 68–9.
58. Anderson, *Imagined Communities*, p. 178.
59. Sulter, *Zabat*, p. 68; if the word is a typographical error, it is a fortuitous one.
60. Sulter, *Zabat*, p. 69.
61. Sulter, *Zabat*, p. 66.
62. Sulter, *As a Black Woman*, p. 12.
63. Sulter, *As a Black Woman*, p. 14.
64. These 'forms of exclusion' are from Connell, 'Modes of Marginality', p. 42.
65. Kay, Jackie, *Chiaroscuro*, in Lynette Goddard (ed.), *The Methuen Drama Book of Plays by Black British Writers* (London: Bloomsbury, 2011), pp. 59–117.
66. Hall, 'New Ethnicities', p. 166.
67. Kay, *Chiaroscuro*, p. 91.

68. Kay, *Chiaroscuro*, pp. 64, 91.
69. Kay, *Chiaroscuro*, p. 72.
70. Kay, *Chiaroscuro*, pp. 63, 69.
71. Goddard, *The Methuen Drama Book of Plays by Black British Writers*, p. x; the first performance of the play featured Bernardine Evaristo in the role of Beth.
72. Kay, Jackie, *The Adoption Papers* (Tarset: Bloodaxe Books, 1991), p. 6.
73. Kay, *The Adoption Papers*, p. 21.
74. Kay, *The Adoption Papers*, p. 14; McLeod, John, 'Adoption Aesthetics', in Deirdre Osborne (ed.), *The Cambridge Companion to British Black and Asian Literature (1945–2010)* (Cambridge: Cambridge University Press, 2016), pp. 211–24.
75. McLeod, 'Adoption Aesthetics', p. 213; the reference is an autobiographical one to Kay's own adoption, which she mentions in her father's obituary; Kay, Jackie, 'John Kay Obituary', *The Guardian*, 9 February 2020, www.theguardian.com/politics/2020/feb/09/john-kay-obituary (last accessed 30 March 2020).
76. McLeod, 'Adoption Aesthetics', p. 214.
77. Kay, *The Adoption Papers*, p. 29.
78. Kay, 'John Kay Obituary', n. pag.; Hames, *Literary Politics*, p. 87.
79. Kay, *The Adoption Papers*, p. 26.
80. Kay, *The Adoption Papers*, p. 46.
81. Kay, *The Adoption Papers*, p. 48.
82. Kelman, James, *Some Recent Attacks: Essays Cultural and Political* (Stirling: AK Press, 1992), pp. 9, 10, 16, 35.
83. Kelman, *Some Recent Attacks*, p. 66; *'And the Judges Said': Essays* (London: Secker & Warburg, 2002), pp. 10, 349, 359–60.
84. Kelman, *Some Recent Attacks*, p. 73; it should be noted this essay was written before the murder of Stephen Lawrence and Kelman's active participation in the campaign to bring his killers to justice.
85. Kovesi, Simon, *James Kelman* (Manchester, Manchester University Press, 2007), pp. 99, 134.
86. Kelman, *'And the Judges Said'*, p. 226.
87. Kelman, *'And the Judges Said'*, pp. 226, 260.
88. Kelman, *Some Recent Attacks*, p. 71.
89. Zagratzki, Uwe, '"Blues Fell This Morning" – James Kelman's Scottish Literature and Afro-American Music', *Scottish Literary Journal* 27:1 (2000), pp. 105–17: 109.
90. See 'Say Hello to John La Rose' in *'And The Judges Said'*, p. 223; 'Kelman and LKJ Speak Out for Black Writers', *The List*, 24 March 1995, https://archive.list.co.uk/the-list/1995-03-24/6/ (last accessed 30 March 2020).
91. Own correspondence, 30 January 2020.
92. Hinds, Donald, 'Busman's Blues', in Andrew Salkey (ed.), *Stories from the Caribbean* (London: Paul Elek Books, 1972 [1965]), pp. 98–103.
93. Hinds, 'Busman's Blues', p. 101.
94. Kelman, James, *A Disaffection* (London: Secker and Warburg, 1989), pp. 336–7.
95. Kelman, *A Disaffection*, pp. 336–7.
96. Kelman, *Some Recent Attacks*, p. 65; *'And the Judges Said'*, pp. 27, 371–2.
97. Kelman, *Some Recent Attacks*, p. 65.
98. Kelman, James, *How Late It Was, How Late* (London: Vintage, 1998 [1994]), pp. 103, 105.
99. Morrison, Toni, *Playing in the Dark* (Cambridge, MA: Harvard University Press, 1992), p. viii.
100. Gilroy, *Small Acts*, p. 20.
101. Welsh, *Trainspotting*, pp. 124–5.
102. Welsh, *Trainspotting*, p. 126.
103. Welsh, *Trainspotting*, p. 127.
104. Welsh, *Trainspotting*, p. 128.

105. Welsh, Irvine, *Marabou Stork Nightmares* (London: Jonathan Cape, 1995), pp. 83, 125.
106. Welsh, *Marabou Stork Nightmares*, p. 125.
107. Welsh, *Marabou Stork Nightmares*, pp. 62, 83.
108. Welsh, *Marabou Stork Nightmares*, p. 15; Gilroy, *After Empire*, p. 102.
109. Welsh, *Marabou Stork Nightmares*, p. 13.
110. Welsh, *Marabou Stork Nightmares*, p. 122.
111. Welsh, *Marabou Stork Nightmares*, p. 157.
112. Welsh, *Marabou Stork Nightmares*, p. 80.
113. Ignatiev, Noel and John Garvey (eds), *Race Traitor* (London: Routledge, 1996), pp. 9–10.
114. Kemp, Arnold, 'The Shame of Sighthill', *The Guardian*, Sunday 12 August 2001, www.theguardian.com/uk/2001/aug/12/immigration.immigrationandpublicser vices3 (last accessed 27 September 2019).
115. Miller, Gavin, 'Welsh and Identity Politics', in Berthold Schoene (ed.), *The Edinburgh Companion to Irvine Welsh* (Edinburgh: Edinburgh University Press, 2010), pp. 89–99: 97.
116. Jones, Carole, 'White Men on Their Backs – From Objection to Abjection: The Representation of the White Male as Victim in William McIlvanney's *Docherty* and Irvine Welsh's *Marabou Stork Nightmares*', *International Journal of Scottish Literature* 1 (2006), n. pag.
117. Football clubs from Scotland's two largest cities are marked by a strong sectarian identity; Hibernian FC is Edinburgh's Catholic club, Heart of Midlothian its Protestant one.
118. Welsh, Irvine, *Filth* (London: Vintage, 1999 [1998]), p. 160.
119. Welsh, *Filth*, p. 46.
120. Welsh, *Filth*, p. 46.
121. Daly, Mark, 'Sheku Bayoh Custody Death Officer "Hates Black People"', BBC News, www.bbc.co.uk/news/uk-scotland-34529611 (last accessed 30 March 2020).
122. Welsh, *Filth*, p. 77.
123. Welsh, *Filth*, p. 390.
124. 'Liam Neeson in Racism Storm after Admitting He Wanted to Kill Black Man', BBC News, www.bbc.co.uk/news/entertainment-arts-47117177 (last accessed 27 September 2019).
125. Welsh, *Filth*, pp. 27, 34.
126. Welsh, *Filth*, p. 142.
127. Welsh, *Filth*, p. 59.
128. Welsh, *Filth*, p. 379.
129. Miller, 'Welsh and Identity Politics', p. 99.
130. Welsh, *Filth*, p. 11.

Chapter 3

The Black Jacobeans: Jackie Kay's *Trumpet*

One vivid memory Millicent Moody has of her recently deceased husband, the jazz trumpeter Joss Moody at the heart of Jackie Kay's *Trumpet* (1998), is of him play-acting with their son Colman at the seaside, as heroic 'Black Jacobeans' who could 'fight any battle'.[1] The expression alludes clearly to C. L. R. James's *The Black Jacobins* (1938), a history of Toussaint L'Ouverture and the Haitian Revolution of the late eighteenth century. The revolutionaries James identifies as the black Jacobins are so named because of their more fundamental embodiment of the principles of the French Revolution, defined against the post-revolutionary hypocrisy of the slave-holding white French colonials. In their statement of sovereignty in the spirit of the French Revolution, and in the name of dispossessed black people across the transatlantic world, San Domingo's Jacobins would 'alter the fate of millions of men and shift the economic currents of three continents'.[2] *The Black Jacobins* was a key source for Cedric Robinson's history of the black radical tradition, *Black Marxism*; Robinson describes it as an extraordinary and seminal work in the field of black radical critique, an ambitious attempt 'to establish the historical legacy of African revolutionary struggles'.[3] *Trumpet*'s reference to black radicalism is not coincidental. The novel touches on diverse subjects of radical thought: Afrocentrism, neoliberalism, nationalism and the gendered dimensions of black politics in Britain. The core of a black politics in the novel, however, is hiding in plain sight: jazz music, what Fred Moten has called the aesthetic of the black radical tradition.[4]

This is a radical politics with a social and historical context, and the playful collocation of 'black Jacobeans' has its own local national dimension too. Joss's evocation of Jacobeans is a suggestive reference to British constitutional history, to James Charles Stuart, the Union of the Crowns, and the seventeenth-century infancy of what would become the United Kingdom. The image of Joss and Colman, swathed in tartan, striding up the beach, 'playing at being chieftains', is also plainly suggestive of 'black Jacobites', reminiscent of the iconography of Stuart return that threatened the Union state at various points in the eighteenth century and which remains linked in the popular imagination to the Scottish independence movement.[5] The novel's coincidence of black radicalism beyond the First Republic with the monarchic imagery of the Stuart dynasty initially seems strange, but the contradictory implications of *Trumpet*'s black Jacobeans are coherent with contemporary Scottish party-political nationalism, which has involved a compact between a reformative republicanism and cautious strains of monarchism, albeit supportive of the contemporary Hanoverian royal family.[6] However, liberal nationalism of the contemporary Scottish type, even in its most civic manifestation, remains at odds with the modern tradition of black radicalism. James and Robinson are more readily associated with a transnational structural critique that has eschewed what Kehinde Andrews calls 'narrow nationalism', either in the form of autonomous black-majority nations in the Caribbean or Africa, or the black cultural nationalism of Amiri Baraka and a US-style 'nation within a nation'.[7] The textual moment of the black Jacobeans, therefore, frames a conundrum in devolutionary Scotland: how to resolve the injunction towards a transnational black radicalism, with the potential for radical political change constituted by Scottish nationalism, to the British national, and to a larger neo-colonial, status quo.

Trumpet's genealogical narrative spans three generations of black men – John Moore, Joss Moody and Colman Moody – who each have a distinctive relationship both to blackness and to Scotland. These intergenerational relationships are marked by ruptures, to the smooth transmission of a cultural inheritance and to the stable, biocentric assumptions of nativity. John Moore emigrates to Scotland, a '[g]host country' of 'no colour' peopled with 'long pale faces', as a six-year-old boy, his birth country indeterminate and consigned to the lost past of his life in the early twentieth century.[8] Moore's son Joss has a developed black political consciousness, a profound knowledge of jazz music and musicians, and a sharply articulated Scottish national loyalty; his relationship to the black diasporic formation his father represents is to a 'fantasy Africa', an adaptable and repurposable cultural inheritance. By contrast, Colman Moody represents the unknown 'black British' quantity of the novel. An émigré from Scotland to England but socially excluded from both, Colman has a racial and national disaffection and disorientation, contrasted distinctively against his father's apparent cultural confidence. The contingency of intergenerational memory is built into the novel formally in the heavily mediated narrative, in which the lives of the fathers are told from the temporally displaced perspectives of the sons, displaced further by the spectral presence of a 'ghost writer' who re-presents the narrative: 'The trouble with the past', Joss recalls John Moore saying, 'is that you no longer know what you could be remembering'.[9] The biological determinations of birth are similarly made provisional. Joss Moody, born female and living his entire adult life as a man, stands against gender assignation. Likewise, the Moodys' adoptive family re-evaluates kinship, privileging social relations over biological consanguinity, registering the way that adoption '[puts] into crisis normative notions of race and culture' established through metaphors of 'common blood'.[10] Elective kinship is profoundly connected to black history too. Achille Mbembe says that the history of slavery ensures that 'loss is first of a genealogical order'; the 'kinlessness' of slavery thus directly drives the elective formation of black collectivity.[11]

Analysing the biocentric, nativist and taxonomic assumptions upended by the narrative has powered much of the critical work on *Trumpet* to date. But this methodological assault on essentialism, particularly against both national and racial reification, has offered scant resistance or even modification to continuity Britishness. Indeed, much of the critical analysis of *Trumpet* has reinforced Britishness in a number of ways: by co-opting the novel into the plasticity of British national reinvention and 'reinvigoration'; by supplanting its disruptive Scottish national dimensions with a permanently exilic, diasporic Afrocentrism; or surmising from it a post-racial universalism which shares features with British neoliberal multiculturalism. By contrast, I argue that *Trumpet* proves Femi Folorunso's proposition of a qualitative national difference between an 'after Empire' England and Scotland, and a nationally specific black experience, which thwarts any attempt to naturalise the novel as reformatively British.[12] This is emblematised by the moment of the black Jacobeans, but the novel's attempts to get purchase on the question of blackness in devolutionary Britain go further than this iconic moment. Scotland is set apart both from territorial England and from the neoliberal project of the British state, and situated within a larger transnational framework of black radical thought.

'Scottish and/or black cultural energies': renewing Britishness

The constitutional consciousness discernible in *Trumpet*'s Jacobean moment makes sense in the light of its publication in 1998. After the election of New Labour and the 1997 referendum, but before the recommencement of the Scottish Parliament, the novel emerged in a moment of national reimagination defined by an as yet unrealised potential. The result of the referendum, in which 74.29 per cent of voters supported the establishment of a new Parliament, showed resounding popular support for a new configuration of government that would extend Scottish national autonomy in various ways. Furthermore, it settled any outstanding doubts resulting from the narrowness of margin in the 1979 referendum. Viewed from Westminster, meanwhile, the period following the 1997 referendum was crucial if the overall ambition for devolution, following the recommendations of the Kilbrandon Commission, was to be realised: namely, that the political concession of a devolved Parliament would secure rather than further corrode the Union. The ambition was to settle devolution as a new identitarian constitutional arrangement – modern, flexible and responsive. However, the ultimate levers of power would remain securely in Westminster, and state-led efforts to naturalise Britishness as the master category of nation would be redoubled.

Part of reaffirming that 'naturalised' Britishness was the new government's vision of a reformative political multiculturalism. In an echo of the Scarman Report, policy was once again being driven by activism resulting from street-level violence directed at black people. The racist murder of Stephen Lawrence in Eltham, Greenwich, in April 1993 was the defining racialised event of the decade. Much as in the case of the New Cross fire a decade before, inadequate investigation by the same state agencies – the Metropolitan Police and the Crown Prosecution Service – led to the mobilisation of a sustained campaign for justice, headed by Lawrence's parents Doreen and Neville. Surrounding the Lawrence case was a 'mediatized public crisis', triggered by the CPS decision not to prosecute the main suspects in the case. The injustice of the Lawrence murder and its aftermath threatened to destroy the narrative of British equality, justice, anti-racism and tolerance – the terrain upon which New Labour was to build its 'elaborated Britishness' – as 'baseless myth or, worse, cynical sham'.[13] Consequently, one of the first acts of Jack Straw as Home Secretary after the general election of 1997 was to establish an inquiry into the death of Stephen Lawrence four years previously. As part of a process that Simon Cottle describes as 'civil society renewal', this gesture helped to restore a sense of equilibrium in Britain's popular anti-racist conscience, assuaging the public shame of Lawrence's unsolved murder. It was also part of a broader strategy that, combined with a new 'Race Relations Forum' comprised of black and Asian professionals, sought to demonstrate New Labour's proactive stance on racism.[14]

In the context of devolutionary Scotland, the ideological cast of blackness imagined as part of a 'reinvented Britishness' is starkly apparent. The fact that *Trumpet* has been coded as both black and Scottish means it is perfectly positioned for the cultural work entailed in supplementing, rejuvenating or reinventing millennial Britain. Consequently, the critical response to *Trumpet* provides a striking example of the way that literary studies have remained in step with the imagination of this new model Britishness, in an otherwise progressive attempt to oppose racism and pay due critical attention to marginalised subject positions. One such example is Catherine Lyn Innes's *A History of Black and Asian Writing in Britain*, which sets out the general framework of this new Britain via a series of contemporary hyphenated 'multiple identity' categories, in which writers are simultaneously 'black *and* British, or African and English, or Indian and English, or Caribbean and Scottish'.[15] Innes shows the way that diverse racialised and national markers can be blended with Britain's constituent national formations without ever threatening their classification as 'within Britishness'; these are national 'identities' in a pure sense, as elective rather than politically activated positions. Her analysis of *Trumpet*, where the novel is characterised by both individual and national reinvention, illustrates this recuperation:

> Like so much of the writing by black and Asian people in Britain through-out the previous two centuries, it [*Trumpet*] allows the reader to understand the extent to which individual selves as well as visions of Britain may be continually invented and reinvented.[16]

'[V]isions of Britain' are not simply perspectives, but imply a holistic national reconception; Joss's self-creation, the 'individual reinvention' registered in his gender performance, expressive jazz and the negotiation of both national and diasporic affiliations, is subordinated to a larger dynamic of British adaptation to racial difference. After 1997, this 'continual reinvention' of the individual subject self, standing in for British national adaptability, speaks more to the national-political requirements of a neoliberal, post-imperial and devolutionary conjuncture than to anything specific to *Trumpet*. Meanwhile, the syncretic logic by which black and Asian writers facilitate the reinvention of Britain is recognisable as normatively 'multicultural', in which cultural admixture is a restorative, modernising process which remakes the national fabric of British life.

The language of hybridity in which these readings are couched often drifts back towards a quasi-biological metaphor in which the cultural body of the nation is replenished via the infusion, grafting or intermixture of genetic material provided by racialised others defined against a white majority. For example, Peter Clandfield's reading of Kay frames her 'black Scottish writing' as 'potentially a very potent form of hybrid cultural vigour' and 'a potential source of rejuvenation for British culture'.[17] Such 'hybrid vigour' is suggestive of a racial-genetic metaphor, in which black-ness offers a health-giving injection of genetic material, and is underlined by the reference to black 'potency' familiar from colonial discourse, which persists in the mediatised discourse of 'strength', 'power' and even 'mon-strosity' routinely applied to black people.[18] Clandfield's argument, that 'Kay's Scots voice functions [. . .] as a sign of the hybridity that is part of Britishness itself', is celebratory, and returns to the logic of Defoe and his defence of the 'het'rogeneous' Union.[19] The larger national consequence of this argument comes to the fore when Clandfield observes that Kay's work serves the 'reinvigoration of Britishness by Scottish and/or black cultural energies'.[20] This amplifies Innes: the black writer in Scotland now provides the metabolic 'reinvigoration' of Britain, a neat illustration of the way that national Scotland, and Britain's racialised minorities, are first incor-porated into Britishness, and then redeployed as legitimating and health-giving influences. Alongside the celebration of what Scotland can offer British culture, Clandfield quotes both Paul Gilroy and Stuart Hall to establish that 'non-English and ambiguous nationality' is another part of Britain's 'resident hybridity'.[21] There is no suggestion that Clandfield sees the Union as a cause to be defended, but just like devolution, this British cultural nationalism co-opts Scotland as a distinctive restorative national influence, while keeping England as assumed and undefined.

The obverse of *Trumpet* as a revitalising influence on post-imperial Britishness is the heavy prosecution of its African diasporic qualities. Militating against a putative ethnocentric Scottish nationalism, Alan Rice's 'Heroes across the Sea' presents Joss as a figure of diasporic aliena-tion and dislocation: 'Moody [. . .] self-invents, but does so on the basis of his own African diasporan identity, of having a home somewhere else that he is in exile from and a home in Europe he is stranger to'.[22] In Rice's reading of *Trumpet*, blackness not only signifies an imaginative transna-tional link to the African diaspora but implies a condition of intrinsic exile that precludes national participation – a forced 'unhoming' that equates blackness to European marginality. Rice psychopathologises Joss as having a 'schizophrenic identity', wherein 'jazz, paradoxically, enables Moody to be at home when thinking about Scotland', and it is 'only natural for a black man in Scotland to use it [jazz music] to tell his own specific and similar story of exile'.[23] These arguments are at odds with Joss Moody's explicit Scottish national affinity in *Trumpet*. They may be more appro-priate to a reading of John Moore: Moody's memories of his father in the penultimate chapter of *Trumpet*, 'Last Word', certainly convey a sense of Moore's diasporic yearning, if not active estrangement in Scotland. Moore is 'haunted' by the loss of his childhood, in the memory of 'my country, my own one', reiterating how 'he missed his mother, his country, his mother-country'.[24] However, even the pronounced diasporic consciousness of John Moore does not neatly conform to the picture of 'schizophrenic' exile drawn here. Rice's 'heroes across the sea' are the black jazz musicians of the United States that inspire Joss Moody. But John Moore has a 'wonderful singing voice and could sing from memory just about any folk song', including Scottish folk songs; the idea of heroes across the sea thus chimes with the novel's playful Jacobean reference, acknowledging the 'king over the water' through folk music such as the 'Skye Boat Song' and 'My Bonnie Lies Over the Ocean'.[25]

For Rice, the key to Joss Moody's 'estrangement' is the intrinsic whiteness of Scotland understood as a form of racial nationalism: Moody struggles to 'find his identity in a Scotland that has no place for an African presence, that builds its Scottish identity at least in part through a racialized mythology of Celtic whiteness'.[26] The emphatically 'Celtic' character of Scotland's national whiteness is juxtaposed implicitly against the long history of black presence in a racially diverse Britain which forms the initial launchpad for 'Heroes across the Sea'. Evidencing this ethnic Celticism at work in *Trumpet* does not proceed with reference to the novel. Instead, Rice uses a quotation from a *Guardian* interview with Kay herself, omitting the way Kay 'roars delightedly' as she relates the story of being called a 'foreign-looking bugger' by a Glaswegian woman in London to change the tone subtly; nevertheless, this story makes no reference to the Celticist whiteness Rice describes.[27] Neither is there much evidence of this 'mythology' contemporaneously: the political purchase of 'blood and soil' white Celticist groups like Sìol Nan Gàidheal has been very marginal in contemporary Scotland. Rice's observation of Scotland's whiteness is correct, but in terms of white mythologies, any 'ethno-Celticism' is dwarfed by a Scottish history of racially defined Unionism within and after Empire, much of which has sought actively to downplay and minimise the role of Highland Scots and Gaelic speakers in the Scoto-British national community.

These theoretical positions form a complete whole that is recognisable as serving the needs of an elaborated Britain, championing the absorptive and plastic qualities of modern Britishness. Concurrently, Scottish nationalism is delegitimised via the insinuation of an ancestral-archaic ethnocentrism or racial exclusivity, which takes its lead from the prevailing devolutionary discourse of New Labour. Such national assumptions are largely ideological; they fit the template of Michael Billig's 'banal' nationalism, where 'nationalism' describes social movements that 'threaten the existing status quo' – like the movement for Scottish independence – while the social reproduction of 'established' nationalisms like Britishness necessarily goes unremarked, maintaining their quotidian, and consequently hegemonic, properties.[28] A literary-critical preoccupation with the 'reinvention' of Britishness is itself a nationalistic intervention, but is seldom recognised or named as nationalism. Meanwhile, the easy association between Scotland and 'Celtic whiteness' reflects the way that the first recourse when presented with 'threatening nationalisms' is to home in on their ostensible ethno-purist characteristics.

'Ignite the paparazzi': British mediations

These critical accounts miss the tension in *Trumpet* between an absorptive, elaborated Britishness and a territorially and nationally distinct Scotland. The dramatic action of the novel coheres around a choice with strong national co-ordinates: whether Colman Moody will return to the explicitly Scottish national inheritance of his family, or 'sell his story' by accepting the financial inducements of Sophie Stones, a journalist whose professional practice and personal self-creation emblematise contemporary Britishness in a mediatised and neoliberal form. The initiatory moment of the novel sets up this distinction: Millie Moody, beset by photographers in London, describes on her return to Scotland a sense of sanctuary and recognition of a 'different air', away from cameras likened in their violation to the 'assault of a machine gun'.[29] Such a representation of Britain's mediascape has a historical resonance, where the tabloid frenzy precipitated by Joss's death bears the imprint of the major psychodrama of millennial British public life, the death of Diana, Princess of Wales in August 1997. The prodigious mobilisation of public sentiment around Diana's death had eclipsed, and even threatened to postpone, the Scottish devolution referendum. Even as the televisual spectacle of the funeral presented the opportunity for a narrative of a nation 'united in mourning', her death also seemed to presage a constitutional threat, necessitating the polishing of the 'enchanted glass' of the monarchy into a new, more modern form.[30] The rationale behind Sophie Stones's new project to biographise Joss Moody has its own subtle racial dynamics encoded in the language of the novel. The 'white envelopes' Stones sends to Millie Moody are part of a series of signifiers that give a racial dimension to the whole tabloid exposé: the camera flash is both 'blinding' and a 'raging white light', and all the journalists pursuing the Moody story possess the 'same white, sharp face'.[31] These references reinforce the racial politics of a white journalist vigorously monetising the salacious hunger for tabloid stories of black deviation from cherished British 'norms', realised vividly by treatment of high-profile figures such as Frank Bruno or Naomi Campbell, and recognisable contemporaneously in the media disdain – a kind of 'raging white light' – directed at figures such as Raheem Sterling and Meghan Markle.

A cursory examination of the tabloid media in Scotland would indicate that this racial discourse is not exclusive to England. What secures Stones as representative of a recognisably British state-national formation is the way she demonstrates a Thatcherite neoliberal subjectivity. Stones exaggeratedly conforms to Wendy Brown's typology of the neoliberal subject self, one of those 'rational, calculating creatures whose moral autonomy is measured by their capacity for "self-care" – the ability to provide for their own needs and service their own ambitions'.[32] Her rationalism and ambition are strongly evidenced and given their proper economic character by her exhaustive accounting of her personal wealth via her account books, or 'blue bank babies'.[33] Like all good neoliberal subjects, however, Stones is also wholeheartedly dedicated to consumption; her meticulous economism is periodically rewarded by shopping sprees she describes as a kind of 'savagery'.[34] Stones is a particular vision of self-realisation: referring to herself in the third person, constantly pep-talking and obsessively marshalling her resources, 'playing tricks on my mind, putting up pictures round my flat, repeating radical words', and dieting as a response to her feelings of inferiority and sibling jealousy.[35] In this regard she is a perfectly rendered example of what Sara Farris and Catherine Rottenberg describe as a neoliberal or 'righted' feminist, one who is 'not only individualised but entrepreneurial in the sense that she is oriented towards optimising her resources throughout incessant calculation, personal initiative, and innovation'.[36] Synchronised with this entrepreneurialism is the gradual effacement of discourses of equal rights, liberation and social justice, which has its starkest racial inscription in the way that women's rights have become weaponised in anti-immigrant and Islamophobic rhetoric across Western Europe.[37] Joss provides a counter-example to Stones in his subtle advocacy for a womanist politics, conveyed in moments such as those when he suggests to Colman that '[b]lack men need to be more gentle', that '[t]hey could learn a lot from women'.[38] In the language of British reinvention, Stones is *Trumpet*'s alternative vision of post-1979 British self-creation, the transformation into the entrepreneurial subject.

The connection to the British state has more dimensions than the general Thatcherite thrust of transformative entrepreneurial feminism. Beyond the economic logic of profit-oriented ghost-writing, Stones's 'Interview Exclusive' emphasises her acquisition of representational power over the Moody story: 'It is my book really. [. . .] I am Colman Moody's ghost writer. His psyche. I like the idea of finding his voice'.[39] Any appropriation of voice in this way has an implied political character in relation to both the devolutionary and multicultural strands of elaborated Britishness. Stones's would-be white mediation of black experience underlines many of the dynamics of publishing that mean black writers are excluded in favour of white writers doing the representing; David Dabydeen's *A Harlot's Progress* (1999), published a year after *Trumpet*, engages with the same question of white mediation, allegorised through the competing interests of the abolitionist and the slave in the composition of slave narrative. This problematic of representation is sharpened by the literary-economic field. As Corinne Fowler has observed, even black writers who are published in Britain are already party to an editorial compact that applies a stringent test of economic viability targeted at a book-buying market that is largely metropolitan and white.[40] Further, the struggle for representational power also has a direct political correlation in the increasing usefulness of black visibility in the media and arts to the New Labour agenda, not only to establish its 'one nation' credentials but also as a functionalist approach to culture that models, and consequently 'achieves', social inclusion.[41] The acquisition of proprietorial rights over Joss Moody's story, and the structuring and ordering of Colman's biography to match, is suggestive of a dynamic of 'multicultural laundering' that the New Labour spin machine was already putting in motion between the 1997 election and *Trumpet*'s publication in 1998. But this multiculturalist appropriation had its deeper roots in the ways that black life had been appropriated to serve the ends of politicians and parties of all stripes in Britain during the 1980s. Thatcher's Conservative Party, for example, had used a Saatchi and Saatchi advertising campaign depicting a black man in a suit, and declaring that 'Labour says he's black. Tories say he's British', an early deployment of a familiar trope of post-racial meritocracy.[42]

Representational deficits, or the deficiency of representational democracy itself, have their own inscription in Scottish politics and Scottish letters. A sharp awareness of the 'stateless nation' and the disjunction between Scottish voting patterns and the larger British electoral map – the democratic deficit – was manifested in Scottish literature after 1979 through a marked examination of the politics of representation, acts of 'speaking for' that engaged at both a parliamentary-democratic and literary-aesthetic level.[43] Sophie Stones's book never comes to pass, but her would-be acquisition of narrative control from a position of dominance over Colman, both in her level of articulacy and her relative economic strength, is part of the same representational struggle, including scepticism over some of the fundamental assumptions of representative parliamentary democracy itself associated with James Kelman.[44] The partiality of representation, and the limits of literature as 'representative' either in a political or collective sense, is provided by the 'Editorial' sections of the novel, voiced by an unidentified editor who has the same relationship to *Trumpet* as Stones has to her own book project. Just as Stones's objective is to collate testimonies of Joss Moody's life into a coherent and saleable narrative, the 'Editorials' connect that 'ghost-writing' process to the aggregation, selection and presentation that structure the novel as a whole. Alice Ferrebe has commented that the idea of voice constitutes an 'emancipatory potentiality' in *Trumpet*.[45] As in *Trainspotting*, the apparent democratic polyvocality of the novel suggests some 'writing back' to the constitutional structure of the United Kingdom, but unlike in *Trainspotting*, the regulating and organising principle behind *Trumpet*'s diverse voices is made perceptible. This editor is more rumina- tive than Stones, and awakened to the ethical implications of ghost-writing, or more broadly, literary mediation: 'Many ghost writers believe they are the real authority on their subject and not the ghost themselves'.[46] The resolution of voice in *Trumpet* is not simply the wresting away of represen- tational rights from a political, cultural and economic 'centre' in metropoli- tan England, imperfectly personified in Sophie Stones, and subsequently distributed around manifold narrative perspectives in a performance of vernacular democratisation. The editorial voice concedes its own authorial sovereignty, which acquires representational authority in the same manner as British representative democracy; writers, like the imperial rulers, 'tend to get irritable if their subject disagrees with them'.[47] This recognition of the limited radical potential of literary representation as 'voice' is in step with a critique of devolution as a form of political management: as Scott Hames writes, '[c]onceiving devolution as a granting-of-voice [. . .] tends to reinscribe the containment logic of 1970s UK centralism'.[48] *Trumpet*'s rep- resentational caveats acknowledge the way that such a centralism operates in representational terms: for black writers avoiding political appropriation while carrying a burden of collective representation, and also for Scottish vernacular narrative or devolutionary 'voice' being received as a surrogate for a more activated form of democracy in Scotland.

Malt fanatics and talentless fuckwits: *Trumpet*'s nations

What adds bite to any national-constitutional reading of *Trumpet* is the novel's explicit representation of national belonging and *ethnos,* with a particular focus on the national association conferred by birth and the counterclaim of an overarching Britishness. As with Millie Moody's sense of relief at her return, Scotland is imagined as an affective territory, one which is definitively bordered. Colman Moody unexpectedly finds that his ambivalence about 'crossing a border' on his journey back to Scotland from London transforms over the course of the train journey, and the 'thought of arriving at Glasgow Central fills him with excitement'.[49] Exilic return to territorial Scotland is emphatically desirable for Joss Moody, who knows he is in his 'own country' from the moment the train reaches Carlisle; the traversing of the border itself is the point at which his 'heart starts beating'.[50] Sharply contrasted to Rice's claim of national estrangement, each of these journeys sets up Scotland as a site of diasporic return that is correlated formally with the hereditary influence of the previous generation. Joss Moody's affective responses are mediated through Colman's recall of his father, amplifying the echo of Joss's excited return in Colman's own. The reported language Colman uses to describe his father's reaction to Scotland, his 'own country', is similar to the language Joss himself in 'Last Word' uses to describe his own father's sense of national longing, for 'my country, my own one'. It remains unresolved as to whether Joss has inherited the language of exilic loss from John Moore, or whether his own experience of national exile inflects his memories of his father in the final correspondence with his son Colman. But the mutual framing of diasporic longing and territorial return, far from suggesting Joss's fundamental estrangement from Scotland, instead points to an equivalence between his exile from Scotland and that of his father from his 'mother country'.

In the case of Joss, this national-territorial affiliation is augmented by a series of cultural markers which he uses to designate himself as a committed Scot. Linguistically, Colman recalls his father speaking Scots and idiomatic Scottish English, such as 'eedyit' and 'coorie in'.[51] After moving to England, Joss 'clung on to his' Scottish accent, '[d]etermined that everyone would know he was Scottish'.[52] This 'determination' manifests itself in a form of commodity nationalism: Joss is a 'malt fanatic', who 'liked them all to have Scottish things, daft naff Scottish things to keep them in touch', 'packets of tattie scones, slices of square sausage, bottles of Barrs irn bru. Shortbread. Black bun' and black pudding.[53] Supplementing the nostalgic sensory triggers of home, Joss consciously aligns himself with an idea of 'Scotland the Brand', where commodities form a differentiating element for a heritage nationalism. This is both literally 'branding' in the product placement of Barr's soft drinks, and the nostalgic brand of the Scottish nation conveyed by the domesticity of 'tattie scones' and 'square sausage'. Hidden within the list of Scottish foodstuffs is a ludic appropriation of a common narrative trope in writing coded as black British – a culinary nostalgia for foods from the West Indies, South Asia or Africa. This performance or protestation of national belonging has some semblance of racialised precariousness, of a blackness that lies 'beyond' the nation. But Joss's commodity-oriented nationalism had already been identified as a larger historical tendency in *Scotland – the Brand*, where David McCrone, Angela Morris and Richard Kiely argue that this mode of national enactment, fetishising a 'panoply of material and symbolic inheritances [. . .] hardly older than the possessor', has 'uncommon power in Scotland because it is a stateless nation', motivated by 'the fear, or rather the threat, of submersion into a much bigger British state'.[54] Joss's 'cling-ing' on to 'daft', 'naff' objects associated with his life in Scotland, and his active reproduction of linguistic and cultural markers of that life, hint at resistance to the hegemonic injunctions of Britain's cultural centre: in his case, to be black and British.

Joss's hunger for the salty, fatty materiality of Lorne sausage is diametri-cally opposed to the ambivalence with which John Moore regards the por-ridge, 'fog with lumps in it', he is given after stepping off HMS *Spiteful*.[55] In the space of a generation, the gently mocked 'cuisine' of Scotland has metamorphosed from a Sulterian ethereal 'fog', closely linked in John Moore's account to the 'ghostly' quality of white Scottish people, to a concrete identification, an embodied relationship that carries a particular linguistic connotation. The punctuation of the list with 'black bun' and the reference to 'black pudding' are not coincidental. They share the same playful alignment of the black signifier with exaggerated Scottish cultural and culinary artefacts as the black Jacobean moment. This pattern is estab-lished early on when Joss's blackness is articulated as a familiar kind of Scottish commodity by his wife Millie, who muses that '[h]is skin was the colour of Highland toffee'.[56] Colman's recitation of the list of his father's 'brand Scotland' items also includes a copy of comic strip *The Broons*, a Scottish cultural vehicle for a burnished representation of working-class life which Kay had already hijacked in various poems. In 'The Broons' Bairn's Black', for example, Scotland's national 'heart attack' is caused by the sudden revelation promised by the poem's title: the scandalous inter-ruption of white homogeneity by the black Scottish baby.[57]

These national markers are then linked via Scoto-British kitsch to Joss's clothing-based 'passing', his gender performance, as Colman scornfully asks his dead father, 'Why don't you get a kilt and play your horn in a kilt? The jazz world would love that'.[58] The kilt is a pre-eminent part of the compensatory heritage nationalism McCrone et al. describe in *Scotland – The Brand*. This welds Joss's enactment of nation to Colman's perplexity at the disconnection between his father's gendering and his sex organs; Joss's gender and nationality are both forms of performance. Aside from the com-mercial novelty of the kilt-wearing jazz trumpeter, the precept that Scots wear nothing under the kilt means that implicit in wearing one is the threat of exposure of the biological, the reintroduction of the 'real' sexed body that lies under what Colman sees as the fabric, and fabrication, of Joss. However, as the question posed by the fictional Transvestite Action Group in *Trumpet* after Joss's death and 'exposure' goes: 'What is the force of that reality?'[59] The question translates directly to a Butlerian understanding of performance not as re-presenting or masking a hidden reality but as the reality itself. In the case of Joss's nation and gender, brought together in the kilted jazz performance, the performance is the reality.

Where Joss Moody models the transnational black Scot, the representation of his son Colman plots the vexed relationship between Scottish and 'black British' constituencies. With his racialisation and internal migration between Scotland and England as a child, Colman represents a unique subject position that takes on a key representative function in terms of national relationships within the Union:

> We moved to London when I was seven. I got rid of my Glasgow accent.
> Well, almost. [. . .] It was a fucking nightmare moving down here with that accent. I got ribbed. Non stop. Got it both ways. London was seething, racist. I don't remember much about Glasgow.[60]

As a black Scot who '[g]ot it both ways', Colman's national and racial differences in England compound one another. He describes himself as ending up 'practically schizophrenic', thus hinting at both the psychopathologisation of blackness and the 'split self' which recurs through Scottish cultural criticism.[61] His nightmare dislocation involves both an attempt to 'stay Scottish' to please his father, and a recognisable process of periphery-to-centre adaptation. The adjustment is twofold, accentual and lexical, as Colman's willed self-erasure of the Glaswegian speaking voice and Scots language positions him within a long genealogy of anglicised Scots for whom linguistic conformity is a condition of successful adaptation to Union. However, this is not configured as the loss of an organic, native or inherited Scotland but as a more profound deracination: 'My father kept telling me I was Scottish. Born there. But I didn't feel Scottish. Didn't feel English either. Didn't feel anything'.[62] The national differentiation here points towards 'British' as an unspoken and empty category, the 'anything' which follows procedurally from the actually experienced national formations of England and Scotland.

Despite his comment that he remembers little of Glasgow, Colman does pointedly remember one crucial encounter from his time as a young boy. He experiences his own moment of childhood racialisation, by witnessing racist abuse on a bus in Glasgow that provokes his own epiphany of race.

> I was on this bus with my mother and this black man got on. This was in Glasgow. So I'd be six or something like that. And somebody said something horrible to him, called him a fucking ape or some shit like that. [. . .] I was scared people were staring at me. It made me look at my own colour of skin when I got home. Maybe that was the first time I really noticed it. And I was sort of surprised by it.[63]

'This was in Glasgow' has the plain tone of recollection, a geographical marker to assist the ghost writer in lining up the chronology, but as a declarative statement taken in isolation it also emphasises that the encounter is undeniably one of Scottish racism and race formation, not to be confused with his later experiences of racism in London. Colman's detailed recall, more than thirty years after the event, reinforces the powerful formative significance of the moment, which is configured in precise, Fanonian terms. Fanon describes the way that racialisation entails a 'suffocating reification' that denies subjectivity and renders the black man 'an object in the midst of other objects'.[64] The epiphanic moment Fanon describes is provoked by a child's reaction to meeting him in the street, when his race becomes an 'objective fact': '"Mama, a Negro!" [. . .] the little white boy throws himself into his mother's arms: Mama, the nigger's going to eat me up'.[65] *Trumpet* repositions the psychoanalytic players of Fanon's staged encounter so that it is the child who experiences the revelation of objectifying racialisation, rather than the educated émigré who moves from colonial margin to centre. But further, as an adoptee, and the child of a white mother, Colman's particular situation has profound consequences. Racial objectification not only materialises broader social difference in his body, but blocks the progressive implication of 'adoptive' social organisation at both familial and national levels.

Recurrently, Joss's insistence on natal nationhood is countermanded by Colman's reiterated lack of national feeling: 'His father was always telling him: you are Scottish, you were born in Scotland and that makes you Scottish. But he doesn't feel Scottish'.[66] Colman's explicit Scottish racial objectification partly explains his scepticism of the value of his natal connection to Scotland, but this scepticism also translates into a constitutional context too. It is incongruous that Joss, the adoptive father whose life is defined by the rejection of the biologically deterministic conditions of his birth, should be the primary advocate for national affiliation premised on birth location. Instead it is Colman, born in 1961, who has the clearer perspective on the interrelation between the affective and the constitutional implications of nationhood in late twentieth-century Britain. The question of nativity has specific purchase in a context that unifies both the racial and Scottish national dimensions of *Trumpet*: the evolving question of enfranchisement. Matthew Brown translates Joss's assertion as holding that a 'Scottish origin bestows Scottish citizenship'.[67] This is true in the understanding of 'citizenship' in an informal sense, as part of an imagined community. But a Scottish native origin does not confer much in the way of official citizenship in two important senses. First, Scotland does not have the ability to issue formal citizenship or exert influence over immigration policy, as those powers are reserved to Westminster. Second, the Scottish parliamentary franchise – a fair measurement of Scotland's 'official' citizenship – is residency-based and does not come with birth conditions attached.[68] This breaks down along ethnic versus civic lines, where a historical link like birth translates into *ethnos* – the 'feeling' of Scotland which Colman lacks and Joss works so hard to preserve – versus the *civis* defined by living and participating in life in Scotland, traceable in the stress that *Trumpet* places on the border-crossing back into Scotland the 'place'. Under this franchise, 'affective' or natal Scottishness is not enough: constitutional decisions are a matter for people in Scotland, a point of divergence between Scotland and the British state. Conversely, British citizenship laws in the post-war period have moved away even from rights based on location of birth towards genealogical or patrial requirements, which, as Ian Baucom has pointed out, are de facto racialised laws: 'most of those who would qualify as patrials [under the British Nationality Act 1981] would be the children or grandchildren of whites who had moved abroad rather than the children of Indians, Pakistanis or Nigerians whose parents or grandparents had been born in the colonies'.[69] Extending the wilful self-creation of Joss, it is through Colman, the adoptee, that the importance of lived experience both in affective and constitutional terms for Scotland is most explicitly registered: in Joss's own formulation, 'related the way it mattered'.[70]

Setting up the juxtaposition with Scotland, Colman's life in London provides an index of post-war black migration to the capital, and his experiences replicate many of those represented in other writing coded 'black British'. His conditions of dwelling, in a flat afflicted with 'wonky electrics', 'the smell of rotting mice', 'damp peeling paint' and decrepit linoleum, is a call back to what James Procter describes as 'the very real conditions of squalor that black settlers were subjected to in the early postwar years'.[71] Meanwhile, his young adulthood, growing up in the context of the 1970s and 1980s, 'picked up by the police countless times [. . .] for doing fuck all', occurs in the era of moral panic around mugging, and of *Policing the Crisis*.[72] Colman's concept of blackness is rooted in a larger national discursive practice that *Policing the Crisis* identified, particularly in the equivalence drawn between black people, threat and criminality.[73] 'Mugging' recurs a number of times in *Trumpet*. Colman observes that, when growing up, 'practically every black guy my age that I saw on TV had just been arrested for something. Or was accused of mugging. It's like we only had the one face to them. The same face'.[74] *Policing the Crisis* notes that the British mediascape is an important load-bearer for racial ideology that informs and is informed by policing, 'made active and realised [. . .] in the practices and apparatuses of news construction'.[75] Neither had this process of news construction significantly changed by the middle of the 1990s. Colman is struck by the realisation that his arrival at his grandmother's house in Scotland still fits the prototype of racialised criminality: 'Men that look exactly like Colman are always in the news. Some top arsehole in the police said recently that black guys were more likely to be muggers than white guys'; the reference here is to comments made by Metropolitan Police Commissioner Paul Condon in 1995, that 'most "muggers" in London are "black"'.[76] Colman's self-conception as black becomes hyper-determined by the persecution of state and media agencies directed towards him as representative of the threatening, fungible black man: 'It is not easy to travel in this country. Black guys like him'.[77] Like Joss Moody's posthumous relationship with the recurring 'red pen' of the National Health Service, which reiterates his femaleness via a biopolitics of classification that mirrors Condon's comments, Colman's relationship with the police is a reminder that the British state itself has historically been the primary actor in the taxonomising and persecution of black people.

Colman's self-doubt is sharply contrasted against what he sees as the confidence and success of his father as an iconic black man. Matthew Brown suggests that Colman 'perceives himself through an economy of representation redolent of Gilroy's problem/victim dynamic', in which black people are either a threat to British life or perennial victims of an inevitable racism, as 'homeless refugees'.[78] However, Colman's particular 'problem/victim' conception takes on some characteristics of resistance in the late 1990s, standing diametrically opposite to a discourse of a normative 'multi-ethnic Britain'. As Arun Kundnani observes, in British political multicultural discourse '"ethnic" communities are always "vibrant", always making "positive contributions", always to be "tolerated"'.[79] Like the besuited black man of the Saatchi and Saatchi campaign for the Conservative Party, black people were strategically deployed – and in some cases deployed themselves – as illustrative of the new Britishness. One thing noticeably absent from Colman's testimony is the counter-example of the prevailing media image of a young black man in the historical moment of *Trumpet*: the resonant picture of Stephen Lawrence, whose symbolic inclusion in the nation was as fixed as the equivalent casting out of his murderers. Steven Blevins points to the example of the bespoke tailor Ozwald Boateng, exuding entrepreneurial confidence and paying due reverence to Savile Row as a nostalgic icon of Victorian British commercial-cultural life, who presents himself 'as a product of Cool Britannia – if not its very emblem'.[80] Colman, however, is not the handsome face of British harmony, entrepreneurial success and a pluralistic 'Cool Britannia' in the Boateng mode. The foregrounding of his lack of ability – as a 'talentless, ordinary fuckwit' in contradistinction to Joss Moody – is itself resistant to a certain vision of black success as an aspect of elaborated Britishness, as well as to the black-positive codes of representation that had defined an earlier era of black arts in Britain.[81] In a national context where minority rights are increasingly imagined as contingent on cultural-economic contribution, upstanding moral conduct and an allegiance to nebulous and shifting 'British values', Colman's characteristic enmity, grievance and failure take on pointed political significance as the right simply to be an independent sovereign subject.

Colman's informed comments on the subject of police profiling, meanwhile, are part of a sociological consciousness reflected in the way he 'likes talking about black people and white people and how they do or do not get on'.[82] His interrogation of his own experiences as a black man are part of a larger examination of black politics in devolutionary Britain. One central element is the thwarted desire for intergenerational masculine approval, Colman conceding that 'I wanted him [his father] to be proud of me as a man, as a black man'.[83] The disruption to gender equivalence presented by Joss's death is concurrently a disruption to the expectations of this black masculinity, unwinding a 'core' blackness that had been at the centre of British Black Power – Afro-Caribbean, male and heterosexual – signalled in Hall's 'New Ethnicities'. Colman's struggle to find a fitting replacement black politics is textured further by his explicit rejection of pan-Africanism:

> Colman doesn't feel as if he has a history. Doesn't feel comfortable with mates of his that go on and on about Africa. It feels false to him, mates that get dressed up in African gear, wank on about being African with a fucking cockney accent, man. Back to Africa is just unreal as far as Colman is concerned. He's never been to Africa, so how can he go back?[84]

Beyond Colman's anomie, his puzzlement at the prospect of going 'back to Africa' – either geographically or politically – speaks to the dissipation of historical modes of black organisation both in Britain and transnationally, and the way that, in Gilroy's terms, by the 1990s 'the public sphere seems to have been entirely abandoned' by a 'voguish Africentrism'.[85] His consternation is born of his own experience of racism and social exclusion encountering the realisation that, in Kalbir Shukra's unflinching account, '[r]adical black politics in Britain is dead'.[86] That death had taken place in the decade or so preceding the publication of *Trumpet*. Colman's challenge is that of developing new political literacy and strategies in a 'multi-ethnic' moment when even the *Daily Mail* had swivelled around to champion the cause of Doreen and Neville Lawrence, without much change to the racism embedded in underlying economic and institutional structures.

'The passage I'd like to take you to is music': black radicalism

Colman's sociological imagination, his understated literacy in a state politics of race, his reflections on racialisation in Scotland and his desire for relational black 'approval' from his father all point towards an attempt to grasp the roots of his racialised experience: in short, his struggle to find a mode of radical critique. This is configured as a political inheritance; his memories of Joss Moody are of a man with a more purposeful sense of black consciousness, who observes the axiomatic link between black collectivity and black music, that '[a]ll blues are stories. Our stories [. . .] our history. You can't understand the history of slavery without knowing about the slave songs'.[87] The emphatic 'our' stresses the collectivism at the heart of Joss's conception of blackness. However, much of the critical analysis of *Trumpet* has espoused an opposite position, that the vision of reinvention offered by Joss's re-gendering is a testament to an individuated worldview, a 'post-racial' perspective in which his blackness is an infringement of a fully realised subjectivity. Matthew Brown, for example, gauges Joss's 'radical self-authorship' as foundering on race as a persistent 'interpellative stranglehold on individual identity'.[88] Sara Upstone suggests that *Trumpet* imagines a way of living that is '[p]ost-racial, post-gender, post-identity'; that when Joss plays the trumpet, it is 'not just the space in which Joss is without gender, it is also the space in which he is without race'.[89] These accounts cohere around the crucial passage at the heart of the novel, 'Music', which depicts the intensity of a single jazz performance. The passage is bracketed by a moment of deconstruction, as Joss 'loses his sex, his race, his memory', and reconstruction, as he 'brings himself back', 'slowly, piecing himself together'.[90] There is no doubt that a form of radical renegotiation is at stake in 'Music', a section that, in its prenatal and posthumous visions, breaks the mainly naturalistic narrative mode of *Trumpet*. However, the indelibility of blackness is noted in the same section: the stripped-back Joss becomes a 'small, black mark', a mark that is simultaneously 'representational' and '[invested] with racial meaning'.[91] This is commensurate with the ambivalence in the novel towards the dissolution of political and social formations into universalism. For example, as Carole Jones has noted, *Trumpet*'s post-gender credentials have been oversold, Joss's 'passing' tends towards the socially conservative, and it contains little by way of 'radical proliferation' of gender.[92]

Rejecting race understood as biocentric taxonomy does not mean rejecting blackness as a political collective. However, Upstone also seems to step back from the possibility of black collectivity in *Trumpet* when she comments that 'Joss is not black, but mixed race'.[93] On one level, this is an acknowledgement of 'mixed racedness' as a lived experience, or as a taxonomy with significant social history and purchase, discursively produced, and with its own specific characteristics. This includes an anxiety around eligibility for a black political category; for example, in one of many moments of self-excoriation, Colman describes himself as 'yellow'.[94] However, the mutual exclusivity between 'black' and 'mixed race', the 'not blackness' that this claim entails, is untenable in the abstract, let alone in a literary-cultural field where such signifiers are constructed and contested. The assertion suggests an unexpected return to a quasi-biocentric understanding of race that jars with Upstone's extensive rejection of biocentrism earlier in *Rethinking Race*, and her recognition that writing in Britain represents a 'diversity of blackness'.[95] The strict prosecution of racial taxonomies requires that blackness be a pure state, invalidated by 'racial mixing', but, as David Parker and Miri Song write in *Rethinking 'Mixed Race'*, '[t]o merely mix "race" is to concede too much to those who would divide and judge human beings on the grounds of biologically inherited characteristics'.[96] Likewise, Kehinde Andrews argues that '[b]lackness is a rejection of race' understood as biocentric, and consequentially 'makes no claims to unity based on biological purity'.[97] Despite works like *Chiaroscuro* and 'So You Think I am a Mule?', which interrogate various processes of black inclusion and exclusion and present blackness in precisely the terms Andrews outlines, Kay's work has generated readings that position mixed-racedness as both biographical and racial-biological. Peter Clandfield, for example, describes Kay as being of 'mixed black-white (African-British) biological parentage' and consequently, in reading *The Adoption Papers*, notes with an incongruous haemocentrism that the semi-autobiographical character of the daughter 'has Scottish as well as black/ African blood'.[98] Joss, like his son Colman, is black *and* 'mixed-race', part of a series of 'complex combinations [. . .] of affiliations' which provide a more substantive basis for Upstone's local argument that the unintelligibility of race taxonomies in *Trumpet* tends towards their subversion.[99]

Explaining the need to maintain blackness as a political constituency, Kehinde Andrews argues that 'dreaming that we [black people] can be an undifferentiated part of the system is a fantasy', a fantasy that amounts to the re-enactment of discredited integrationist arguments that paper over rather than resolve the structural conditions of racism.[100] Moody's 'Music' should not be construed as that kind of fantasy, in which the dream is of a 'non-racialised' subject position that looks like nothing so much as the right to be what Lentin and Titley describe as 'free like me', or the individuated freedoms enjoyed largely by the white middle classes in liberal developed economies.[101] The representational and collectivist implication of the 'small black mark' makes sense both in terms of the novel and the historical connotations of black music. In *The Black Atlantic*, Paul Gilroy observes that the significance of music for black Atlantic expressive culture grows in proportion to the limits of language: '[m]usic becomes vital at the point at which linguistic and semantic indeterminacy/polyphony arise amidst the protracted battle between masters, mistresses, and slaves'.[102] Contemporary jazz music is thus an extended part of what Gilroy names the 'topos of unsayability'. The implication of this unsayability is twofold. First, it refers to the condition of linguistic mutilation in plantation slavery: the separation of people with shared languages; a culture of enforced silence; the strict prohibition on literacy. Second, 'unsayability' describes the impossible representational task presented by both the brutality of slavery and the extreme partiality of the archive, which reduces the experience of slavery and the lives of enslaved people to the accountancy and the metrics of the slave trade itself.[103] Music hence offers the 'capacity to express the inexpressible and communicate the effects of a history of barbarity that exhausts the resources of language'.[104] Any attempt to express adequately this unsayability in literary form necessitates a form of experimentalism that can capture, only imperfectly, the 'oral structures' and 'distinctive kinesics' of black Atlantic cultural forms.[105] As Joss himself says, '[y]ou can't understand the history of slavery without knowing about the slave songs', making explicit his understanding of the profound connection between music and black history.[106] Rather than wishing for an abolition of blackness or a fantasy of its obsolescence, *Trumpet*'s 'Music' chapter shows a profound comprehension, and a working-through, of the aesthetics of black radicalism.

The interrelation of literary form, jazz music and black history in 'Music' correlates with the cultural project of Fred Moten's *In the Break*, a critical work that, in its own extraordinary methodology, style and structure, lives out its central principle that jazz constitutes the aesthetic of black radicalism. The eponymous essay, 'In the Break', shares some of the formal practices of *Trumpet*'s 'Music'. It is a piece of cultural theory in the form of codified jazz composition. Indeed, 'In the Break' is grounded in a period of jazz history and black literary politics that overlaps with *Trumpet*: Moody's debut album *Millie's Song* is released in 1958, the same year as Miles Davis's *Milestones*. For Moten, the '[s]yncopation, performance, and anarchic organization of phonic substance' of jazz performance delineates 'an ontological field wherein black radicalism is set to work'.[107] This radicalism is characterised by an 'abundant refusal of closure', the 'reconstructive improvisation of ensemble' that mediates between two polarities of being, the singularity and the totality. Moten's literary-political examples are, for singularity, what he calls the 'devolutionary aesthetic individualism' of Ralph Ellison, and for totality, the strong collectivist and historical-materialist orientation of Amiri Baraka's black cultural nationalism.[108] It is thus 'in the break' of the music that the ongoing negotiation of a radical black politics in America is not played out, but played on, an ongoing improvisation found in a 'location of interplay' between Ellison and, particularly, Baraka. Moten's exemplars and argument prove a case applied to the particular racial context of the United States, but the aesthetic-political principles of 'In the Break' also speak to *Trumpet*, not only in the novel's inheritance of American musical forms but in its relating of those forms to the historical, political, national context of devolutionary Scotland and England.

Shifting to focus on Davis's 'So What?', Moten's seminal example of modal improvisation as a compositional form, he remarks that '[t]he passage I'd like to take you to is music'.[109] This serendipitous phrasing indicates the way that *Trumpet* itself anticipates elements of Moten's codification of black radical aesthetics. Read in the context of a black radical tradition, the indelibility of the black mark at the epicentre of Joss's performance connotes less a natal or biocentric essence than the inscription of blackness as a principle of improvisational disruption, what Moten calls 'the extended movement of a specific upheaval, an ongoing irruption that anarranges every line'.[110] Considering the chronological and geographic distance between 'In the Break' and *Trumpet*, the novel's anticipation of Moten's black radical aesthetics demonstrates a strong conceptual continuity in black radical expression. Embedded in Moten's improvisation is the prospect of a radically deconstructive 'active forgetting', as when Moody manages to 'get down deep enough, he loses his sex, his race, his memory'.[111] *Trumpet*'s eschewal of biological determinism, its adoptive and gender-destabilising characteristics, correlate to the rejection of both biocentric race and the fetishisation of 'originarity' that is key to black radicalism, 'the natal occasion that our musico-political tradition must evade'.[112] When Moten speaks of the '(elegiac) resurrection' of ensemble, to be found 'in music, in utopian desire, in institutions strange and peculiar, and in their echoes and aftermaths, deconstructions and reconstructions', his conceptualisation speaks not only to the unique narrative configuration of the 'Music' passage itself, but to the whole of *Trumpet*: the tension between polyphonic perspectives and organising narrative agent; the contingency of lives reconstructed through memory and testimony; and the subversion of 'institutions' both public and conceptual.[113] The 'ungendering and re(en)gendering' or sexual dimension of jazz performance interrupts the 'smooth, false interinanimations of manhood, nation, race' that, as Andrews describes, have particularly troubled American black cultural nationalism, 'patriarchal and heteronormative at its core'.[114] These heteronormative and patriarchal attributes have also troubled black political organisation in Britain, a fact alluded to in *Trumpet* through Colman's fantasies of sexual potency, part of a larger 'austere, Spartan masculinity' which Gilroy calls 'disastrous for black men', which merge with his reverence for his father's blackness.[115] Attempting to make sense of his own gender disorientation after Joss's death, he feels certain that if Joss had had a prosthetic penis, 'he would have rammed it in, I promise you'.[116]

Like 'In the Break', 'Music' is an examination of the dynamic negotiation between the individual and the collective. Even in the throes of his own solo performance, in the midst of his subject-centred self-destruction and reconstruction, Joss Moody acknowledges the 'galloping piano behind him', and the give-and-take interlocutions and musical exchanges of the jazz band in action, the improvisatory act oscillating between the singular and the ensemble.[117] Moten's formations of singular and ensemble are not purely abstract but have their roots in an actually existing black history, in racism, in black America's 'political despair' and in the aesthetic modes of Ellison and Baraka emergent from and part of that history. Likewise, Joss Moody's call-and-response, and *Trumpet*'s meditation on the relationship between the individual and the collective, has its own historical co-ordinates. Among many other operations, 'Music' applies to the distinct context of national Scotland: two of the polarities between which Joss improvises are 'Scotland' and 'Africa'.[118] The significance of race in Scotland, and of national differentiation within Britain, throughout *Trumpet* opens up the prospect that Joss Moody is the black soloist playing through a relationship with the 'ensemble' national formation of Scotland, at the point of incipient devolution. After all, Colman reminisces that his father thought of his band as 'all part of some big family. Some of them were white, some black'.[119]

One immediate difficulty that arises from this interpretation is the exclusivity between the various modes of black radicalism represented by C. L. R. James, Cedric Robinson, Amiri Baraka and Fred Moten, and the more conservative political project of a devolved Scotland. As a form of constitutional containment that remodels the archaic Union state, devolution does not represent the achievement of radical change. Even modern nationhood on the European social democratic model affords no fundamental break from the capitalist, neo-imperial world system, nor any guaranteed means to address the structural conditions or historical inequities that power contemporary racism. While the black Jacobeans are politically playful, staging a symbolic invasion of the staid and settled territory of the Union, they do not present a coherent political programme. Nevertheless, it is clear that *Trumpet* identifies some prospective black political organisation contingent on the changing constitutional face of Britain. While historical forms of organisation such as pan-Africanism are rejected either as fantasy or as pretension, the novel alludes to the need for devising a new understanding of black politics that considerably extends the contemporary 'black British' frame. In a similar manner to the improvisational dialectics of singularity and ensemble that Moten describes, *Trumpet* poses an open-ended question about black lives in the space of potential change – both constitutional and imaginative – represented by devolution, in which the shape and character of the 'ensemble' subtly shifts. As Murray Pittock identifies, Jacobitism itself presented a critique of parliamentary corruption and of a 'centralized and centralizing state and its thirst for war and Empire'.[120] There is something 'radical', in the sense of grasping structural conditions at the root, in the novel's identification of national differentiation within the Union itself, the disruptive potential of independence implied by that differentiation, and in the tartan-clad black Jacobeans striding out of the past.

Notes

1. Kay, *Trumpet*, p. 99.
2. James, C. L. R., *The Black Jacobins: Toussaint L'Ouverture and the San Domingo Rebellion* (New York: Vintage, 1989 [1938]), p. 25.
3. Robinson, Cedric, *Black Marxism: The Making of the Black Radical Tradition* (Chapel Hill: University of North Carolina Press, 2000 [1983]), p. 265.
4. Moten, Fred, *In the Break: The Aesthetics of the Black Radical Tradition* (Minneapolis: University of Minnesota Press, 2003).
5. Kay, *Trumpet*, p. 99.
6. See Kidd, Colin, 'From Jacobitism to the SNP: The Crown, the Union and the Scottish Question', Stenton Lecture, 2013, University of Reading, www.reading. ac.uk/web/files/history/From_Jacobitism_to_the_SNP.pdf (last accessed 20 August 2019), pp. 3–4.
7. See Andrews, Kehinde, 'Narrow Nationalism' in *Back to Black: Retelling Black Radicalism for the 21st Century* (London: Zed Books, 2018), pp. 1–34.
8. Kay, *Trumpet*, pp. 271–2.
9. Kay, *Trumpet*, p. 273.
10. McLeod, 'Adoption Aesthetics', p. 214.
11. Mbembe, *Critique of Black Reason*, p. 33.
12. Folorunso et al., 'In the Eyes of the Beholder', p. 84.
13. Cottle, Simon, 'Mediatized Public Crisis and Civil Society Renewal: The Racist Murder of Stephen Lawrence', *Crime, Media, Culture* 1:1 (2005), pp. 49–71: 51.
14. Shukra, *Changing Pattern*, p. 94.
15. Innes, Catherine Lyn, *A History of Black and Asian Writing in Britain, 1700–2000* (Cambridge: Cambridge University Press, 2002), p. 2.
16. Innes, *History of Black and Asian Writing*, p. 244.
17. Peter Clandfield, '"What is in My Blood?" Contemporary Black Scottishness and the Work of Jackie Kay' in Teresa Hubel and Neil Brooks (eds), *Literature and Racial Ambiguity* (Amsterdam: Rodopi, 2002), pp. 1–25: 5, 16.
18. One recognisable example is in contemporary sports coaching and journalism; see King, Colin, 'Is Football the New African Slave Trade?' in Daniel Burdsey (ed.), *Race,*

Ethnicity and Football: Persisting Debates and Emergent Issues (London: Routledge, 2011), pp. 36–49.

19. Clandfield, 'What is in my Blood?', p. 4.
20. Clandfield, 'What is in my Blood?', p. 6.
21. Clandfield, 'What is in my Blood?', p. 4.
22. Rice, Alan, '"Heroes across the Sea": Black and White British Fascination with African Americans in the Contemporary Black British Fiction of Caryl Phillips and Jackie Kay' in Heike Raphael-Hernandez (ed.), *Blackening Europe: The African American Presence* (London: Routledge, 2004), pp. 217–33: 228.
23. Rice, 'Heroes', p. 228.
24. Kay, *Trumpet*, pp. 274, 275; Iain Lambert has described the way that John Moore's narrative is an adaptation of Amos Tutuola's *My Life in the Bush of Ghosts* (1954): 'This is Not Sarcasm', p. 200.
25. Kay, *Trumpet*, p. 275.
26. Rice, 'Heroes', p. 227.
27. Brooks, Libby, 'Don't Tell Me Who I Am', *The Guardian*, 12 January 2002, www.theguardian.com/books/2002/jan/12/fiction.features (last accessed 30 June 2019).
28. Billig, *Banal Nationalism*, pp. 10–11.
29. Kay, *Trumpet*, p. 2.
30. Nairn, *After Britain*, p. 50.
31. Kay, *Trumpet*, pp. 3, 152, 155.
32. Brown, Wendy, *Edgeworks: Critical Essays on Knowledge and Politics* (Princeton: Princeton University Press, 2005), pp. 42–3.
33. Kay, *Trumpet*, p. 129.
34. Kay, *Trumpet*, p. 232.
35. Kay, *Trumpet*, p. 124.
36. Farris, Sara and Catherine Rottenberg, 'Righting Feminism', *New Formations* 91 (2017), pp. 5–15: 11.
37. Farris and Rottenberg, 'Righting Feminism', p. 6.
38. Kay, *Trumpet*, p. 192.
39. Kay, *Trumpet*, p. 170.
40. See Fowler, 'A Tale of Two Novels'.
41. See Nwonka and Malik, 'Cultural Discourses'.
42. See Phillips, Caryl, *A New World Order: Essays* (New York: Vintage, 2002), p. 247.
43. Gardiner, Michael, *From Trocchi to Trainspotting: Scottish Critical Theory since 1960* (Edinburgh: Edinburgh University Press, 2006), p. 171.
44. Hames, *Literary Politics*, pp. 290–1.
45. Ferrebe, Alice, 'Between Camps: Masculinity, Race and Nation in Post-Devolution Scotland' in Schoene (ed.), *Edinburgh Companion to Contemporary Scottish Literature*, pp. 275–82: 278.
46. Kay, *Trumpet*, p. 262.
47. Kay, *Trumpet*, p. 262.
48. Hames, Scott, 'On Vernacular Scottishness and its Limits: Devolution and the Spectacle of "Voice"', *Studies in Scottish Literature* 39:1 (2013), pp. 201–22: 202.
49. Kay, *Trumpet*, pp. 190–1.
50. Kay, *Trumpet*, p. 187.
51. Kay, *Trumpet*, pp. 56, 68.
52. Kay, *Trumpet*, pp. 50–1.
53. Kay, *Trumpet*, pp. 213, 139, 198.
54. McCrone, David, Angela Morris and Richard Kiely, *Scotland – the Brand: The Making of Scottish Heritage* (Edinburgh: Edinburgh University Press, 1995), pp. 1, 196, 197.
55. Kay, *Trumpet*, p. 274.

56. Kay, *Trumpet*, p. 11.
57. Kay, Jackie, 'The Broons' Bairn's Black (A Skipping Rhyme)', *Off Colour* (Newcastle upon Tyne: Bloodaxe, 1998), p. 61.
58. Kay, *Trumpet*, p. 192.
59. Kay, *Trumpet*, p. 160.
60. Kay, *Trumpet*, pp. 53, 51.
61. Kay, *Trumpet*, p. 53.
62. Kay, *Trumpet*, p. 51.
63. Kay, *Trumpet*, p. 54.
64. Fanon, *Black Skin, White Masks*, p. 82.
65. Fanon, *Black Skin, White Masks*, pp. 85–6.
66. Kay, *Trumpet*, p. 190.
67. Brown, Matthew, 'In/Outside Scotland: Race and Citizenship in the Work of Jackie Kay', in Schoene (ed.), *Edinburgh Companion to Contemporary Scottish Literature*, pp. 219–26: 225.
68. The Scottish parliamentary franchise, which was also (excluding the expansion to include 16- and 17-year-olds) in operation for the 1997 devolution referendum, differs from the Westminster and European parliamentary franchises in the United Kingdom. In the former, absent British nationals with a historical residency connection to Scotland – most commonly expatriates – cannot vote; in the latter, some legal residents such as EU citizens are excluded from voting while non-residents with status are able to vote; see Shaw, Jo, 'Citizenship and the Franchise' in Ayelet Shachar et al. (eds), *The Oxford Handbook of Citizenship* (Oxford: Oxford University Press, 2017), pp. 290–313: 307–8.
69. Baucom, *Out of Place*, pp. 12–13.
70. Kay, *Trumpet*, p. 58.
71. Kay, *Trumpet*, p. 180; Procter, *Dwelling Places*, p. 24.
72. Kay, *Trumpet*, p. 51.
73. Hall et al. (eds), *Policing the Crisis*, p. 20.
74. Kay, *Trumpet*, p. 162.
75. Hall et al. (eds), *Policing the Crisis*, p. 83.
76. Kay, *Trumpet*, p. 224; Shukra, *Changing Pattern*, p. 114.
77. Kay, *Trumpet*, p. 189.
78. Brown, 'In/Outside Scotland', pp. 221, 226.
79. Kundnani, 'Rise and Fall', pp. 105–6.
80. Blevins, Steven, *Living Cargo: How Black Britain Performs Its Past* (Minneapolis: University of Minnesota Press, 2016), pp. 197, 209.
81. Kay, *Trumpet*, p. 45.
82. Kay, *Trumpet*, p. 192.
83. Kay, *Trumpet*, p. 49.
84. Kay, *Trumpet*, p. 191.
85. Gilroy, *Small Acts*, p. 8.
86. Shukra, *Changing Pattern*, p. 110.
87. Kay, *Trumpet*, p. 190.
88. Brown, 'In/Outside', p. 225.
89. Upstone, *Rethinking Race*, p. 109.
90. Kay, *Trumpet*, pp. 131, 136.
91. Kay, *Trumpet*, p. 131; Jones, Carole, *Disappearing Men: Gender Disorientation in Scottish Fiction 1979–1999* (Amsterdam: Rodopi, 2009), p. 114; Brown, 'In/Outside', p. 225.
92. Jones, *Disappearing Men*, pp. 109, 113.
93. Upstone, *Rethinking Race*, p. 107.
94. Kay, *Trumpet*, p. 48.
95. Upstone, *Rethinking Race*, pp. 48, 88.

96. Parker, David and Miri Song (eds), *Rethinking 'Mixed Race'* (London: Pluto Press, 2001), pp. 6, 11.
97. Andrews, *Back to Black*, p. 290.
98. Clandfield, 'What is in My Blood?', pp. 1, 11; it is particularly striking that Clandfield uses haemocentric racial proportionality to read 'So You Think I Am A Mule?', a poem that explicitly rejects gradated racial taxonomies and haemocentrism.
99. Parker and Song (eds.), *Rethinking 'Mixed Race'*, p. 8; Upstone, *Rethinking Race*, p. 108.
100. Andrews, *Back to Black*, p. 169.
101. Lentin and Titley, *Crises of Multiculturalism,* pp. 85–122.
102. Gilroy, *The Black Atlantic*, p. 74.
103. See Hartman, Saidiya, 'Venus in Two Acts', *Small Axe* 12:2 (2008), pp. 1–14.
104. Gilroy, *Small Acts*, p. 5.
105. Gilroy, *The Black Atlantic*, p. 75.
106. Kay, *Trumpet*, p. 190.
107. Moten, *In the Break*, p. 85.
108. Moten, *In the Break*, pp. 85–6.
109. Moten, *In the Break*, p. 100.
110. Moten, *In the Break*, p. 2.
111. Moten, *In the Break*, p. 90; Kay, *Trumpet*, p. 131.
112. Moten, *In the Break*, p. 2.
113. Moten, *In the Break*, p. 98.
114. Moten, *In the Break*, p. 108; Andrews, *Back to Black*, p. 128.
115. Gilroy, *Small Acts,* p. 8.
116. Kay, *Trumpet*, p. 169; Moten, *In the Break*, pp. 155, 108.
117. Kay, *Trumpet*, pp. 131, 136.
118. Kay, *Trumpet*, p. 136.
119. Kay, *Trumpet*, p. 58.
120. Pittock, Murray G. H., *Jacobitism* (London: Macmillan, 1998), p. 136.

Chapter 4

White Ethnographies:
Luke Sutherland's *Jelly Roll*

Like *Trumpet,* Luke Sutherland's *Jelly Roll* (1998) is about jazz, but where Joss Moody moves to England 'for work', Sutherland's novel is claustrophobically focused on Scotland as a territory on the eve of devolution. In this frame, 'jelly roll' has its own colloquial significance. It evokes a nostalgic sign of urban Scottish childhood, echoing the kitsch 'Jeely Piece' song, a Scots faux-folk number from the 1960s about parents dropping sandwiches from the open windows of new high-rise housing blocks.[1] *Jelly Roll* interrupts this sentimental vision of working-class Scotland, through its explicit connection to Glaswegian drug culture, the inclusion of a semi-fantastical Highland frontier that lies beyond the Central Belt, and Scotland-wide representations of racist violence. That interruption channels the second registration of the title, a knowing reference to the metabolic effects of withdrawal from the benzodiazepine temazepam – 'jellies' – the use of which was widespread in Glasgow in the 1990s. The temazepam dependency of the narrator, Roddy Burns, translates into psychotropic effects which shape the novel at a formal level. Following the shift from opioid allegories in Irvine Welsh's *Trainspotting* to the club-drug scene of *Ecstasy* (1996), *Jelly Roll* is embedded in a particular moment in Scottish literature, of 'culture caught up in transition' between the hyper-individual heroin abuse of the 1980s and the new, empathogenic ecstasy scene.[2] The racism depicted in the novel also seems to face in two directions that map onto that pharmacological transition, back towards hard-edged chauvinist abuse, and forward towards erotic fixation, what Alice Ferrebe calls the 'fetishisation of the organic mystery' of blackness.[3]

  Trumpet is in part a retelling of the Billy Tipton biography, and *Jelly Roll* similarly alludes to the biography of an earlier figure in jazz: the title of the novel is a clear call back to the seminal figure of Jelly Roll Morton.[4]

'Jelly Roll' is one of the black names that, as Joss Moody chastises Millie in *Trumpet*, '[w]hite people always laugh at'.[5] The principle of jazz renaming at work here underlines the idea of literary personae; like both Joss and Colman, Morton underwent a transformative name-change from his birth name, Ferdinand Joseph LaMothe, that accompanied a moment of self-authorship. Colloquially, Morton's 'Jelly Roll' nickname, 'a throwback to the days when jazz and sex were practically inseparable', refers to his erotic interest in female genitalia, his virility and his occasional pimping.[6] Morton's nomadic life and volatile personal relationships, including with would-be band members and collaborators, provides a template for the narrative action of *Jelly Roll* itself. Beyond the persona encoded in the 'Jelly Roll' soubriquet, Morton made a crucial tripartite contribution to the history of jazz music: as a piano-player of exceptional range and virtuosity; as a composer of some of the most popular jazz pieces of his era; and as the first recognised arranger of jazz music, who grasped and codified its 'underlying syntax'.[7] His 'Jelly Roll Blues' is often cited as the first piece of notationally recorded jazz music.[8] Morton is thus an apt totemic figure to name alongside *Jelly Roll*'s literary exploration of jazz, and the fraught process of representing the linguistic 'unsayability' of black history, which is the absent centre of the novel. Furthermore, the self-aggrandising and hyper-masculine posture of his name is in keeping with the novel's Welshian machismo, its anxious male homosocial–homophobic oscillations and sexual hypocrisy. A Glaswegian 'jeely piece' might even have been made using a bread roll from Mortons bakery in Anniesland.

Taken together, these entanglements index three of the novel's main recurring motifs: the relationship between black experience and jazz music; a critical interrogation of contemporary Scotland; and a dialogue with the prevailing tropes of devolutionary Scottish fiction. Published in the same year as *Trumpet*, *Jelly Roll* touches on many of the same broad questions of racialisation, citizenship and consanguinity, and resilient ideas about the heritability of national culture. After deliberation, argument and sullen compromise, the 'Sunny Sunday Sextet', a Scottish jazz band comprised of five white musicians, admits into the group a black Irish saxophonist, Liam Bell. Liam replaces the violent and unpredictable Malc, provoking in the latter a mixture of racist anger, slighted masculinity and envy. Interspersed with narrative flashbacks to dark scenes in Glasgow, the Sunny Sundays embark on a promotional tour of the Highlands, experiencing first-hand the varied stripes of racism in Scotland. As Graeme Macdonald observes, this racism is displayed with a 'shocking publicity [that] is provocatively aimed at a society that trades and thrives on a hospitable, "open" image, one distanced from the "British" (that is, English) "problem" with racism'.[9] These range from microaggressions –

Duckie's diagnosis of Liam's 'devilish mystique', or the sound engineer who demands Liam speaks 'Inglish' – to a constant vocabulary of racist abuse terms throughout the dialogue: 'Leroy', 'Bananas', 'black bastard' and 'nigger'.[10] Liam is a catalytic figure, whose signifying blackness the novel's white Scottish characters react against, establishing a baseline for a recurring interrogation of racism and anti-racism – conflicting ideologies occurring simultaneously sometimes within the same characters – via an ethnography of white Scotland that combines historical forms of 'Scottish journey'. However, he is not simply a cipher: occasionally glimpsed through the white narrative perspective is the burden he carries as a representative load-bearer for a purported black subjectivity or culture. Partially obscured by the narrative perspective and psychotropic haze of the novel, therefore, Liam registers one example of the lived experience of blackness in Scotland. The novel's implied struggle is for a liveable present, the condition Achille Mbembe describes as 'belong[ing] fully in this world', to 'pass from the status of excluded to [. . .] rightholder', and to 'participate in the construction and the distribution of the world'.[11] Set against that project is a condition of ontological reduction that keeps Liam as the 'object' of the novel's contestation between Scotland's racists and anti-racists, excluded from the arena in which inclusion and belonging are negotiated by enfranchised political subjects.

Welshian analogies

Unlike *Trumpet*, *Jelly Roll* has little to say about the racist actions of state agencies such as the police, the social and political practice of black collective organisation, or the affective conditions of Scottish national belonging. In this respect, the novel is also distinct from other millennial works coded 'black British' which set community relations and cultural encounter as a primary platform, such as the paradigmatic *White Teeth*. One of the ways that *Jelly Roll* presses a claim for the fresh recognition of racism in Scotland is through the way it writes back to a contemporary Scottish literary tradition, reopening the imaginative failure of Alasdair Gray's *Lanark*, the white Scot, to grasp the spiny stem of racial history and contemporaneity. Where *Trumpet* substantially addresses the race politics and prevailing ideological configuration of the British state, *Jelly Roll*'s anthropological lens is turned towards establishing Scotland's pathologies of whiteness in the context of a 'dramatic loss of cultural anchorage' recognisable in the 'splintered urgency' of *Trainspotting*.[12] With its subcultural drug motif and anxious machismo, it is unmistakably responding to a Scottish literary moment defined by the aftermath of Welsh's *Trainspotting*, but *Jelly Roll* is also marked by, and modifies, the semi-fantastical or surreal Scotland created by other writers and artists such as Alan Warner and John Byrne.

The relationship between *Jelly Roll* and *Trainspotting* provides a route into decoding some of its national-devolutionary implications. Welsh's novel casts a long shadow over Scottish literature both before and after 1999; the question of its constitutionality, and its position vis-à-vis devolution, has been a vexed one. An initial orthodoxy emerged that read the novel as a critique of British state ideology embedded in the social and economic behaviour of heroin addiction: in Cairns Craig's description, a 'community [. . .] whose descent from communitarianism into egotism, from community into isolation, is itself the mirror image of the pragmatic and egotistic [Thatcherite] society of which it is the underclass'.[13] Beyond this generalised critique of Thatcherism and constitutional paralysis, Michael Gardiner has also pointed to Welsh's early novels, in their local and postcolonial dimensions, as together 'a fairly determined move away from remaining Greater British culture and its cultural backbone, English Literature'.[14] However, with *Trainspotting* further distant in the rear-view mirror, new readings have textured this post-British analysis. Compared to the novel, Danny Boyle's *Trainspotting* film has been associated with 'Cool Britannia', and the co-opted, streamlined commodification it entailed. But Scott Hames has argued that Welsh's novel itself also stands for 'the commodification of Scottish identity and "voice", enabled by a postmodern valorisation of "difference" and marginality', 'a key means by which Scottishness was promoted and re-fashioned in the 1990s'.[15] It is this 'refashioning' on the basis of a valorised marginality, and its concomitant mythology of anti-racism, that is unstitched in *Jelly Roll*. Sutherland's novel trades on an association with Welsh as part of the moment that Hames describes, but also offers a corrective, resisting the narrative of Scottish marginality via a renewed focus on Scotland's centre–margin divisions, internal heterogeneity and racism. The 1990s Scottish literary politics of 'a distinctively Scottish language and "voice"', that constitutes a 'rhetoric of cultural empowerment and national self-representation', cannot remain unaffected by the ethical and moral transgression of the racial slur 'nigger' repeatedly voiced in a manner reminiscent of the dialectal work of Welsh or James Kelman.[16]

Jelly Roll has many explicit and implicit intertextual links to *Trainspotting*. Both share the kind of atomised community described by Craig: both take forward the experiments in transliteration inherited from James Kelman and other precursors; both have a studied perspective on homosocial and homoerotic dynamics; and both feature a narrative that represents, and is formally modified by, pharmacological excesses. *Trainspotting*'s opioid addiction has commonly been read in constitutional terms as affecting the body politic, either through division into individualised units of self-interested consumption, or as typifying a condition of suspended time or constitutional paralysis that echoed Scotland's post-1979 democratic suspension, summarised in Iggy Pop's resonant observation that '[Scatlin] takes drugs in psychic defence'.[17] Like the Edinburgh heroin scene of the 1980s that provided the raw materials for *Trainspotting*, *Jelly Roll*'s eponymous 'jellies' or benzodiazepines are drawn from Scotland's urban epidemiological history. At the point of *Jelly Roll*'s publication, benzodiazepines were statistically and by reputation the most misused category of drug in Scotland, particularly in Glasgow.[18] Benzodiazepines are used both as a primary drug and as a supplement to other drugs, catalysing the metabolic effects of smoking or injecting heroin, 'bringing down' users from the effects of amphetamines and cocaine, and either generating a hedonic effect when combined with alcohol or relieving anxiety induced by chronic alcohol use; in high doses, benzodiazepines 'can themselves provide a "kick"'.[19] There is a certain neat logic in reading Glasgow's temazepam epidemiology as an equivalent constitutional metaphor, positing devolution either as a political sedative that provides its own little representative 'kick' or as an expedient that amplifies and augments the 'primary' constitutional effects of a more powerful, dominant pharmacology. Read alongside the novel's recurring references to ghosts of the imperial past and to Scotland's everyday racism, one compelling 'national' reading of temazepam addiction is in its amnesiac qualities. What is dulled and forgotten in the psychotherapeutic use of temazepam, the force to be repelled by its 'psychic defence', is the violence of an imperial past and its inscription in the present, a Scottish national-colonial 'amnesia' that has been identified by several recent historical and literary-critical studies.[20]

The narrator Roddy Burns is the novel's primary temazepam dependant. 'Jellied up', 'giddied, or 'dazed', Roddy's self-administration of benzodiazepines in *Jelly Roll* provides an anxiolytic mediation of social experience in Scotland.[21] Sedatives not only suppress the anxiety caused by Malc's spontaneous violence, but also Roddy's dysfunctional romantic life with Gemma, and provide therapeutic relief from the exaggerated drudgery of his work as a fly-poster. Like *Filth*'s Bruce Robertson, the near-homophone of Robbie Burns implies a parodic Scottish national character. That equivalence lines up the disciplinary formation of Scottish literature, structured around Robbie/Roddy Burns as the centrepiece, with the amnesiac qualities of his sedative addiction and the racial politics outlined in the narrative. Roddy's stridently voiced anti-racist position-taking is a contemporary remodelling of the homely liberal humanism of his namesake's 'Is There for Honest Poverty' (1795). However, Roddy is also recognisably modelled on Mark Renton, a 'fuckin snooty manipulatin cunt', in his class pretensions and educational failure, and in his amoral behaviours exemplified in his attempted temazepam-drugging and rape of Gemma.[22] Like Renton's drug habit, Roddy's addiction is a thinly veiled analogy for neoliberal individualism, meaning he '[w]on't do anythin fir nuthin, no even fir his mates'.[23] His obsession with styles, and with the lacerating classification and hierarchisation of musical genres and subcultural groups reminiscent of edgy music journalism, makes him a natural fit for 'Cool Britannia', with its heavy emphasis on surfaces:

> [n]erd core and twee clique, fanzine hacks and scene swallowers, sensitive men in Paisley pattern with the occasional pinstripe and layers of flares; the suede and corduroy cats spearheading the Glam heist, swimming in kiss curls[24]

Such vituperation, taking in fans at a Cardigans concert, is one of many examples in the novel of Roddy's orientation towards taxonomic ordering. These litanies of 'cool' condemnation disclose a fixation on an unrecoverable authenticity, one that particularly accords with Roddy's obsession with Liam's blackness. In the zeitgeist of the late 1990s, Roddy hints at what Jason Arday calls the 'weaponised exclusion' underlying a broader narrative of euphoric, multicultural cool.[25]

In Malc, the band's first saxophonist, Roddy's Renton has his own Francis Begbie equivalent. Following the examples of Begbie, Roy Strang from *Marabou Stork Nightmares*, *Ecstasy*'s David Thorn, or Rob Catto from Orkney-based Duncan McLean's *Bunker Man* (1995), Malc supplies *Jelly Roll* with its clearest example of contemporary Scottish literature's 'pathological manifestations of masculinity'.[26] All of the bandmates – Roddy, Mouse, Paddy, Duckie and Fraser – represent some kind of male-life crisis, but Malc is a grossly exaggerated 'hard man' of short temper and sadistic violence, part urban legend, a nihilistic, demonic figure. Parallels between Malc and Begbie – particularly Robert Carlyle's film representation – are immediately apparent. He is bound to the band by a code of homosocial honour, the scratched-in-stone tenet that 'ye dinni [. . .] shite on yir mates' even if 'they spend half thir fucking time threatenin tae kick yir cunt in', recognisable from Tommy's description of Begbie threatening him with a knife in the *Trainspotting* film: 'Beggar's fuckin' psycho, man . . . but he's a mate, so what can ye do?'.[27] Both share a homophobic–homoerotic oscillation: Malc despises 'poofs' but uses a broken bottle to coerce a teenage boy into fellating him; Begbie's hyper-masculinity is subtly undercut in certain moments, such as when he blows cigarette smoke erotically into Renton's face before an immediate cut to them lying side by side in bed. Indeed, Malc's gender-inflected violence outstrips even that of Begbie, such as in the moment – channelling the final 'penectomy' scene in *Marabou Stork*

Nightmares – when he apparently attempts to castrate one of his antago-
nists in a Glasgow bar.[28] Like the adaptive process that transforms Robert
Burns's moralising humanism into Roddy Burns's bourgeois sanctimony,
Malc serves to draw out some of the contradictory logic of a racial hierar-
chy that remains largely dormant or unstated in the broader tableau of the
Scottish 'hard man'.

As well as recognisable pivots in the Scottish literary moment, Roddy
and Malc are the political poles of an allegorical 'micropolitics' that, in
Graeme Macdonald's reading, stands in for a Scottish national community in much the same fashion as the apparently communitarian aspect
of *Trainspotting*. In Macdonald's account, the band's future as a 'progressive collective' depends on the negotiation of the admissibility of
Liam as symbolic outsider, defined by his blackness. Liam's admission
cannot be neatly resolved as a result of a 'struggle for executive control',
mirroring Scotland's situation within the United Kingdom, where control over citizenship and immigration remain reserved in Westminster.
Consequently, the reaction to Liam 'exemplifies the speculative, hesitant
manner in which the discussion about race, ethnicity and citizenship is
pursued in an unclear, devolved context'.[29] The micropolitics of the band
involve a division between the founding, enfranchised band members – a
self-titled 'democracy' – and Liam, the would-be recruit whose nominal
Irishness compounds his racial difference to the band, and establishes him
as a test case in migrant alterity.[30] This analogy can be drawn out further.
The absence of state-level levers of public policymaking in citizenship has
not, after all, precluded the existence of a public political culture of race
in Scotland. Indeed, the statelessness of Scotland means that discussions
of ethnicity, if anything, have been of exaggerated importance. Michael
Gardiner asks rhetorically how, in the absence of 'fixed citizenship' for
Scots, 'we identify a non-Scot [without] ethnocentric measurements [or]
images'.[31] This is especially significant at a devolutionary point where that
historical ethnic imaginary encountered the newly significant parameters
of a Scottish polity. The formal creation of a Scottish parliamentary franchise after 1997 meant that the moment of *Jelly Roll* was precisely when
that historical and under-examined ethnic imaginary, with accompanying
racial dimensions, was encountering the more technical and legally protected category of rights.

In her analysis of racism and anti-racism in contemporary Europe,
Alana Lentin observes that anti-racism in public political culture is more
than a cause or an orientation, but a 'scientific object' available for analysis
which can take various forms that may be in competition or conflict with
one another.[32] One of Lentin's key symbolic differentiations in European
terms is between a 'majoritarian' anti-racism, closely in alignment with

a liberal-humanist public political culture, and a more radical form. The former is premised on meritocracy, weak integrationism and so-called 'colour-blindness'; the latter comprehends racism as the structural continuation of historical inequality, and defends the principle of difference against assimilationist pressure.[33] The British state typifies this first form of public political culture, in which discourses of 'fair play' and 'British values' lend themselves to a context in which professed anti-racism coexists with the continued rehabilitation of benevolent Empire, neo-imperial economic relationships, anti-migrant populism, racialised policing and, more recently, 'hostile environment' policies which have targeted Caribbean-born people without official status who are nevertheless long-term residents in Britain.[34] In certain key respects, the public political culture of Scotland mirrors that of the larger state form in its anti-racist 'pose'. As Jan Penrose and David Howard have observed, 'for most of its history, Scotland has been imagined by most "White" Scots as a place that is devoid of racism', based on the erroneous assumptions that racism emerged from, and was proportionate to, the presence of 'visible minorities', or even more egregiously, that Scotland's experience of English domination inoculated Scots against the 'practice' of racism.[35] The unexamined imperial history and structural racism that underlie these assumptions is barely interrupted by 'majoritarian' anti-racism, which for Penrose and Howard is 'much less threatening [. . .] to most White Scots' than the prospect of actual racial difference in Scotland.[36]

Get the act thegither: Sunny Sunday racism

The question of Liam's introduction to the band is also the question of Scotland's public political culture of anti-racism, in which an orthodoxy of colour-blindness and meritocracy is ill equipped to deal with the depth of racist logic and colonial-historical amnesia, and which fails to stand even on its own terms. Paddy's initial description of Liam is delivered with all of the hesitation of struggling to find the appropriate language of race, the initial dated gambit of 'Liam's eh, he's coloured y'know', finally alighting on the appropriate signifier of the moment, in the uncertain affirmation that he is 'black. Black y'know'.[37] The uncertainty of Paddy's racial language – a consequence of his realisation of the process of racialisation he is enacting in the moment – is juxtaposed against Roddy's response, a muscular race-blindness that stresses his anti-racism through hyperbole: 'I couldn't care if he's black, white or sky-blue pink'; announcing the possibility of recruiting Liam to the band, Roddy 'didn't tell any of them that Liam was black, not because it didn't cross my mind but because it made about as much sense as telling them he had arms and legs'.[38] Roddy's response relativises racial difference, placing historical divisions of race on the same plane as the fantastical 'sky-blue pink'. Significantly, Liam's race is made irrelevant in the light of his fitness to work, completing the picture of a 'meritocratic' race-blindness in keeping with a mantra of 'skilled immigration' or 'fresh talent': '[t]he point is he might be the man for the job and if he wants it we should give him the chance'.[39] Liam can do the work; he has the requisite skills; he is meritocratically justified: contingencies placed exclusively on racialised migrants in an otherwise 'race-blind' political culture. Not only is this colour-blindness ridiculed by the novel's pervasive racism, but even Roddy himself cannot maintain the facade of not-seeing Liam's blackness:

> Does he even look the part?
> – Christ, I spluttered. – More than any of us.[40]

Roddy's protestations of race-blindness are hollowed out in the face of Liam's desirable racial authenticity, and the persistence of race as a social fact, something noticed in a moment of perceptiveness by bandmate Duckie: 'You just speak about them as if there's nae difference an by denyin that there is, you're kinday fudgin over the question ay race'.[41]

As well as being characterised by the 'hesitancy' of the stateless nation, the band-polity is internally divided along class lines into 'elite' and 'vernacular' constituencies, signalled by typographical distinctions. Roddy, the middle-class liberal narrator, observes the necessary pieties of multicultural tolerance and presumes the band will accept Liam on the basis of his evident ability and, largely unspoken, the greater authenticity he offers. Duckie, resenting the presumption, faults a lack of consultation in explaining the band's hostility towards Liam: 'yous lot were on at me tae go aye nae bother the guys in the band, before we'd even had a chance tae talk about it. It's jist no the way ye go about these things. Ye sit down an talk about it'.[42] This is an orthodox criticism of the social changes labelled as 'multiculturalism', imagined as instrumental and lacking a mandate from the white majority. Meanwhile, the 'structural' racism of the band, and their ruminations on whether Liam will 'fit', have their macro-political correlate in a larger discourse of integration into that majority. As a political subject, Liam is excluded from any discussion, and abrogates his claim to membership rights: 'I'd love to do it, but if you don't think that I'd fit in for whatever reason, that's fair enough'.[43] While the ongoing deliberations of the band throughout do suggest a polity-in-action, in all its imperfect negotiation, the near total suspension of Liam's political agency is a sharp contrast to his narrative centrality.

Liam's exclusion from the participatory discourses of the *demos* is compounded by the novel's representational angle, an echo of a Scottish literary history in which black people have been the subjects but not agents of representation, and a pattern which was crystallised sharply in Welsh's own contemporaneous representational practices. In *Trumpet*, the white journalist Sophie Stones seeks to acquire proprietorial rights over black storytelling, both Joss Moody's life story and Colman's retelling of it. In *Jelly Roll*, this transfer of representational power is built into the perspective of the white narrator, Roddy, whose desire for Liam is one of the novel's key racialised dynamics. As Alice Ferrebe has suggested, with reference to Laura Mulvey's ideas about scopophilia, Roddy's fascination with Liam's race is manifested significantly through gaze, in his erotic appreciation of his 'embodied' saxophone-playing: 'his mouth, licking swiftly [. . .] blood and lust [. . .] His slender fingers tapered [. . .] the curve of his arm, lingering at the shoulder where his neck began, and the vein a smooth tuber, glowing glossy dark'.[44] Roddy cycles through a variety of emotional responses including empathy, guilt, pity, frustration and recurring homoerotic desire. Reshaping Mulvey's original argument around the distinctive gendering of scopophilia, this form of white 'watching' had been recognised in some black critical theory of the 1990s. Kobena Mercer's reading of Robert Mapplethorpe's photography in *Welcome to the Jungle* is one such example, in which he argues that all of the camera's points of view

> lead to a unitary vanishing point: an erotic/aesthetic objectification of black male bodies into the idealized form of a homogeneous type thoroughly saturated with a totality of sexual predicates. [. . .] Black + Male = Erotic/Aesthetic Object.[45]

This form of what Mercer calls 'ontological reduction' into the erotic-aesthetic object is also at work in *Jelly Roll* from the first moment in which Liam is made visible, 'framed' in the manner of a photograph 'in the spiral of banister and skylight', and, commencing the narrator's erotic fascination, described as 'beautiful'.[46] In an English context, works such as Isaac Julien's *Looking for Langston* (1989) had sought to disrupt the white homoerotic gaze, repositioning Mapplethorpe's work in order to foreground the gazing black subject. Roddy's eroticisation of blackness in *Jelly Roll* recalls the racialised psychosexual dysfunction of Bruce Robertson in *Filth*, whose murder of Efan Wurie – itself a radical form of 'ontological reduction' – is driven in part by a mixture of sexual jealousy and thwarted desire, encoded in the way Wurie is 'dismissive' and '[brushes] off' Robertson's approaches.[47]

In terms of political voice, Liam's is inevitably trumped by those of the other band members, emphatically in moments when he expresses his own preferred response to racism only to be shouted down by those who protest their own anti-racist credentials in the strongest and most violent terms. Roddy's vocal anti-racism is amplified in the machismo of Liam's brother-in-law, Paddy, the band's drummer. Paddy's anti-racism is part of a masculine priority to 'stand up' for himself and his 'mates'; he angrily accuses Liam that 'Ye jist fuckin stand there takin shite fae every cunt an do nuthin about it. Ye let they bastarts the night walk aw over ye, as per fuckin usual. [. . .] Ah'm fuckin sick ay yir actin the cuntin chicken aw the time!'[48] The manifold possibilities of an anti-racist stance shrink to the simple requirement that one does not 'act chicken' but instead mete out an escalating, physical response. The disparity between Paddy, the anti-racist, and Liam, the subject of that racism, comes through in the language of 'battling':

> – Fuck. Ye know the way it goes, man. Ye've seen him. He never fuckin sticks up fir himself. Waits until ah'm fucking fightin his battles fir him.
> – But there was no battle needing fought, said Liam.[49]

Paddy represents a culture of machismo in which anti-racism is a further channel through which to express domination; the fact that he is the band's nominal 'junkie' implies a connection between this self-righteousness and the social pathologies manifested in the addicts of *Trainspotting*. In the contradictory preoccupation with the mystique of race and the fierce repudiation of racism, the black figure is emphatically excluded from the conversation about not only citizenship and enfranchisement, but resistance to racism itself.

The strident anti-racism of Roddy and Paddy coexists with, and is consequently hollowed out by, a white supremacist logic at work in the Sunny Sundays. Malc's brazen racism opens up a new dimension in the 'hard man' chauvinism of Scottish literature. The racist abuse he directs towards Liam is a calculated strategy of disempowerment, backed up with the ever-present threat of violence. He goes through a cycle of naming that follows the attribution of specific racist classifications: 'Cunt disni really look like Mike Tyson, eh? Mair like that fuckin Adamski. [. . .] Ah'm gonni call Winston here, Bananas'.[50] Blackness connotes variously sporting skill, physical violence and musical affinity; 'Winston' positions him as a black everyman; 'Bananas' is a clownish return to colonial stereotypes of animalistic sub-humanity. Throughout, Liam is associated in their imagination with crude black stereotypes: sexual potency, propensity for theft, 'bigheidedness' and, significantly, natural ability in jazz. On being informed that Liam is black, Malc's judgement is that '[the] [c]unt'll be fuckin good' on the saxophone.[51] However, this racially defined talent for music is markedly 'in the blood', indicated by Mouse working hard to establish that Liam cannot read music and, consequently, has both a 'natural' and uncivilised 'gift' for music. Duckie and Mouse's persistent nicknaming of Liam – as 'Leroy' or 'Dreidlock', or even 'Monkey' – are racial aggressions that perpetuate what Mbembe calls the 'ontological substitution' of racism, in which the human subject Liam is replaced by the race-representative 'black man', 'a sign of a pathological fixation on the absence of a relationship'.[52] The deep racial history of these interactions is made clear when Duckie suggests that the best way to ensure the continued smooth operation of the band after Liam's admission is to 'convince Malc that he's the lead an that what Leroy's doin is just backin. Master an slave, y'know whit ah mean'.[53]

Despite this panoply of white supremacist tropes and racist behaviours, Malc eschews declaring himself ideologically racist. Malc's protestation, contradicting available evidence, that 'ah'm no a fuckin racist, pal. Ah'll talk tae any cunt', is a clear representation of 'post-racialist' thinking in Scotland.[54] His defence against accusations of racism is completed by his reverence for black jazz musicians, 'totally intae Coltrane, Ornette Coleman, Louis Armstrong an Duke Ellington, [. . .] even intae Marvin Gaye an Bob Marley'.[55] Ben Pitcher argues that 'the field of racial discourse operative in our contemporary societies bears little or no resemblance' to the 'caricature of a jackbooted Nazi' in the anti-racist imagination.[56] Implied in Malc's refutation is the 'pastness' of racism, the way that transcending historical 'totems of overt organised racism' allows for new forms of racism to flourish in their shadow.[57] Lentin and Titley cite slavery, colonialism, Jim Crow, apartheid and Nazism as examples of such totems, but a further salient example of 'totemic' racism in a late twentieth-century British context is Enoch Powell, symbolically imagined as the last 'racialist' thinker before his abjection from the British body politic. It also demonstrates the way that in contemporary racial discourse, as Pitcher observes, 'even the fascists have learnt to use the language of cultural diversity'.[58] His 'willing' interlocution with Liam, peppered with racial slurs and threats of violence, cannot be construed in Malc's mind as racist on the basis of implied and absolute 'standards' of racism inherited from the past and, on the basis of national allusions elsewhere in *Jelly Roll*, associated with the BNP and an explicitly non-Scottish politics.

The co-presence of racism and reverence towards black musicians hints at the novel's engagement with Scotland's larger preoccupation with black music. The narrative premise of *Jelly Roll* shares striking similarities with John Byrne's *Tutti Frutti*: a dysfunctional musical outfit of white men specialising in the performance of historically black musical forms recruits a key new member (an Elvis Presley and John Belushi-inspired Robbie Coltrane as frontman Dannie McGlone), and then embarks on a redemptive 'Silver

Jubilee' tour of Scotland, playing in inauspicious venues, to questionable crowds, and beset by internal and familial frictions.[59] The optimistic band names, 'The Majestics' and 'The Sunny Sundays', belie the fractious social relations between band members. The 'disintegrating' masculinity of *Tutti Frutti*, personified in Maurice Roëves's Vincent Diver, the 'iron man of Scottish rock', is also expressed through the vanity, machismo and infidelity distributed across each member of the Sunny Sundays.[60] The strangeness of Scotland in *Jelly Roll* is in step with what Robert Hewison calls Byrne's 'semi-magical realism'.[61] What is notably missing from *Tutti Frutti*, however, is actual black people. Both *Tutti Frutti* and *Jelly Roll* reflect on the re-situation of black American music into a 'whitewashed' Scottish context, a notable cultural presence considering the prevalence of jazz festivals in Scotland, and the history of Scottish 'blue-eyed soul' in the form of acts like Average White Band or Hue and Cry. The thematic similarities between the two texts serve to emphasise strongly the significance of black characterisation in Sutherland's novel, where the proprietorial relationship between black people and jazz music is the preserve, and persistent anxiety, of the novel's white characters.

Jelly Roll thus conducts a form of anthropological enquiry in which Liam's blackness denaturalises and exposes the racial assumptions, preoccupations and psychopathologies of its white characters, emphasising the 'mutual constitution' of racial definition in devolutionary Scotland. Jazz music is white not only by virtue of its practitioners in Scotland, but also ideologically in this context. Corroborating the various white racist and anti-racist subject positions that make up the Sunny Sundays, Malc represents the jazz band as a white space of purity and order, a threatened colonial, civil territory: 'You fuckin listen tae me Bananas, right. We dinni want yir fuckin law ay the jungle in here, OK?'[62] The place of Malc within Scotland's social and cultural collective speaks to a fundamental incompatibility: by the conclusion of the novel, the perplexing contradiction at the heart of the collective is laid out in bare terms by Mouse, who pointedly asks Roddy, 'how the fuck did ye think ye'd get away wi havin him an Malc in the same fuckin band?'[63] In Macdonald's polity-in-action, the question might be rephrased as: how can Roddy's race-blind political correctness facilitate the coexistence of black life in Scotland with a form of cultural machismo, with Malc's chauvinistic and violent white supremacy?

'SUCK MY PICTISH WICK': the journey north

The allegory of the Sunny Sundays as a 'polity-in-action' is given a further dimension by an epistemological process that maps a heterogeneous Scottish national territory at a critical devolutionary point. In *New Geographies of Race and Racism*, Clare Dwyer and Caroline Bressey have observed that certain key 'racialised imaginative geographies' have dominated the framing of race discourses in Britain: northern towns like Bradford or Rotherham; urban London; and rural areas dominated by migrant labour, such as Lincolnshire.[64] For Dwyer and Bressey, Scotland is one of the 'new' geographies, affirming James Procter's observation that the cultural formation black Britain has historically been an 'uneven landscape' with its hegemonic centre in metropolitan England, set against an undifferentiated 'north' that includes both Bradford and Scotland.[65] Geographically, then, Scotland is a national frontier within black Britain. The proof of this national project lies in the conception of the tour itself, rooted in the need to differentiate in national terms from England; Duckie's 'first thought wis just tae head fir Ingland, y'know', but the risk of 'Ingland' is that the band would 'just get fuckin swallowed in amongst it'.[66] The geographical scope of the novel establishes Scotland as a distinct critical object, to be separated out conceptually from being 'swallowed up' into a larger framework. Alice Ferrebe has argued that the cartographic process at work in the novel is 'one of division, backtracking, and disorientation' that seems to stand against the 'picaresque narrative assemblage of varied locations' into a 'conceptually whole nation'.[67] The tour thus achieves the opposite effect to a detailed mapping and ordering of Scottish territory, but nevertheless effects a new *knowing* of the racial terrain of national Scotland.

The tour itself is a vividly realised and theatrical odyssey through the Highlands, suggestive of an internal colonial adventure into the 'hinterlands' of Scotland. Mouse remonstrates that the band are 'gonny get fuckin lynched' out in the 'fuckin backwater shitholes' of provincial Scotland, an ironic note that serves to draw attention to the 'backwardness' of Glaswegian racism, while the language, steeped in the history of post-bellum racist violence, foreshadows later developments.[68] The band are guided in their exploration of the lands that lie beyond Glasgow by the 'wafer thin *Guide to Scotland*', a document that suggests not so much shallowness as a series of unexplored frontiers, an epistemological limit, a lack of national self-knowledge.[69] The touristic register of the entries from the *Guide* is at odds with the broader excavating ambitions of the narrative, and its 'thinness' indexes the absence, exclusion or non-recognition of the 'national character' and of the imperial past. Union history supplies the template through which that epistemological lack is to be addressed, in the form of a modern 'stepping westward', a surreal, psychotropic retelling of the eighteenth-century Highland tour, inflected by the contemporary literary move towards reimagining Scotland's 'peripheries', in which the narrator's accelerating drug use mirrors the growing strangeness of the Highlands as a geography of racism.

Representing the Scottish Highlands as white space involves the adaptation of historical and literary representations which have imagined them first as a form of racial-colonial frontier. In the eighteenth century, Highlanders were depicted as having a 'common savagery' with colonised and racialised people of Empire, which would later be transmuted into a romantic cultural difference in the writing of Walter Scott.[70] Nigel Leask describes the way the Highland tour was likewise of an explicitly 'exotic' cast, involving 'natural history, primitivist ethnography, and landscape aesthetics', and that 'travellers ventured beyond the boundaries of "polite" civil society into a heterogeneous cultural and linguistic "contact zone" that resembled colonial conditions'.[71] This anthropological tourism formed part of Samuel Johnson's *A Journey to the Western Islands of Scotland* (1775), followed by later iterations from Romantics such as the Wordsworths, Samuel Taylor Coleridge and John Keats. These journeys sought to map, to make sense of and make use of a Scottish geography and set of social relations which had largely eluded absorption into British modernity. In *Jelly Roll*'s conception of Scotland beyond Glasgow as an unexplored or 'virgin' land, it provides an echo of these earlier travelogues of the Highland tour, a link made explicit by a reference to Johnson's *Journey* in Fraser's *Guide to Scotland*.[72] The Sunny Sundays tour is a parody of the 'westward journey', insofar as its spirit of discovery is premised more on the stultified lives of the Glaswegians than on a fundamental schism of modernity between metropolitan and Highland Scotland.

In the spirit of the old Highland tour, *Jelly Roll* represents the Highlands as a space of unlikely or weird encounter, a semi-fantastical or carnivalesque mode, filtered through the narrator's continued use of psychoactive compounds, and centred on *ethnos*, racist acts and a racialised imaginary. The penultimate stage of the tour, in the summer heat at Gairloch, provides a good illustration of these weird aesthetics: a 'sprayed gold angel in a white-winged gold helmet with boots to match' with 'WOGS OUT! columned in white paint down his back'; a 'bearded pap in a gold sewn cloak' wearing a medallion inscribed 'ALL LOWLANDERS CAN SUCK MY PICTISH WICK!'; '[j]ewelled belly dancers' and 'a circus offshoot cribbed in a dell'.[73] By this point, the narrative is clipped into passages of varying lengths, including snippets of perspective and memory that suggest the amnesiac effects of Roddy's increasing dependence on his rapidly depleting stash of drugs, and the effects of withdrawal. As a pathological reminder of the consumption that lies in the background of the tour, Roddy 'sneezed and blood burst from [his] nose, the start of an hour-long torrent' that continues on and off until the end of the novel.[74] The racism in this section is not hyper-realised in the sense of its impossibility, or in terms of a lack of precedent; on the contrary, the racism dramatised in the novel has plenty of precedent in colonial and post-colonial history. The weird elements penetrating the mists of Roddy's pharmaceutical daze are spectres of post-colonial melancholy at work and start to take on new significance in a devolutionary context.

Kirsty Macdonald has described the way that the Gothic trope of the 'journey north' has particular purchase in the context of the historical Highland tour, where the region is conceived as a 'Gothic topography' that 'accommodates an internal other: Celtic, Gaelic-speaking and primitive'.[75] Macdonald reads contemporary representations of Highland Scotland – from Iain Banks, Alan Warner, David Mackenzie and Neil Marshall – as extensions of a historical Gothic that 'shades' or haunts a narrative of unified, integrated Scottish nationhood.[76] In these texts the emphatic 'strangeness' of the Highlands manifests formally as a 'semi-magical realism'; *Jelly Roll* could easily be included in such a list. Warner's work in particular overlaps with the aesthetic and social dimensions of *Jelly Roll*; his early novels *Morvern Callar* (1995) and *These Demented Lands* (1997) offer what Duncan Petrie calls a 'vibrant new mythic vision of Scotland' beyond the Central Belt.[77] Cairns Craig reads the 'disjunctive and disorienting effects' of Warner's mythic style as encoding the 'alternative narrative trajectories' of Scottish literature, which cannot be fitted into a British 'unified national narrative'.[78] These accounts position Warner's work as achieving some condition of national definition even as it erodes both the 'total' and the 'stable'; Schoene describes Warner's strange and decentralised representation of Scotland as a 'multifaceted, unpredictable and ineradicably subjective experience, brimming with uncharted ways of national being and belonging'.[79] The mobility at the heart of Warner's later novel, *The Man Who Walks* (2002), in which the elusive Uncle's 'uncoordinated and apparently desultory itineraries [. . .] bring about a conspicuously random remapping of Scotland, both territorially and historically', is reminiscent of exactly the peripatetic and re-historicising narrative of *Jelly Roll*.[80]

While the direction and the rhetoric of the band's journey is in keeping with the Highland Tour of the late eighteenth century, the ethnographic ambitions of the novel as a whole are more national-conceptual in scale. Hence, the oblique 'Scottish journey' hidden within *Jelly Roll*, that emerges through and beyond the Johnsonian 'frontier' narrative, is more reminiscent of Edwin Muir, an Orcadian like Sutherland himself. Muir's *Scottish Journey* (1935), one of the most influential travel narratives of modern Scotland, provided an Orcadian perspective on the mainland.[81] In *Scottish Journey*, Muir, 'an outsider who was also an insider' with a propensity for commentary on the subject of Scotland's 'races', attested to the radical difference between the extremes of the urban, industrial Central Belt and the rural geography of Scotland, which he had experienced first-hand.[82] His contrarian spirit in Scottish literary-national terms, describing Burns and Scott as 'the sham bards of a sham nation', has an echo in Roddy Burns, 'no the poet, jist the tosser'.[83] The novel's culmination at the far north point of mainland Scotland, the 'gentle blue promontory of Orkney' visible in the distance, suggests both the mainland limits of Scotland and the symbolic distance of Orkney.[84] The exclusion of Orkney from the cartographic frame aligns with the question of Orcadian sovereignty, and its vexed relationship with a Scottish Government geographically and politically distant to the islands. The absent Scottish 'wholeness' of the tour can then be read as a form of national decentralisation that has a particular resonance in the devolutionary context where Orkney, for example, was the municipality with the lowest level of support for devolution in the 1997 referendum.[85] Rather than an encounter with the promise of the pre-modern in the rural communities of the Highlands, as the band expect of their own 'Highland Tour', the discovery is instead of the national landscape of contemporary Scottish racism that looks as much to an unsettling post-industrial Glasgow as to the spaces further north.

Damn'd in Hell: white Scotland

Jelly Roll imagines Scotland as a racial phantasmagoria, a descent into the 'hellscape' promised by the novel's epigraph from Marlowe's *Doctor Faustus*, in which racism is represented in ever more amplified and performative ways.[86] The Glasgow sections of *Jelly Roll* are subtitled as 'Limbo', a reference back to Muir, whose memoirs framed the difference between his Orcadian childhood and later life in Glasgow as between Eden and hell. The novel's anthropological study of whiteness is partly conducted through the form of a travelogue that promises some condition of knowledge of Scotland, clearly signalled in the Highland geography covered by the tour, but initiated in Glasgow. Cairns Craig has already elaborated on what might be called the 'hellscape aesthetic' of Scottish literature, with a particular focus on Glasgow as an 'industrial hell' in which 'the forward trajectory of narrative turns into an eternity of repetition'.[87] The novel's depiction of Glasgow is *noir*-ish, 'dark most of the time and nothing opening out', populated by 'hysterical peasant hordes and xenophobic hypocrites'; as though to establish distance from *Trainspotting* as a precursor, Roddy pointedly observes that 'Edinburgh it is not'.[88] Malc, the hyper-extension of a Clydeside urban aesthetic, is a minor lord in this social order, and the seat of his fiefdom – the Greyhound bar, located significantly in Ibrox – is populated with:

> The canon fodder that won the Crimea and marched for Charlie in the 45. Braveheart extras in shell suits. The zit glitter of glue sniffers, Kwik Save cholera and hallowed leper complexions. A whole kingdom built on a diet of salt and batter sandwiches, pie rolls and meths, and they wonder why they die in their fifties.[89]

These figures are fodder, literally the raw 'stuff' of the Scottish canon, which in a short passage ranges across a full Scottian *oeuvre* from Jacobite romance to heroic British imperial sacrifice, to *Braveheart* and the commodified markers of class difference that provided the basis for Clydesideism, and which had been heavily monetised via *Trainspotting* over the preceding few years. They are also a white constituency. As Gavin Miller has observed, phenotypically 'it is trivially easy for "white" Scots to pass between "Catholic" and "Protestant" so long as they can obscure their immediate descent'.[90] The clientele of the Greyhound, despite the bar's suggestive location close to the home of Glasgow Rangers, seem to share characteristics associated with both sides of Scotland's sectarian divide: having 'won the Crimea' they represent British imperial interests, and in the same breath 'marched for Charlie', showing Jacobite sympathies against the Protestant Hanoverian succession. The scorning of romanticised martial Scotland directly echoes the reminders in *Trainspotting*'s 'My Brother Billy' and 'A Scottish Soldier' that Scots have been pre-eminent in fighting British colonial wars.

The descendants of H. Kingsley Long and Alexander McArthur's *No Mean City* (1935), the urtext of Clydesideism, are thus brought together in their 'hallowed leper complexions' as unified by a common imperial whiteness. Roddy's cynicism, self-hatred and obsession with superficiality make him an apt vehicle for the novel's lacerating imagination of white Scots, epitomised in the clientele of the Greyhound but a recurring feature of the Scottish tour. The 'leper complexion' is only one of a range of images that evoke the chromatic quality of white skin: 'stunningly beetroot faces glistening'; 'corned beef bald patches'; 'doughlike [. . .] bleached skin'; 'topless butchers baked red and freckled'.[91] This 'surface reading' is a kind of epidermalising aesthetic that returns to the skin as the signifier of the raced body, in an attempt to make whiteness available for representation. Whiteness has always had a quality of 'invisibility', what Howard Winant has described as 'the easy elision with "racelessness" that accompanies racial domination', a reading of America that has particular purchase when exported to an overwhelmingly white-majority Scotland.[92] The image register of white skin tone – 'beetroot', 'baked red', 'dough', 'corned beef' – places whiteness in the same field of epidermal gradation as more commonly racialised bodies.

What makes the visual denaturalising of whiteness effective in *Jelly Roll* is the way it is partnered with the system of racial dominance contingent upon it. This is starkly realised when the band plays to an upper-middle-class audience near Crieff. After the performance, the Sunny Sundays are entertained by Robert Forbes and Andrew Lamont, jazz aficionados and members of Perthshire's landed gentry. An authentic claim of Scottishness in such company rests on markers laid down by clan membership and a delineable Jacobite heritage: Forbes is 'a real Highlander', a member of 'Clan Campbell' with ancestors '[t]raceable to the first Kings of Argyll', whose 'great great great great granduncle [. . .] fought for Charlie in the Forty-Five'.[93] The reservation of such a political identity as markedly white is suggested by the persistent questioning of Liam, who is expected to answer for his 'own culture':[94]

> – Alright Liam, where are you from? [. . .]
> – Ireland.
> – I mean where were you born?
> – Ireland.
> – Originally. Where are your parents from?
> – Ireland.
> – You don't understand, said Lamont. – He's asking what your origins are? [. . .]
> – He's Irish, said Fraser. – Scottish extraction probably, with a name like Bell.
> Forbes frowned. – He's not Scottish, that's ridiculous.[95]

The exchange progresses through a series of models of citizenship – civic or 'place-bound'; nativist; patrial – which all give way to the racial logic for which these other forms of social classification are simply euphemisms. The implied exclusivity of Celtic nationalism has a further intertextual link here, to James Joyce's *Ulysses*, where Leopold Bloom is quizzed as to his nationhood: '– What is your nation if I may ask? says the citizen. – Ireland, says Bloom. I was born here. Ireland'.[96] Neither is such a link merely coincidental, given Roddy's critical reflections elsewhere in *Jelly Roll* on 'the myth of psychic community between the Scots and the Irish', sharing the 'Pan-national struggle of noble races'.[97] Race as the ultimate correlate to Scottish nationhood is then crystallised in Lamont's account of the 'history and culture bound up with race', via an anecdote of his local Indian restaurant:

> When I go into an Indian restaurant in Perth say, even though the waiters may be speaking with perfect Scottish accents, and have lived here all their lives, I don't think of them as Scottish and neither, I doubt, do they.[98]

In the mind of the anglicised, landed Scot, the nation is defined in ethnic rather than civic terms, taking full advantage of what Michael Gardiner describes as a consequence of the intervening multi-ethnic category of Britishness, where 'Scottish, English or Welsh ethnocentric descriptions of "our" ancient culture are able to go unchecked'.[99]

Making his racist position fully explicit, Lamont, backed into a corner, offers an absurd non sequitur: 'name me five great coloured men of letters or science or politics from the last five hundred years of western history'.[100] The explicit reference here is to David Hume's footnote in 'Of National Characters', stipulating that 'I am apt to suspect the negroes to be naturally inferior to the whites' and speculating that there 'scarcely ever was a civilized nation of that ["negro"] complexion, nor even any individual eminent either in action or speculation'.[101] *Jelly Roll* thus offers an early recognition of what Cairns Craig has called Scotland's 'darkening Enlightenment': the realisation that 'Scotland's Enlightenment, like its economy, had its feet sunk deep in the moral morass of slavery'.[102] This forms part of the distinctly pedagogical quality of the Crieff encounter, which establishes a firm connection between Scottish national history and white domination. The counterpoint to Lamont's racialised clannish and Scottish national superiority is twofold. Fraser, the band's sober intellectual, offers a detailed critique of the historical misdemeanours of the Campbell clan, while Fran, a young student – significantly a progressive from London – provides an orthodox argument-by-heterogeneity against ethnic nationalism, and an observation on Scotland's own economic reliance on slavery. While the substance of these arguments is antithetical to the racially exclusive nationalism of the elite (itself positioned as both 'Jacobite' and 'British imperial' in keeping with the literary inheritance of Walter Scott), the staging of the argument itself is shadowed by the presence of Liam, who sits silent and uncomfortable, and at its conclusion 'rested his head on a hand, the little finger circling at the corner of his eye'.[103] Barely concealed in this didactic narrative mode is a sense of wrangling over a Scottish national self-conception, in which Liam's peripherality reinforces the idea that even the conversation around Scotland's racial past and ethnic present is largely conducted between white stakeholders.

'Fuckin lynched' in Inverness

The Joycean overlap between the ethnocentric Celticism of Scotland and Ireland continues in the racialised encounter in the Labyrinth bar in Inverness. Before the performance, Liam is antagonised by a 'topless skinhead' whose head and hands 'shone snow-white', covered in leaf tattoos and wearing 'Glasgow Celtic' shorts.[104] This folkloric 'Green Man' or contemporary woad-wearer seems to personify a Scoto-Irish white commonality, 'the myth of psychic community [. . .] united not just by common blood, but by oppression at the hands of the English', which Roddy has already diagnosed in the sectarian streets of Glasgow.[105] The racial-territorial energy of the man, who confronts Liam with 'flexing biceps', 'gnashing' and 'roaring', makes him a fitting personification of Celtic ethno-nationalism in the mode of minority political organisations like Sìol nan Gàidheal, and sets up the social context in which other members of the crowd deliver a display of racism in 'high-spirits':

> six men, arms locked in a knot, chanting over and above the jazz as they reeled from one side of the floor to the other.
> [. . .]
> > You black bastard.
> > You black bastard.
> The front row split laughing, buffeted by the six boys bounding [. . .][106]

Despite the rambunctious vocal and communal character of racism directed at Liam, the bar manager Pluto suggests that the chants were 'just some of the boys going a wee bit over the score. It's not like they're members of the BNP'.[107] Inverness's geographic distance from the apparent English 'home' of racism translates into an acute form of Celtic exceptionalism, a national problem reinforced by Roddy's whispered apology to Liam, that '[i]f this was England even, there's no way you'd have had even half the hassle I've seen you get here'.[108]

This models, in Scottish national terms, the way that racism is minimised by reference to its ostensibly more egregious, or politically organised, forms. One target here is the complacency generated by the idea that racism in Scotland is exclusively a problem of Britishness and British chauvinism. The gig ends with the band setting fire to the exaggerated mural of a Rastafarian, a 'Highland refined Jah', and trashing the Labyrinth's kitchen facilities in a symbolic show of anti-racist solidarity. The dramatic conflict between the racist and the anti-racist of the preceding evening is only a precursor to the following morning, however, which brings the revelation of a surreal 'mock lynching' perpetrated by an unknown vigilante group against the six 'bounding boys':

> Liam stepped back pointing up at a naked man hanging by his feet from the cross spar of the streetlight. His face was blackened with soot or charcoal, and fat watermelon white lips were smeared on oversized. His head was shaved almost to the wood and a footwide red paint stripe, starting halfway down his thighs, ran over his cock and balls. A lynched nigger minstrel.[109]

The arrangement of violated bodies in space bears some resemblance to the vengeful staging at the conclusion of Welsh's *Marabou Stork Nightmares* and *Filth*. The uncanny scene is disquieting in its evocation of racist murders in the American South, an amplified and hyper-real moment which gestures towards one of the most violent historical consequences of racism. Meanwhile, the reference to minstrelsy and the blacking of the faces can be coherently read as a reference to the blackface performance associated particularly with a music-hall tradition in the nineteenth century.[110] Consequently, the mock lynching attempts a re-historicisation and amplification, directly linking the contemporary expression of anti-black racism to historical forms of racialised pastiche and its correlates in the regimes of white supremacy of the post-bellum American South.

The quid pro quo of the mock lynching is instigated by other attendees at the aborted Sunny Sunday performance, who had already confided in Liam that 'they were ashamed to be white, that what happened wouldn't be forgotten and that they'd do something about it'.[111] The lynching is conspicuous not just for its violence against the bodies of the men, but in its pronounced demarcation. All are 'epidermalised', their taboo behaviour and ideology made instantly visible at surface level, and marked out or struck through by a censorious 'red line'. The scene models a particular discourse of 'national abjection', one that Anne-Marie Fortier describes as central to the acting-out of multicultural toleration, where the designation and ejection of a racist minority is a strategy for consolidating a constituently anti-racist national ideal: '[t]hey, the racists, are the source of "our" shame: the meanings of shame are seen to originate from, and reside in, the actions of these subjects'.[112] As Fortier argues, the operation of this consolidating and distancing effect, perceptible in the mock lynching, involves the literal projection of 'shame and guilt on individual bodies', permitting a '"decent majority" to emerge as naturally tolerant and inclusive'.[113] The continued salience of the Stephen Lawrence case in British public discourse is illustrative here of the way that the consolidation of racism into a nominated group – his killers, marked out as exceptional racist thugs – allows for their expurgation from the psychologically 'healthy' population spearheaded by the crusading *Daily Mail*, leaving the underlying structure of racism in Britain un-interrogated. Likewise, the recreation of minstrelsy and symbolic punishment of the racists in *Jelly Roll* is simultaneously the expunging of racist practice from Scottish public political culture.

It is instructive that, after the Labyrinth brawl, Liam draws an equivalence between the 'crusading' violence of his anti-racist bandmates with the actions of the Inverness crowd, arguing that '[y]ou're no better than those fucking wankers out there tonight!'[114] This equivalence accords with a critique of 'orthodox anti-racist dogma' presented by Pierre-André Taguieff, who says that '[w]hen antiracists denounce the return of racist regressions into modernity, they hold orthodox dogma, they stigmatise the racist as the Other in the same way as the racist stigmatises the Other'.[115] Under Taguieff's critique of anti-racism in France, 'antiracist postures mirror the differentialist racist ones and lead to a "Nazification" of the enemy [. . .] essentializing it. The denunciator becomes the very category of its denunciation'.[116] The blackening and mock lynching of the racists enacts exactly this metamorphosis, as the 'ashamed' white men of Inverness 'become the very category' of the lynch mob, 'inflicting' blackness as part of a retributive, anti-racist justice, in which the 'blackened' perpetrators are tormented by being forced to share the fate of the subjects of their actions. Lynching as a violent process of anti-racist equalisation supports Paul Gilroy's concern that 'the brutal simplicity of racial typology remains alive even in the most deliberate and assertive of antifascist gestures'.[117] It is the determinedly racial quality of the retributive justice that maintains this 'brutal simplicity', particularly in its stated objective – not to overcome racism, but to address white shame.

This reading is not offered as a defence of the racism of the 'bounding boys', but as a critique of a logic of anti-racism that centres white sensitivity, policing individual utterances and responding to them with a self-glorifying and exculpatory violence: in short, one that expels, violently, the symptoms of racism as a kind of 'national shame' without addressing root causes. Violent anti-racism is amplified as the psychotropic narrative filter of Roddy's drug addiction becomes more pronounced. Reaching Ullapool, the passages drawn from the *Guide to Scotland* have been attenuated to a sparse few words: '*Ullapool 1788 herring*'. The oblique message, with its implication of coding or encryption, introduces a scene which similarly invites 'decoding', where temporal and spatial solidity begin to dissipate into an oneiric landscape of striking imagery, of a 'gold bull thrashing at a brass gate', the besuited protagonists outrunning horses and witnessing men harried by a pack of wild dogs. The passage culminates with another scene of anti-racist violence:

> The swimmers appeared as the two of us lay chatting. Big Baywatch types, they strode past spitting, Fucking niggers or Bob Marley or Seal or something. I don't remember, I don't remember, but Paddy whacked them with the baseball bat. I gasped, laughing at how I'd only seen Polo Neck's nose so mushed and we stepped back watching them squirm in the sand. I helped cram them into a portacabin and Mouse bound it shut with rope. Paddy lit up a Silk Cut, stuttering into a shuffle, nigger this nigger that as we dragged the booth into the sea. Liam looked on.[118]

The hazy indeterminacy of the encounter, implicitly caused by Roddy's drug-induced stupor, introduces a further sense of moral indeterminacy. Roddy's recall of the actual racist utterances of the 'Baywatch types' is indistinct, perhaps lost to benzodiazepine amnesia. Conversely, Paddy's 'nigger this, nigger that' mimicry – recalling the simulation of lynching that sought to punish the racist through the recreation of the racism – has more clarity. As in Taguieff and Gilroy, the actions of the putative racist and the assertive anti-racist bleed into one another, and in this instance, it is clear that the actions of the latter are those that reanimate the 'brutal simplicity' of race. The logic of social cleansing and of national abjection is made clear as the band drag the portacabin into the sea and set it adrift, a de facto act of murder; the bobbing cabin, 'a far off dot' sent out into the sea, perfectly represents the symbolic expulsion of the racist 'problem' from an otherwise healthy Scotland.[119]

Language in the flesh

As the swimmers are expelled from the national body, 'Liam looked on'.[120] Such impassive brevity is in keeping with the novel's wider representation of Liam, casting him in the role of perpetual spectator to an anti-racism that remains the preserve of literal 'white knights', and silenced within the self-scrutiny of a *demos* in the midst of addressing its own historical reconception. Like the perspectival shifts in *Trainspotting*, which puncture the narrative self-control of Renton, Liam's occasional contributions pointedly diminish the authority of Roddy, and signal an ineffable 'backstory' that highlights the way black stories in Scotland remain largely untold, especially by black voices like Liam's. Following the brutal bar fight in Cicero's in Glasgow, when the break-up of the band seems unavoidable, Liam chides Roddy that he 'didn't join this band because you asked me'.[121] The chastisement foregrounds the 'white burden' Roddy carries, which obliges him constantly to recentre the question of racism into his own emotional framing. The narrative mystery around Liam's motivations for joining the band, enduring their racist abuse and completing the tour is never resolved. The solemn 'looking on' during the beach scene is one of several points at which the lack of dialogue attributed to Liam suggests the silencing of black voices, the conditions of 'unsayability' attached to black history, and an eschewing of the autobiographical critical mode often attached to black British writing. Furthermore, the maintaining of emotional distance and the subdual of response via Liam's reserve effects the novel's sustained focus on the racial operations of white Scotland. In the very partial expression of his interiority, Liam is not made available for analysis as a representational load-bearer for black experience.

Neither heroised nor villanised by *Jelly Roll*'s representation of his words and actions, Liam's textual inscrutability means he is resistant to having larger racial discourses 'pinned' to him, and gives an added dimension to the terrible act of violence which Malc perpetrates on him in Glasgow, scarring the word 'nigger' into his stomach with a knife. The violence of the act underlines the violence of the word itself, and the long history of racism in the anglophone world to which it refers. It has an indelible connection to slavery, to white supremacy, to acts of racially aggravated assault and murder, and to the linguistic enforcement of race hierarchy. In line with Mercer's 'ontological reduction' of the voyeuristic gaze trained on the black subject, Kimberly Benston describes the word as ontologically and semiotically transformative:

> Allotting black people the brand of 'nigger' indicates a desire to void the possibility of meaning within the 'blackened' shell of selfhood, thereby reducing substance to the repetitive echo of a catachresis. 'Nigger' is a mechanism of control by contraction; it subsumes the complexities of human experience into a tractable sign while manifesting an essential inability to *see* (to grasp, to apprehend) the signified.[122]

The slur empties out subjectivity and experience and leaves only the racialised and 'denigrated' 'shell'. Benston's qualification of the visual metaphor is necessary, because this mechanism of control actually rests on a surfeit of visibility. Historically, race has been 'written' in the body: Fanon's epidermalisation is a signifying process by which a series of social characteristics inhere phenotypically. As well as a physical violation, Malc's attack is a semiotic act that 'literalises' the subsumption of experience, of human 'depth', into the shallow grooves in Liam's stomach. It is less the creation of a sign, through the combination of signifier and signified, and more the forcible redefinition of the black body once again into a signifier itself, marked out textually. This is a desire for significatory certainty, an attempt to overcome the slippage of racial meaning. The carving is of supreme permanence. In the context of a changing economy of racial language and identification, such slippage is not simply a linguistic trend but has social correlates, and Malc's act seeks the reaffirmation of the stability of hierarchised race categories and black inferiority. This is the novel's final irony, a signifying act that exists in opposition to the wordlessness of the novel's musical expression and to the 'topos of unsayability' that describes the way music stands in for the linguistic mutilation and expressive limits of the black Atlantic, in Liam's saxophone-playing performing '[d]eep flights words wouldn't allow'.[123] Liam is forced into a representative position, not just as the carrier of

Malc's racial hatred, but as the bearer of an epidermalised history of racial violence now available for reading.

To turn away from the forced hermeneutic availability of the black body is to return to the novel's interrogation of white Scotland. While the revelation of the attack comes at the end of the novel, in chronological terms the scarring happens before the Sunny Sundays tour. When Liam eventually confides in Roddy, he has been carrying the scar 'for months', bearing the inscription of racist violence while his would-be white champions prosecute their own anti-racist crusade, ignorant of his injuries.[124] The powerful dramatic effect of the word and the medium of the scarring establishes the profound distance between the psychological and embodied experience of racism, a history of radical social exclusion, and those would-be sympathisers or 'white knight' defenders for whom anti-racism is structured around their own affective responses. Roddy's own failure to intervene as Liam is knifed transforms his generalised anti-racist 'position-taking' into the guilt of the bystander; his immediate confession that '[t]his is my fault' describes a white guilt that recentres the white subject while remaining peripheral to the violent operations of racism.[125] This is borne out immediately after Liam reveals his scars: Roddy weeps, and Liam cradles him as though to comfort him. Malc's attack on Liam thus becomes an opportunity to reassert starkly the normalised racial-affective relationship in which the violated black subject is obliged to provide comfort for the guilty white subject.

In Malc's case, the resignification inherent in the knife-scarring is most obviously an attempt to re-establish the racial hierarchies of slavery through exactly the kinds of violence acted out in plantation society, to ensure the relationship between the two is unquestionably that between 'Master an slave'.[126] The slavery reference foreshadows the heavy subtext of colonial violence implicit in the malicious scarring of the black body. But there is another salient reference, very close to the beginning of the novel, that when '[y]e play in a band fir three years an yir part ay a team fir fucksake. Anythin ye've got tae say ye dae it in the flesh, y'know'.[127] This binds together the apparent *demos* of the band, and the mythology of political enfranchisement implicit in their vernacular speech, with Malc's communicative act enacted precisely 'in the flesh' of Liam's body. That what Malc chooses to 'say' is 'nigger' introduces a note of white supremacist violence into the vernacular moment of late twentieth-century Scottish literature represented by the 'team' and the intimation of local-communal affinities suggested by the band-as-polity. Stripped of the euphemism that has facilitated the proliferation of 'colour-blind' racism, the scarring act is the indelible concentration of all of the novel's recurring uses of the word 'nigger', by Malc and others, an ideological, structural and deeply historical racism that cannot be veiled by protestations of personal affection, the appreciation of black expressive culture or a public political culture of tolerance.

The gentle blue promontory

The novel's resting place within sight of Orkney's 'gentle blue promontory' completes the arc of a distinctive Scottish journey, and chimes with T. C. Smout's observation that for Edwin Muir, Orkney remained a sort of Arcadian dreamworld which could not be regained.[128] However, any readers of Sutherland's second novel, *Venus as a Boy* (2004), part-set in South Ronaldsay, would quickly identify that contemporary Orkney should not be idealised as a comparative Eden in comparison to the infernal racism of mainland Scotland. Muir himself saw mainland Scotland as degraded, but not irreversibly so. Crucially, *Scottish Journey* suggests that the consolation offered by a 'benign nationalism' in the 1930s did little to address what Muir saw as the persistent structural failures of Scotland, which could only be solved by socialism. *Jelly Roll* works in a similar way, in a context where the benign tone of a new, post-Thatcherite national politics obscures the stubborn structural questions of race and post-imperial melancholy in Scotland. Becalmed in John O'Groats, the novel ends on an ambiguous note. Liam calls his wife Christine in order to tell her about the scarring, the hiding of which has resulted in their estrangement. He is relieved to find that the line is engaged, promising the possibility of a reconciliation to come. The resolution of the scarring, the conclusion of the tour and the prospect of genuine subjective knowledge of Liam all remain contingent and paused, questions posed for Scotland in the devolutionary moment.

Notes

1. 'The Jeely Piece Song', Scottish Book Trust, www.scottishbooktrust.com/songs-and-rhymes/the-jeely-piece-song (last accessed 24 February 2020).
2. Schoene, Berthold, 'Welsh, Drugs and Subculture', in Schoene (ed.), *Edinburgh Companion to Irvine Welsh*, pp. 65–76: 71.
3. Ferrebe, 'Between Camps', p. 279.
4. Sutherland, Luke, *Jelly Roll* (London: Transworld, 1998).
5. Kay, *Trumpet*, p. 5.
6. Reich, Howard and William Gaines, *Jelly's Blues: The Life, Music, and Redemption of Jelly Roll Morton* (Cambridge, MA: Da Capo Press, 2003), p. 137.
7. Reich and Gaines, *Jelly's Blues*, p. 39.
8. Reich and Gaines, *Jelly's Blues*, p. 45.
9. Macdonald, 'Scottish Extractions', pp. 90–1.
10. Sutherland, *Jelly Roll*, pp. 158, 345.
11. Mbembe, *Critique of Black Reason*, p. 176.

12. Hames, *Literary Politics*, p. 273.
13. Craig, *Modern Scottish Novel*, p. 97.
14. Gardiner, *Cultural Roots*, p. 120.
15. Hames, *Literary Politics*, pp. 296–7.
16. Hames, *Literary Politics*, p. 25.
17. Welsh, *Trainspotting*, p. 75.
18. Ashton, C. Heather, 'Benzodiazepine Abuse' in Woody Caan and Jackie de Belleroche (eds), *Drink, Drugs and Dependence: From Science to Clinical Practice* (London: Routledge, 2002), pp. 197–212: 204.
19. Ashton, 'Benzodiazepine Abuse', p. 200.
20. For example, Tom Devine's *Scotland's Empire* and *Recovering Scotland's Slavery Past*; or Carla Sassi's 'Acts of (Un)willed Amnesia'.
21. Sutherland, *Jelly Roll*, pp. 79, 85.
22. Sutherland, *Jelly Roll*, p. 116.
23. Sutherland, *Jelly Roll*, p. 116.
24. Sutherland, *Jelly Roll*, p. 123.
25. Arday, Jason, *Cool Britannia and Multi-Ethnic Britain: Uncorking the Champagne Supernova* (London: Routledge, 2020), pp. 5–6.
26. Whyte, Christopher, 'Masculinities in Contemporary Scottish Fiction', *Forum for Modern Language Studies* 34:3 (1998), pp. 274–85: 282.
27. Sutherland, *Jelly Roll*, p. 17; *Trainspotting*, dir. Danny Boyle (Film4 Productions, 1996).
28. Sutherland, *Jelly Roll*, p. 309.
29. Macdonald, 'Scottish Extractions', pp. 91–2, 93.
30. Sutherland, *Jelly Roll*, p. 61.
31. Gardiner, *Cultural Roots*, p. 44.
32. Lentin, Alana, *Racism and Anti-Racism in Europe* (London: Pluto Press, 2004), p. 4.
33. Lentin, *Racism and Anti-Racism*, p. 12.
34. See Kundnani, 'Rise and Fall'.
35. Penrose and Howard, '*One Scotland, Many Cultures*', pp. 95–6.
36. Penrose and Howard, '*One Scotland, Many Cultures*', p. 108.
37. Sutherland, *Jelly Roll*, p. 32.
38. Sutherland, *Jelly Roll*, p. 33.
39. Sutherland, *Jelly Roll*, p. 33.
40. Sutherland, *Jelly Roll*, p. 53.
41. Sutherland, *Jelly Roll*, p. 109.
42. Sutherland, *Jelly Roll*, p. 106.
43. Sutherland, *Jelly Roll*, p. 97.
44. Sutherland, *Jelly Roll*, p. 93; Ferrebe, 'Between Camps', p. 279.
45. Mercer, *Welcome to the Jungle*, p. 174.
46. Sutherland, *Jelly Roll*, p. 44.
47. Welsh, *Filth*, pp. 1, 390.
48. Sutherland, *Jelly Roll*, pp. 245, 246.
49. Sutherland, *Jelly Roll*, p. 246.
50. Sutherland, *Jelly Roll*, p. 292; Adam Paul Tinley, 'Adamski', is a white English producer and DJ known for his collaboration with Seal, a black singer-songwriter.
51. Sutherland, *Jelly Roll*, p. 266.
52. Mbembe, *Critique of Black Reason*, p. 32.
53. Sutherland, *Jelly Roll*, p. 112.
54. Sutherland, *Jelly Roll*, p. 297.
55. Sutherland, *Jelly Roll*, pp. 111, 297.
56. Pitcher, *Politics of Multiculturalism*, p. 19.
57. Lentin and Titley, *Crises of Multiculturalism*, p. 68.
58. Pitcher, *Politics of Multiculturalism*, p. 19.

59. John Byrne, *Tutti Frutti*, dir. Tony Smith (BBC Scotland, 1987).

60. David Hutchison, 'The Experience and Contexts of Drama in Scotland' in Ian Brown (ed.), *The Edinburgh Companion to Scottish Drama* (Edinburgh: Edinburgh University Press, 2011), pp. 200–10: 207.

61. Hewison, Robert, *John Byrne: Art and Life* (Farnham: Lund Humphreys, 2011), p. 68.

62. Sutherland, *Jelly Roll*, p. 293.

63. Sutherland, *Jelly Roll*, p. 407.

64. Dwyer, Claire and Caroline Bressey (eds), *New Geographies of Race and Racism* (London: Routledge, 2008), p. 2.

65. Procter, *Dwelling Places*, pp. 162–3.

66. Sutherland, *Jelly Roll*, pp. 26–7.

67. Ferrebe, 'Between Camps', p. 279.

68. Sutherland, *Jelly Roll*, p. 59.

69. Sutherland, *Jelly Roll*, p. 160.

70. Pittock, *Celtic Identity*, p. 25.

71. Leask, Nigel, *Stepping Westward: Writing the Highland Tour* c.*1720–1830* (Oxford: Oxford University Press, 2020), p. 9.

72. Sutherland, *Jelly Roll*, p. 232.

73. Sutherland, *Jelly Roll*, pp. 382–3, 393.

74. Sutherland, *Jelly Roll*, p. 382.

75. Macdonald, Kirsty, '"This Desolate and Appalling Landscape": The Journey North in Contemporary Scottish Gothic', *Gothic Studies* 13:2 (2011), pp. 37–48: 37.

76. Macdonald, 'This Desolate and Appalling Landscape', p. 47.

77. Petrie, Duncan, *Contemporary Scottish Fictions: Film, Television and the Novel* (Edinburgh: Edinburgh University Press, 2004), p. 100.

78. Craig, *Modern Scottish Novel*, pp. 238–9.

79. Schoene, Berthold, 'Alan Warner, Post-Feminism and the Emasculated Nation' in Schoene (ed.), *Edinburgh Companion to Contemporary Scottish Literature*, pp. 255–63: 262.

80. Schoene, 'Alan Warner', p. 262.

81. Muir, Edwin, *Scottish Journey* (London: Flamingo, 1985 [1935]).

82. Smout, T. C., 'Introduction', in Muir, *Scottish Journey*, p. xi.

83. Quoted in Watson, Roderick, 'The Modern Scottish Literary Renaissance', in Ian Brown and Alan Riach (eds), *The Edinburgh Companion to Twentieth-Century Scottish Literature* (Edinburgh: Edinburgh University Press, 2009), pp. 75–87: 76; Sutherland, *Jelly Roll*, p. 68.

84. Sutherland, *Jelly Roll*, p. 414.

85. Dewdney, Richard, 'Commons Research Briefing RP97-113: Results of Devolution Referendums 1979 & 1997', *House of Commons Library*, p. 12, https://commonslibrary.parliament.uk/research-briefings/rp97-113/ (last accessed 30 March 2020).

86. Sutherland, *Jelly Roll*, p. 9.

87. Craig, *Modern Scottish Novel*, p. 132.

88. Sutherland, *Jelly Roll*, p. 73.

89. Sutherland, *Jelly Roll*, p. 67.

90. Miller, 'Welsh and Identity Politics', p. 92.

91. Sutherland, *Jelly Roll*, pp. 118, 242, 335, 382.

92. Winant, Howard, 'Theoretical Status of the Concept of Race' in Les Back and John Solomos (eds), *Theories of Race and Racism* (London: Routledge, 2000), pp. 181–90: 187.

93. Sutherland, *Jelly Roll*, pp. 197, 204, 195.

94. Sutherland, *Jelly Roll*, p. 203.

95. Sutherland, *Jelly Roll*, pp. 200–1.

96. Joyce, James, *Ulysses*, ed. Hans Walter Gabler (London: The Bodley Head, 1986), p. 272.
97. Sutherland, *Jelly Roll*, p. 119.
98. Sutherland, *Jelly Roll*, pp. 201, 201–2.
99. Gardiner, *Cultural Roots*, p. 106.
100. Sutherland, *Jelly Roll*, pp. 202–3.
101. Craig, *Wealth of the Nation*, p. 105.
102. Craig, *Wealth of the Nation*, p. 107.
103. Sutherland, *Jelly Roll*, p. 205.
104. Sutherland, *Jelly Roll*, p. 238.
105. Sutherland, *Jelly Roll*, p. 119.
106. Sutherland, *Jelly Roll*, pp. 238–9, 242–3.
107. Sutherland, *Jelly Roll*, p. 247.
108. Sutherland, *Jelly Roll*, p. 254.
109. Sutherland, *Jelly Roll*, p. 258.
110. See Maloney, Paul, *The Britannia Panopticon Music Hall and Cosmopolitan Entertainment Culture* (London: Palgrave Macmillan, 2016) for an example of blackface as popular entertainment in Scotland.
111. Sutherland, *Jelly Roll*, p. 259.
112. Fortier, Anne-Marie, *Multicultural Horizons: Diversity and the Limits of the Civil Nation* (London: Routledge, 2008), p. 31.
113. Fortier, *Multicultural Horizons*, p. 31.
114. Sutherland, *Jelly Roll*, p. 246.
115. Lentin, *Racism and Anti-Racism*, pp. 87–8.
116. I am indebted to Sophie Body-Gendrot's analysis here, as Pierre-André Taguieff's *La République Menacée* (Paris: Textuel, 1996) is unavailable in English translation; Body-Gendrot, Sophie. 'Race: A Word Too Much? The French Dilemma' in Martin Bulmer and John Solomos (eds), *Researching Race and Racism* (London: Routledge, 2004), pp. 150–61: 157.
117. Gilroy, *Against Race*, p. 51.
118. Sutherland, *Jelly Roll*, pp. 336–7.
119. Sutherland, *Jelly Roll*, p. 337.
120. Sutherland, *Jelly Roll*, p. 337.
121. Sutherland, *Jelly Roll*, p. 311.
122. Benston, Kimberly, 'I Yam What I Am: The Topos of (Un)naming in Afro-American Literature', *Black American Literature Forum* 16:1 (1982), pp. 3–11: 5.
123. Sutherland, *Jelly Roll*, p. 412.
124. Sutherland, *Jelly Roll*, p. 403.
125. Sutherland, *Jelly Roll*, p. 401
126. Sutherland, *Jelly Roll*, p. 112.
127. Sutherland, *Jelly Roll*, p. 16.
128. Smout, 'Introduction', p. xii.

Chapter 5

Mad as a Nation: Suhayl Saadi's *Psychoraag*

In 1998, the same year as *Trumpet* and *Jelly Roll* were published, Asian Dub Foundation (ADF) released 'Black White' as a single from the album *Rafi's Revenge*.[1] Six years later, Zaf, the DJ narrator of Suhayl Saadi's *Psychoraag* (2004), carefully notes the name of the band and song on his working playlist as he reflects that, on an Asian radio station, it is appropriate to play '[a]ll the bits, past an future, that daily jostled and sang the state of Asianness into being, that reconstructed somethin that wasn't real from somethin that wis'.[2] 'Black White' appears a curious choice given the racial signification of the title, repeated in the song itself, which proclaims that 'Black and white here has united / Building this community of sound', channelling the spirit of anti-fascist unity inspired by Rock Against Racism and echoing slogans like the Socialist Workers' Party's 'Black and White Unite and Fight'.[3] By 1998, the splintering of 'Asian' from the political constituency of 'black' had already mostly taken place. Writing in 1997, Michael Eldridge argued that even at the high point of 'Afro-Asian' black Britain in the early 1980s, Asian perspectives had been 'persistently under-recognised', and dominated by Afro-Caribbean interests wherein '*black* meant – well, black'.[4] Meanwhile, the rapidly developing culturalism of New Labour's state politics of race meant that, by the time of *Psychoraag*'s publication, not only was 'Asian' no longer part of 'black' in census terms, but now both were open to further state-defined taxonomic division according to national or religious hyphenation. ADF's 'Black White' sounded a hopeful but nostalgic note in 1998, and by the time Zaf plays the CD, it seems his emphasis is firmly on returning to a past moment in the history of the formation 'Asian'. Throughout *Psychoraag*, however, it becomes clear that blackness remains part of the twenty-first-century 'state of Asianness' in Scotland, as a critical cultural resource, as an imposed taxonomy and as a threatening contaminant within 'shadeism' or hierarchal gradations of skin colour.

Britain's shift towards multicultural governmentality had a longer history, but *Psychoraag* emerged near the apogee of the development of multiculturalism within the lexicon of politics, popular discourse, literary genre and literary criticism. In the literary-cultural field, multiculturalism has lent itself to a genre of fiction that occupies an ambiguous space. On one side, writing coded as 'multicultural' has been exploited as an exotic commodity, and deployed as a symbolic reinforcement of benign 'Greater Britishness' which sidelines race and racism. This is Graham Huggan's articulation of multiculturalism, as a 'wilfully aestheticizing discourse' which 'inadvertently serves to disguise persistent racial tensions within the nation; and one which, in affecting a respect for the other as a reified object of cultural difference, deflects attention away from social issues'.[5] On the other hand, such writing urgently communicates the continuing centrality of race in Britain, often via an explicit registration of the limitations of its multicultural politics. Offering for some a symbol of Scotland's 'achieved' multiculturalism, *Psychoraag* is indisputably a cultural product coded as multicultural, while containing various strategies of resistance. Using Stuart Hall's taxonomy, the novel negotiates commercial multiculturalism, which 'exploits and consumes difference in the spectacle of the exotic "other"', and resists corporate multiculturalism, which 'manages difference in the interests of the centre'.[6] We might recognise the policy and discourse of government as the most important 'centre' in British corporate multiculturalism, but beyond the state the devolved Parliament of Scotland itself adopted multicultural discourse, and many elements of policy, from Westminster in the first years of its existence. The same is true of the literary consumption of the multicultural product, which is driven by centralised commercial interests in London and, to a lesser extent, metropolitan Scotland. *Psychoraag* interrupts multicultural governmentality and codes of exoticism in a similar way to textual precursors, by writers alternately coded 'black British' and 'British Asian', such as Hanif Kureishi and Salman Rushdie, whose works provide routes to circumnavigate their own marketing tropes via what Huggan identifies as their own 'staged marginality'.[7]

While *Psychoraag* shares a larger governmental and commercial context with Kureishi and Rushdie, its response to British multiculturalism is impelled distinctively by a Scottish national context, and a series of engagements with literary antecedents from elsewhere in Scottish literature. The novel carries the imprint of the kinds of formal experiments pioneered by writers like Tom Leonard, Alasdair Gray, James Kelman, Janice Galloway and Irvine Welsh: orthographic and typographic rebellions;

vernacular aesthetics; embodied action; and temporal–spatial disruptions. These experiments have been taken together as a form of resistance to the class structure and value system that defines Britishness, and which has often been carried forward by the discipline of English Literature itself.[8] *Psychoraag* shares that broader critique: Great Britain is, for Zaf, a '[m]ad duchess riding a pig'.[9] But its own specific multicultural critique is significant in national terms too. Multicultural governmentality involves the recognition and safeguarding of ethnic identities within state-sponsored communities and the individual realm of the personal-affective, much as the British state designates Scottish nationhood as a 'regional identity' to be managed via the strategic concessions of devolution, keeping the fundamental questions of Union beyond the political horizon. To 'write back' to this form of governmentality is simultaneously to intervene in the national politics of Britain, facing both the cultural-political context of 'Britishness' and the ongoing critical interrogation of Scotland itself.

The era of multicultural governmentality has brought about a 'post-racial' common sense in which, as Alana Lentin and Gavan Titley ironically observe, '[o]ne of the certainties [. . .] is that racism no longer exists'.[10] That is to say, as in the racial logic of Malc in *Jelly Roll*, anything short of a stated political commitment to a biocentrically organised hierarchy of human 'races' cannot by definition be racism; all else is culture, and the legitimate target of criticism. Refuting the 'post-racial' implication of British multiculturalism is at the heart of *Psychoraag*. Through an extensive intertextual relationship with Frantz Fanon's *Black Skin, White Masks*, the novel reintroduces a psychopathology of race that is grounded in its embodied character, in the process of epidermalisation that reduces the subject to taxonomies of skin colour with associated cultural values, wherein black critical thought is deployed to articulate the racialised experience of the 'state of Asianness' in devolved Scotland. *Psychoraag*'s language of madness refers on one level to the psychic costs of racism, and to the psychiatry of racialisation in which Fanon was such a pioneering force. Figuratively, madness is also a form of counter-Enlightenment, a wilful and unmanageable 'unreason' opposed to a rational 'control-system' of culturalist logic, a manifestation of what Ghassan Hage describes as the 'ungovernable intercultural and transnational relations that interrupt nation-based multicultural governmentality'.[11] The seminal 'Scottish multicultural novel', with all that this coding entails, sharply introduces the problematic of British-brand multiculturalism into the literary moment of a devolved Scotland, and exposes its expedient elisions and control strategies both in elaborated Britishness and as a managerial tool of the new Scottish Government.

'Rivers of Blood' to 'One Scotland, Many Cultures'

The sheer breadth of definitions and connotations attached to multiculturalism seems to make the concept itself psychoactive. In a series of lectures in which he attempts to work through the complexity of the term, Hall describes multiculturalism as a '*maddeningly* spongy and imprecise, discursive field: a train of false trails and misleading universalities'.[12] The 'sponginess' that Hall flags up is part of the political usefulness of multiculturalism for nation-states, as a floating concept that euphemistically captures various disparate qualities, of cultural difference, migration policy or social transformation, but without the need for concrete definitions or courses of action. Multiculturalism can be a 'glittering generality', representing the newly confident pluralism of the post-imperial state, or the world-facing Scottish nation. Alternatively, it can be a rhetoric of failure, 'zombified', invoked only to be disavowed, a political programme that has 'gifted us the pathologies that gird our new certainties' – the certainty of social crisis.[13] As a discursive strategy, it lends itself naturally to the British state, with its technocratic post-war footing, its requirement to balance imperial continuity with neo-imperial adjustment, and its long-held suspicion of determinate legal codes and accountable definitions.[14]

Britain's multicultural governmentality has its roots in post-war migration and the moment of political reckoning instigated by Enoch Powell's 'Rivers of Blood' speech in 1968. As Martin Barker argues in *The New Racism*, Powell's speech marked a watershed moment that consigned explicit enunciations of biocentric racist thought to the past, and which led the Conservative party directly to mobilise a new form of racial categorisation during the 1970s, what Barker describes as a 'pseudo-biological culturalism'.[15] In this discourse, race as biological destiny is replaced by essential culture – 'Afro-Caribbean culture'; 'Indian culture'; and the paradigmatic contemporary example, the Muslim – defined most often against the soft-focus cultural core of the nation-state. These shifting taxonomic practices did mark some form of progression. As Hall pointed out, the movement away from races towards ethnicity at least entailed the recognition of the importance of cultural and linguistic distinctiveness.[16] But such cultural groupings were often still premised on intractable features, especially in governmentality, in which 'the return of the biological theme is permitted', leading to the 'elaboration of new variants of the "biological myth" within the framework of a cultural racism'.[17] Constant attention is required to modify the function of ethnicity 'in the dominant discourse', as Hall says, to guard against its 'equivalence with nationalism, imperialism, racism, and the state'.[18]

Psychoraag emerges from a period of New Labour multiculturalist discourse that extended and elaborated Thatcher's state-national Anglo-Britishness. The novel provides an early and pronounced comment on the culturalist turn, that 'it wis all rubbish, this stuff, this ascribing of characteristics to a whole group of people based on their tribe or their religion or the *mulk* from which they'd journeyed'.[19] Although New Labour's brand of multiculturalism offered an enthusiastic endorsement of British pluralism, it retained its own 'white heart' beset by contradictory impulses and neo-imperial tensions, a government 'compromised by its attempts to placate racism and xenophobia within its increasingly disenchanted electorate'.[20] So while New Labour engaged in 'flirtations with multicultural democracy', it simultaneously made 'appeals to the remnants of racially exclusive nationalism and the phantoms of imperial greatness', evidenced in the language of swarming and swamping, anti-migrant rhetoric and the attempted rehabilitation of the imperial past.[21] Given that the Scottish Labour party dominated the first eight years of the new Parliament after 1999, it is not surprising that much of New Labour's multicultural strategy was adapted for use by Scottish Labour, to establish a common inclusive-pluralist tone that conformed to the demands of Greater Britishness for social and political stability. Peter Hopkins has noted that the British state's control over immigration, nationality, employment and equal opportunities under devolution meant that 'legislation relating to black and minority ethnic groups tend to be matters reserved to Westminster'.[22] However, the Scottish Government was also responsible for implementing requirements placed on national public bodies, such as those provided in the Race Relations (Amendment) Act 2000.[23] Reservation to Westminster also left considerable scope for intervention in other areas, such as education, the arts, and in public marketing campaigns articulating a particular vision of race in Scotland. For example, Scottish Executive materials from 2003 require that schools 'promote race equality' through 'curriculum programmes' and 'monitoring access, progress, and achievement'.[24]

One major public relations platform was the 'One Scotland, Many Cultures' campaign, dating from 2002. This featured, among other promotions, a prototype *One Scotland, Many Cultures* website launched in 2004, complete with links to the 'New Laws for Race Equality' leaflet in multiple languages, a 'History of Migration', contact details and a list of events and initiatives around racism and diversity.[25] This site later developed into 'Scotland Against Racism' in 2008, and then into a new incarnation, *OneScotland.org*.[26] The sites provide a gauge of the Labour-run Parliament's multiculturalist position from 2002, indicating the way in which anti-racism becomes co-opted into the political-multicultural 'management' of race advanced through public relations. Malcolm Chisholm,

Communities Minister, stated that the *One Scotland, Many Cultures* campaign

> [. . .] celebrates the cultural diversity of Scotland and challenges racist attitudes and behaviour which have such a negative impact on individuals and society. We want Scotland to be at ease with its diversity, a place of innovation and creativity to which people want to come and are welcome.[27]

Chisholm's analysis deploys the 'whole panoply of multiculturalist clichés' identified by Kundnani and common to political discourse in Britain.[28] The narrative of enrichment recurring throughout the various incarnations of *One Scotland* aligns the Executive with Westminster, where 'ethnic communities' are defined instrumentally by contribution, which implicitly justifies their continued toleration.[29] Multicultural acceptance of this sort is always guarded and provisional, dependent on 'good behaviour' and the metrics of national economic contribution, of 'creativity' and 'innovation', rather than a commitment to equality without conditions. Racism, meanwhile, is reduced to a series of individuated 'attitudes' and 'behaviours', made the moral responsibility of individuals and subject to policing, education and policy intervention. Without a more radical attempt to grasp racism in Scotland, the political vacuum is filled actively by a form of recognisably British multicultural governmentality, against which *Psychoraag* reacts.

Psychoraag and the 'multicultural novel'

As Huggan's description of multiculturalism as an 'aestheticizing' discourse hints, the novel form is itself a site in which multicultural aesthetics are reinforced or contested. Multiculturalism as a commodity in literary publishing around the millennium has been tracked by Corinne Fowler, whose 'Tale of Two Novels' meticulously compares the commissioning and marketing of Zadie Smith's *White Teeth* and Joe Pemberton's *Forever and Ever Amen* to establish the 'commercial and (multi)cultural logic by which novels are coded as worthy of national and international readerships'.[30] Fowler observes that certain key material and thematic factors affected the respective successes of the two novels: promotional budgets and strategies (which primed *White Teeth* for acclaim); imaginative geography (metropolitan London against the northwest of England); and Smith's ostensible 'universalism' versus Pemberton's locality. Fowler argues that *White Teeth* 'proved amenable to a process of domestication that at least partially serves a celebratory cosmopolitan agenda' with Smith herself 'an apparent success story of British multiculturalism'.[31] Fowler's article alludes to, without directly articulating, the role of such a cosmopolitan agenda in state-national terms and in a New Labour project of elaborated Britishness. One effect of coding writing as 'multicultural', either in terms of marketing or scholarship, is to render it into a form of affirmative culture for the British status quo in constitutional terms.

Psychoraag occupies a conflicted place in this literary economy. Just as *White Teeth* acted as a piece of affirmative culture for elaborated Britishness, *Psychoraag*'s commissioning and commercial success in Scotland owes something to a particular historical need, coinciding with the rise of Scottish political multiculturalism, to showcase the newly devolved nation in language and a conceptual register in debt to British multiculturalism. Review copy used to promote the 2005 paperback edition is indicative in this respect: 'not just *Midnight's Children*-meets-*Trainspotting* because Saadi is more thoughtful than Welsh or Rushdie'; 'an enchanting and colourful novel that combines magical realism with the gritty reality of Glasgow's urban scene'; no less than 'one of the most original and powerful novels to come out of Scotland for years'.[32] These quotations suggest how the novel conforms to Huggan's idea of 'staged marginality', the process by which 'marginalised individuals or social groups are moved to dramatise their "subordinate" status for the benefit of a majority or mainstream audience'.[33] Implicit in the metaphor of Zaf's precarious late-night radio show broadcasting to a tuned-in audience, directly from the Glaswegian urban periphery, is the acknowledgement of just this form of staging. Staged marginality does, however, allow for the exposure of dominant structures of power, and *Psychoraag* differs from *White Teeth* in significant ways. Marie-Odile Pittin-Hedon has pointed out that explicit references to multiculturalism in *Psychoraag* often have an ironic tone, where the invocation of the term itself is a parody of its inability to gauge, map or manage culture.[34] It matches many of the peripheralising characteristics of *Forever and Ever Amen*, geographically 'north' and writing back to a metropolitan and multicultural centre in a British publishing sense. The comparison to *Trainspotting* is apt in the respect that *Psychoraag* makes use of a politically transgressive embodiment, heroin metaphors and taboo language that distance it from the liberal universalism attributed to *White Teeth*. This 'cultivated exhibitionism' can then be read as a critique of the novel's own saleability, a subversion of its commodity multiculturalism.[35]

Much criticism on *Psychoraag* has to date been concerned with reading its multicultural attributes, and with a nebulous critical concept of 'identity'. This mode of analysis internalises and privatises race and leaves multicultural governmentality largely undisturbed. For Sara Upstone, *Psychoraag* is primarily identity-based, concentrating on Scottishness, biculturalism and the 'mutability of cultural reference points'.[36] In the

'Scottish-Asian' identity category Upstone references, to be 'bicultural' is 'not to be alienated, but to be an embodiment of modern culture, with a multi-faceted, multifarious identity that is represented as one to be celebrated', a multicultural cliché that loops back to Scottish 'identity' and hence to the management of cultural distinctiveness within British nationalism.[37] Pittin-Hedon quotes Upstone on *Psychoraag* as a novel that 'examine[s] identity "from perspectives broader than race"', emphasising the elaboration of hyphenated identities, but which simultaneously advocates a 'destruction of a series of constructed ideas of identity'.[38] Elsewhere, *Psychoraag* is presented as evidence of Scotland's achieved multiculturalism, or serves as the basis for cultural quantification. Carla Rodríguez González, in her Lefebvrian 'rhythmanalysis' of the novel, describes it as 'Scottish multiculturalism', an example of 'high-quality multicultural urban writing' that represents a Scottish 'intercultural encounter';[39] Kirstin Innes sees the novel as drawing on 'at least three cultural backgrounds', focused on a protagonist with 'intrinsic cultural multifacetedness'.[40] The tension between countable cultures and the dimensional proliferation implied by 'multifacetedness' evidences the cognitive dissonance incurred by modes of analysis that rely on both destroying and celebrating 'identities'. One thing lacking in these accounts is the perpetuation of race under multiculturalism as a state enterprise and a social reality, and its relationship to the specific context of devolved Scotland: what Huggan would describe as the 'underlying political mechanisms through which more "traditional" racial/-ethnic hierarchies are preserved', and precisely what is often obscured by multicultural discourse.[41] While at pains to avoid referencing essential cultural taxonomies, these arguments return to fluid or hyphenated identity categories that have similar effects in their de-privileging of race and racism, and which operate within the rhetoric of celebration laid down by multicultural governmentality. Hence, Pittin-Heddon's suggestion that *Psychoraag* is concerned with something 'broader than race', while accurate, moves the frame of analysis away from one crucial thrust of the novel: the return to the persistence of racism in resistance to the never-ending elaboration of cultural or 'identity' definition.

One of the clearest signals of *Psychoraag*'s position within British culturalism is its rejection of a celebratory post-racial harmony through its mobilisation of the radical race critique of Fanon. An opposition between the racial and post-racial is presented early on, where Zaf's response to ADF's 'Black White' encapsulates the post-racial contradiction inherent in multiculturalism: '[t]oo much of all that lovey-dovey stuff depended on there being some kind of level playing field to start with. It depended on a delusion'.[42] The 'lovey-dovey stuff' imagines anti-racism as celebratory, an orientation, a pose or mood, rather than a radical critique that identifies and addresses historical structural inequalities and ideological racial hierarchies. *Psychoraag*'s return to epidermalisation, via explicit references to Fanon's psychopathological examination of race, is a key mode of disruption that tries to illuminate a racial topography, the unevenness of that structural 'playing field':

> [H]e had hated himself so much, he had deliberately avoided mirrors. [. . .] [I]f you were in between, now that was the real locus of purgatory. [. . .] It wis right down inside of your skin and it turned and twisted until you were turned and twisted and you couldn't think straight any more. Until you were so fuckin crazy.[43]

The heavily emphasised epidermal quality of Zaf's racial angst, 'Right down inside of your skin', leading to a twisting, turning 'craziness', testifies to the psychopathological effects of his racialisation in Scotland, a description of the 'massive psychoexistential complex' surrounding race as articulated by Fanon.[44] Like Fanon's 'The Fact of Blackness', the normalisation and privileging of whiteness as the aspirational standard for racialised people, to 'come close to being a real human being', can be read in Zaf's conscious desire literally to become white:[45]

> he had wanted to obliterate himself, to merge his being in their white-ness. He had wanted, so badly, to be accepted and loved that he would've been willin to have scraped the blackness from his skin, cell by fuckin cell, until all that would've been left would've been the bones. And they were white. *Burzakh*. For a long time, he had wished that he wis white.[46]

The meticulous cultivation of hyphenated identity categories vanishes into the powerful racial heuristic of black and white. The genetic and bodily violence of Zaf's willed whiteness – obliteration, skin-scraping, cells and bones – returns to biocentric race in Fanonian terms, turning the body into an *object* signified through epidermalisation. The use of the black signifier is not accidental: through the novel, it has an ambiguous function that fluctuates between a desire for 'solidity' within a comprehensible racial binary, solidarity with pre- or para-multiculturalist anti-racist organisation, as a term of racist abuse, and as the accentuation of the enduring power of whiteness in Scotland.

The black-and-white aesthetics of *Psychoraag* echo Fanon's poetic-aesthetic sensibility and evokes the psychiatry of racialisation in *Black Skin, White Masks*: '[o]ut of the blackest part of my soul, across the zebra striping of my mind, surges this desire to be suddenly *white*'.[47] This aesthetic continues from examples in Saadi's earlier fiction, particularly the short story collection *The Burning Mirror*, in which the contrast between the political and social classifications of black and white, and the sublimated desire to become white, are displaced back to the visual. Often, this register retains an explicit link to race: for Ruby in 'The Queens of Govan', '[t]he black of her jeans and leather jacket made her skin seem whiter. That an the make up. It wis aw in the contrast'.[48] The black–white aesthetic is more pervasive, though, as the visual contrast expands out, and ostensibly disconnected visuals are cast as black and white: 'Reebok'd legs [. . .] on the quivering asphalt'; 'a line ae crack on black'.[49] Such visual clues that are detached from, but recalling, the binaries of racial signification recur throughout *Psychoraag*: 'white meat' and 'black hole'; strobe lighting emphasising a dichotomous whiteness and blackness; references to mythological figures Shaitan the Black and Iblis the White.[50] Just as Fanon recognises in hegemonic whiteness a corrosive effect that 'burns' him,[51] so too does Zaf '[burn] the night from his skin', or 'feel the moon burn the skin on the back of his neck white'; the bodies of the partygoers at Radio Chaandni 'were skinned, burnin, raw. In the glaring, almost ultraviolet light, everyone wis white'.[52] Zaf's wished-for racial transformation echoes Fanon's imagination of a sorcerous spontaneity, 'a form of salvation that consists of magically turning white'.[53]

The occasion for the sudden surging desire for whiteness that Fanon describes is, augmented by the libidinous subtext, the 'white love' of a white woman.[54] The most acute enactment of Zaf's racialisation occurs in his relationship with Babs, a white Scot, a 'supremacist's miscegenate nightmare' which superficially conforms to the exogamous demands of multicultural integration.[55] This desire is mobilised within multiculturalism. As Anne-Marie Fortier points out, for the post-millenium centre-left in Britain, heterosexual, 'interracial' love, particularly formalised in marriage, is celebrated as the 'ultimate symbol of achieved multiculturalism'.[56] This symbolic union is metonymically Unionist: the myth of a 'fully multicultural nation' is also the overcoming of challenges to British unity under New Labour's elaborated Britishness and a governmental-managerial 'One Scotland'. The relationship dynamic in *Psychoraag* is brought into sharper focus in the light of Paul Laverty and Ken Loach's contemporaneous film *Ae Fond Kiss* (2004), which bears an uncanny resemblance to the novel in its depiction of a relationship between a young aspiring Asian Scottish DJ, Casim, and a white Irish music teacher, Roisin.[57] In *Ae Fond Kiss*, the symbolism of achieved multiculturalism remains: the couple's mutual abandonment of familial and religious obligation (Muslim and Roman Catholic respectively) is presented as freedom within an exogamous 'new liberty', crucially accompanied by workplace success and entrepreneurial encouragement, and breaking from a claustrophobic inheritance of religious observance and labour traditions. In contrast to many other films produced by the Ken Loach–Paul Laverty collaboration, *Ae Fond Kiss* produces an essentially New Labour vision of the future.

However, the socially conservative belief in endogamy that adheres both to Zaf's Glasgow Pakistani family and Babs's white Borders family, the 'whole bloody family thing', exposes the political expedience of that vision.[58] Both are caught up in a reification and exoticisation of racial difference which is given its sharpest definition in a Fanonian racial-psychosexual inheritance:

> Her love takes me onto the noble road that leads to total realization. . . .
> I marry white culture, white beauty, white whiteness.
> When my restless hands caress those white breasts, they grasp white civilization and dignity and make them mine.[59]

A clear precedent of Zaf's desire to 'grasp whiteness' is rendered explicitly in 'Ninety-Nine Kiss-o-grams' in *The Burning Mirror*; the focaliser Sal intends to sell land his grandfather has bought him in Pakistan in order to fund the titular kissograms, fantasising himself 'surroondit by them, their wee white breasts pushin intae his broon face, fillin his mooth, his body so that he couldnae breathe fur the whiteness'.[60] In *Psychoraag*, textual descriptions of Babs continually return to Fanon's metonymic 'white breasts', the character's embodied and sexualised whiteness, her 'light golden hue', her eyes 'translucent blue and moist', her 'limbs, her complexion proportioned to suit the Scottish vista – the etiolated, northern light'.[61] Meanwhile, Zaf's own 'noble road' finds literal form in the motorcycle journeys piloted by Babs, 'grasping' the body of the white woman that offers him the prospect of civilisation, dignity and humanity.

The unspoken racialised premise of the relationship is exposed sharply in an argument that seems to presage its end:

> 'Ye dinnae jis walk away fae me – no aifter two bloody years. Ye fuckin ungrateful black bastard![']
> [. . .]
> She's been tripped up. It had always been there, runnin beneath their relationship, the implicit threat of her takin her white-ness and goin elsewhere.[62]

Babs's 'trip' is to reveal inadvertently her internalised belief in her own racial superiority. This is a logical extension of the racial underpinning of their relationship, which is founded in a logic of racial exoticism and colonial expropriation, where '[s]he needed his brown-ness – just as he needed her white. They were both conquerin territories'.[63] Unlike the resolution of *Ae Fond Kiss*, the latent Fanonian psycho-racial hierarchy of black and white remains embedded in *Psychoraag*'s contemporary social relations. Babs's moment of racist abuse is the point at which Scotland's 'achieved

multiculturalism' implodes, via the return of sublimated British imperial racial hierarchies. Part of the shock of 'black bastard' in this context
is its strong association with British post-colonial melancholy; just as in
Sutherland's *Jelly Roll*, abuse is markedly defamiliarising when it emerges
in a supposed 'tolerant multiculture', within an affectionate relationship,
and voiced in a literary Scots that for the preceding twenty years had
mostly been associated with an anti-colonial politics. It also evidences the
operation of racist signifiers in Scotland, which Maud Sulter had already
written about in 'The Privilege of the Fairskinned', that 'Nigger Darkie
Paki / all means the same to them'.[64] The 'blackness' of *Psychoraag* seems to
modify both the specific, Afrocentric racial history that Fanon articulates,
and to the racial taxonomies operating in multicultural Britain after the
attenuation of 'political blackness'. Zaf's use of 'black' is not coherent with
the sociology of race and the development of political blackness in Britain,
or necessarily acutely sensitive to the defining history of blackness itself. In
'Political Blackness and British Asians', Tariq Modood had already outlined a number of reasons why 'the concept of [political blackness] harms
Asians', and argued that most Asians rejected inclusion in the category.[65]
But to Babs, Zaf is both brown and black, encapsulating his broader racialised experience in Scotland. In accordance with Sulter, that contingent
process of racialisation does not necessarily conform to governmental,
political or sociological categories.

'Charred black': racial Gothic

'Grasping' Babs offers Zaf the promise of white civilisation and escape
from the 'locus of purgatory' determined by his own racialisation. The
prospect of being dragged metaphysically lower, towards the underworld,
is represented by his contrasting past relationship with Zilla, a ghostly
'shadow', a heroin addict and sex worker whose supernatural presence
haunts the studio. Her 'shadow' nickname suggests the way that, like Zaf,
Zilla is enmeshed in a form of shadeism, preoccupied with a hierarchy
of skin tone, 'medium brown and she'd never forgiven herself for it'.[66]
Their relationship is defined by their shared experience of racialisation in
Scotland, but rather than being a source of social or political solidarity,
their common blackness has a pathological quality, 'as though there wis
a danger that they might catch somethin from each other. Mibbee blackness'.[67] In the context of their mutual intravenous drug use, a line is drawn
from blackness to the terror of HIV transmission, casting both as a form of
public epidemiological scare, reaffirmed shortly after by Zilla's appearance
in the radio cubicle in which '[s]he wis all needle and black'.[68] Indeed, as

though to emphasise the disjunction between the 'extra-discursive refer-ent' of skin colour and the massive social architecture of race, Zilla is not only 'medium brown' but has a recurring abstract blackness; she is 'a tree charred black by lightning' whose 'eyes [. . .] just got blacker' as she pro-gresses onto harder drugs.[69]

The visitation of Zilla is a Gothic manifestation of the bodily and psychological horror of her own racialised experience. Set partially in the nightscape of urban Glasgow, with the generous proportions of its ten-ement buildings suggesting the monstrous and exaggerated, *Psychoraag* invokes a 'kind of Gothic nightmare' populated by the dead.[70] Maisha Wester has examined the way that the Gothic, historically a sublima-tion of white racial terrors, has been redeployed in the context of African American writing as 'a capable and useful vehicle for expressing the terrors and complexities of black existence'.[71] The Gothic, concerned with the derangement of social order and an uncanny return to the body, is par-ticularly apposite for dramatising anxieties around 'normative and "non-normative" bodies'.[72] The hallucinatory encounter between Zaf and Zilla channels the heroin imagery of *Trainspotting* to generate a sense of hallu-cinogenic transformation, communicated through hyper-sexual, animal, religious and mythological imagery. She represents an amplification of the novel's poetics of madness in Foucauldian terms: 'a freedom to roam amongst the monstrous forms of animality'.[73] The dangerous liberty of Zilla, 'a human beast' who exists outside social normalcy, is conceptualised in monstrous forms: 'Her body wis sleek like that of a porpoise', with a '[w]olf's eyes' and 'a big cat's tongue',[74] a series of unstable animal, sorcer-ous or sacral 'becomings' in Deleuzian–Guattarian terms that do not settle but blend chaotically into one another, *continually transforming [. . .] into a string of other multiplicities*.[75] Her rapid, shape-changing permutations extend into the supernatural, as she becomes a 'gargoyle', a 'djinni', a vampire without a shadow, and a crucified, black-winged archangel with stigmata-like injection wounds.[76] These Gothic elements manifest through Zilla's monstrous embodiment, and constitute both her threatening black-ness, interposing itself between Zaf and his desire to be white, and her threatening liberty, secured in the text's sub-British 'madness' that stands in stark contrast to the reifying control system of multicultural govern-mentality. For Zilla, there can be 'nae appeal tae rationality', and the markedly 'exotic' character of her transformations breaches the 'rational' ordering of culture.[77] In both her transformational shapeshifting and the drug addiction it seems to sublimate, Zilla pushes hard against the param-eters of a prevailing culturalist taxonomy of 'British Asian' and at the racial assumptions that still undergird it.

The encounter with Zilla gives an explicit racialised inflection to significant Gothic tropes from Scottish literary history. Part of this link is found in its use of Robert Burns, with references including Zaf's rumination on 'Tam O'Shanter' and the reproduction of 'The Tarbolton Lassies' within the narrative.[78] Ian Duncan's account of the development of Scottish Gothic as a distinctly national genre in the late eighteenth and early nineteenth century makes clear the significance of Burns's work, particularly 'Tam O'Shanter', in moving the Gothic frame away from a ghostly and elegiac Ossianism towards a vernacular or popular storytelling form, which accords with the manic communitarianism and spontaneous address of *Psychoraag*.[79] Meanwhile, Zaf's encounter with Zilla is suggestive of the embodied immediacy and social implications of 'Tam O'Shanter' that stood in opposition to early British 'official cultural registers [and] decorum', with the heroin provocations of *Trainspotting* as an obvious contemporary point of reference; like Tam's witches, Zilla's sexual assault on Zaf, and the forced injection of heroin which leaves its mark on his body, has a 'carnal solidity' despite the drunken-hallucinatory quality of the encounter.[80] With Zaf in the role of Tam, a resistant 'material world of desires, needs, prejudices, and anxieties', made manifest in the aesthetic mode of *Trainspotting*, is juxtaposed against the 'ghostly past' of fixed anterior culture – a contemporary multicultural manifestation of the Ossianic reification of culture in the name of British stability.[81]

Burns fits into the dialectical imagination of *Psychoraag*, where 'some hings – maist hings – exist in two warulds', a nod to Cairns Craig's 'doubling of the world' between myth and reason which he identifies as typical of Scottish fiction.[82] Zaf wonders whether, like 'Auld Rabbie Burns', his listeners have '[i]vir been in two places at wance?'[83] These bifurcations seem an explicit allusion to C. Gregory Smith's 'Caledonian antisyzygy' and the Scottish Gothic tradition of the *doppelgänger*, a central feature in James Hogg's *The Private Memoirs and Confessions of a Justified Sinner* (1824) and Robert Louis Stevenson's *Strange Case of Dr Jekyll and Mr Hyde* (1886).[84] Duncan points out that Hogg's novel, set during the period of parliamentary Union, narrates 'the futility of "union" as a state of collective or psychic being', and thus rejects the ideological commitments of Hogg's literary mentor, Walter Scott, to the unifying of Scotland-in-Britain.[85] The *doppelgänger* motif within *Psychoraag* signals its literary antecedents in Hogg and Stevenson, and connects the racial dimension of the novel's subject-splitting to the new context of 'union' in the national moment of declining Britain and newly devolved Scotland. *Psychoraag*'s Gothic doubling splits along an axis that returns to a racial double-consciousness or 'in-betweenness', the 'black but not black' and aspirational whiteness of Zaf.

The intertextual link to Stevenson is conveyed in the putative moral distance between Zaf the poet-philosopher in the role of Jekyll, and Hyde as reprised by Zafar, 'The Psycho', a Glaswegian-Asian gangster and archetypal Clydeside 'hard man' who grew up in the 'same century but another world'.[86] Following the example of Gil-Martin and Hyde, Zafar is a projection of the subterranean, repressed elements of Zaf's personality: racial self-hatred, violent anger, and sexual possessiveness. While Zaf and Zafar are ostensibly separate characters, the distinction between them is shrouded in uncertainty. Zafar's presence in narrative action verges on the imperceptible, a trick of the light witnessed only by Zaf, and they share a connection which culminates in the taking possession of both the *Junnune Show* and Zaf's body by Zafar: 'Ah can feel iviry inch ae yer corpse. An ye know why? Cause Ah'm better than you in iviry way. Ah'm inside ye. [. . .] Ah am you'.[87] That this Gothic doubling has a racial quality is made clear in the first moment in which Zaf 'possesses' Zafar:

> [Zaf] felt himself slippin into the body of Zafar, into the scars which he had instead of birth lines, into the hate that he had for everythin an especially for himself and into the black-and-white of his blood.[88]

This hate for the 'black-and-white' returns to the psycho-traumatic 'in-betweenness' that Zaf has already identified in himself, the 'in-between [. . .] locus of purgatory' that comes from being between whiteness as a 'state of bliss' and an undeniable blackness that Zaf erroneously thinks is immune to the politics of colour gradation.[89] Carrying on the national refutation of 'union' found in Hogg's early *doppelgänger*, the subject-splitting racial self-hatred of Zaf(ar) emerges in reaction to the celebratory vision of black and white British unity emblematised earlier in ADF's 'Black White', replacing it with the figure of the 'Scottish-Asian' hyphenated man caught between the Gothic dichotomy of whiteness and blackness.

Appropriately, the sign of madness in *Psychoraag* contains an oppositional 'double' to Fanon's articulation of psychopathological race: Zaf specifies that 'only in madness' might the route to a 'colour-blind' future be possible.[90] This is an inversion of the common use of madness to psychopathologise migration policy, or to inveigh against the 'madness' of multiculturalism. The paradigmatic case is Powell's 'Rivers of Blood' speech in which he stressed that '[w]e must be mad, literally mad, as a nation to be permitting the annual inflow of some 50,000 dependants'.[91] This textual madness, aesthetic and metaphorical, is tonally different to the Fanonian 'psychoexistential complex' of race and racism; like the monstrous transformations of Zilla or the double naming of Zaf and Zafar, the sign of madness in *Psychoraag* suggests a playful-serious transgression against the British rational organisation of culture and perpetuation of race. The structuring conceit of the novel itself is the 'show of madness', '[s]ix hours of turntable madness, of laser lunacy, of autohypnosis on the wheel rims of rattly cassettes', which carves out a confined space of liberty arranged against obliquely indicated systems of control: 'thur's nae control oan this last episode ae *The Junnune Show*'.[92] Zaf's own combination of spontaneous philosophy and rambling, contradictory confusion place him in the role of a madman-philosopher, in keeping with Shoshana Felman's recognition that 'the literary madman is most often a disguised philosopher'.[93] This manifests in various forms of the philosopher-madman: as a jester or fool, 'mibbee jist the clown dancing oan the fag ends ae the celluloid'; as an evangelical prophet, from whom 'ye don't get ony lies. Here, ivirythin ye hear is the truth. Goad's ane'; and as an idiot savant, 'an intuitive, illiterate expert in the auld Al-Misr discipline ae Euclidean Geometry'.[94] These mutable roles are interwoven with an explicit recognition of a community brought together in the inclusive medium of the radio broadcast, that 'onywan listenin tae me noo, tae this crazy, this *junnune*, show, must be haufweye *paagal* themselves'.[95]

This allusive social and philosophical madness aligns with a Scottish intellectual tradition associated with R. D. Laing, an attempt to restore social relationality to the hierarchal, coercive and medicalising institution of psychiatric practice. David Cooper's description of psychoanalysis before the anti-psychiatry movement, as the 'compartmentalization of certain states of experience into formally reduced types', resonates strongly with the taxonomic and managerial politics that inform multicultural governmentality.[96] In the context of New Labour governmentality, a 'rational' approach to difference is defined by a series of orderings: reified cultural formations and 'common sense' raciologies, demographic cartograms and standardised language, all perfectly fitted to an overarching, naturalised and frictionless Britishness. The novel's madness, a process of unsettlement which threatens these compartmentalising processes, extends Zaf's psycho-spiritual lexicon through various formal strategies that accord strongly with Scottish literary antecedents: the temporal and narrative disjunctions of the show and its musical index; transgressive embodiment; relationality and the collective; linguistic and typographical experimentation; and a final mind–body separation that offers a redrawn cartogram of Glasgow. Whether *Psychoraag* is also part of a Laingian romanticisation of 'psychic regression' remains open to question, although the novel generally avoids getting too close to the clinical-psychiatric in its elaboration of the 'raag'.[97]

The lyricism of unreason (*Trainspotting* remix)

The music in *Psychoraag* has an apt allegorical value for this kind of disruptive madness. Michel Foucault states that it is the 'lyricism of unreason' which is silenced by the rationalism of Descartes,[98] while for Felman, madness is best expressed as 'a kind of rhythm; a rhythm that is unpredictable, incalculable, unsayable, but that is nonetheless fundamentally narratable'.[99] The novel's attempt to blend narrative, poetics and music together is metaphorically constitutive of a counter-rational sound project, which underlines the significance of the 'psychoraag' itself, a 'melody of the mind'. The track list at the end of the novel provides the opportunity for a multimedia reading experience, as the reader can listen to the music alongside narrative developments. It taps into a rich history of black musical forms as a kind of avant-garde 'radical collage' that has long made political claims in Britain, in opposition to the dictates of established taste.[100] The spoken portions of the text are narrated rhythmically, through Zaf's distinctive speaking voice with its free associations and narrative syncopation, but music tracks themselves are also embedded in an intertextual framework, with their own signifying potential. Zaf's rhyming and rhythmical oral-poetic style (for example, 'like me' // 'Sumjhe?' // 'majestie'; 'button' // 'Ilivin'; 'son' // 'wan')[101] resembles the 'Rabelaisian spontaneity' that Gilroy connects to the politics of hip hop and rap.[102] The music itself plugs in to Kobena Mercer's 'discrepant cosmopolitanism', evoked by the 'postcolonial hybridity [. . .] of a Bally Sagoo remix of Nusrat Fateh Ali Khan'; Zaf airs a Nusrat Fateh Ali Khan remix as his penultimate track.[103] But where Gilroy and Mercer pinpoint the political potential of music within a black British framework, *Psychoraag*'s DJ emphasises cultural connections specific to Scotland. Ali Azmat's voice 'wis like that of an elemental, powering up from deep in the bowels of the burnin Scottish earth'; the Cosmic Rough Riders enact the journey from 'Karachi to Glasgow in twenty easy strings'; 'Lata [Mangeshkar's] song wis the spiritual anthem of the Shiels'.[104] Scotland, already nominated as a 'sound object' available for renegotiation within the text, is itself remixed by the DJ-philosopher.[105]

That this 'remix' is in some sense uncodifiable is embedded within the novel's own paratextual structure. The show's playlist, reproduced as a form of index after the glossary at the end of the book, only imprecisely matches narrative developments; meanwhile, the playlist as a paratextual object represents an attempt to organise and order text and time that slips into blurred unintelligibility in an echo of the novel's own unruly orthography. Orthographic breakdown is one of the defining characteristics of a post-1979 Scottish literary moment, in the font, white space, image intrusion and free indirect discourse of Gray, Kelman and Galloway. On one level, the disintegrating list stands as a parody of Nick Hornby's DJ in *High Fidelity*, a high-water mark of the Brit-pop literary genre, where an obsessive process of self-aggrandisement and authentication is acted out through competitive listing of tracks.[106] Indeed, the process of listing itself – seen in elegiac books by Roger Scruton and Jeremy Paxman and the poetry of John Betjeman, and parodied by Julian Barnes in *England, England* (1998) – has been deployed as a backwards-looking form of English cultural nationalism that has historically stood in for an institutional English nationhood absorbed into Britishness, and which Scotland retains in a more distinct form.[107] Against the national systematising inherent in the English list, *Psychoraag*'s playlist inverts its own managerial and curatorial purpose. Initially legible and coherent, the list soon metamorphoses into 'a hermeneutic form of shorthand, a kind of hidden Hebrew or mibbee a revealed Arabic'; as the night progresses, the list strays further from legibility: 'like some kind of hieroglyphics. Different times, other scripts'; until '[t]he scribbles on his paper had become completely illegible – almost like some kind of lost blue music. Etruscan perhaps. Or Kafiristani'.[108] The transition between each 'lost' and 'hidden' alphabet maps speculative migratory routes buried in pre-Britain, an anti-cartographic 'worlding' Saadi later returns to in *Joseph's Box* (2009), that broadens the temporal and spatial dimensions of migration beyond the foreshortened, amnesiac discourses of contemporary migration to Britain.

Hornby's structuring lists are jettisoned as his narrator reaches a level of respectable middle-class maturity, in the way that the edginess of 'Cool Britannia' has always been a chimerical cultural threat. Conversely, in *Psychoraag* the unmanageable effluvia and viscera of the narrator literally and figuratively soil the playlist, destroying its structuring power and transforming it from white to black: 'His playlist wis almost black with the various stains of the night. Wine, blood, spunk, vomit [. . .] skin, bone, flesh, brain [. . .] Zaf had emptied his body onto the clean white surface of the paper'.[109] Zaf's biofluids and tissue become an incontinent and incomprehensible mark of blackness on the 'clean' paper, a similar racial-representational analogy to the 'small, black mark' of *Trumpet*. Where the bodily, social and moral transgressions of *Trainspotting* have been read by Aaron Kelly as a direct challenge to British 'delimitative parameters of bourgeois discourse', the expulsions, exudations and cellular matter of Zaf's raced body also transgress British state-cultural priorities via a return to race, opposed to an anodyne and celebratory 'culture' mappable through listing.[110]

The playlist is a paratextual metonym of the novel itself, a track listing appendix added after the conclusion of narrative events in *Psychoraag*. Its imprecision moves away from stable, 'knowable' culture towards an insta-bility that more closely resembles the contingency and unpredictability of actual social and cultural lived experience. The gradually increasing unintelligibility of the list is a form of systemic entropy, a disavowal of the tracks as a comprehensible index of culture, culminating in a mess of ink that constitutes a semiotic break:

> The surface of the paper wis almost completely covered in ink. [. . .] the blue had smudged and spread so that, now, the song titles were partially obscured by irregularly shaped blotches. Letters faded into pools of ink and the meanings of the words had grown less distinct with each note of every song he had played.[111]

The obliteration of the list mocks the taxonomic or ordering impulse implied by the written record, while authorial power over meaning is liquefied, 'smudged' and 'obscured'. The 'meanings of words' are smeared away, suggestive of a representational deficit. Such an anxiety of represen-tation calls up a problem interrogated in Kelman's *How Late It Was, How Late*: a distancing from the ascribed role of representative writer.[112] In the case of Sammy Samuels and Ally 'the rep', Sammy's refusal of legal repre-sentation to articulate on his behalf can be read as a refusal of an autho-rial role to speak for, to become the voice of, working-class Glasgow – a role in which Kelman has been repeatedly placed in larger British literary journalism. *Psychoraag*'s representational subtext is similar, situated within the particular context of multicultural writing and the 'first Asian-Scottish novel'. The novel's inchoate cultural politics, deferred by narrative mad-ness and the slippage of meaning and form emblematised in the list, are part of a literary practice that staves off a process of multicultural labelling and the projection of authenticity onto Saadi as a writer of the 'Asian Scottish experience'.[113]

As though consciously positioned in dialogue with the literary experi-mentations that had dominated Scottish writing in the preceding decade, *Psychoraag* has a breadcrumb trail of references to Welsh. Zaf's face 'wis covered in a cold sweat and he wis tremblin', a close approximation of the first sentence of *Trainspotting*; there are references to 'A Scottish Soldier' and Scottish soldiery fighting the wars of the British Empire; the large typeface 'Z' of *Marabou Stork Nightmares* appears as a reference to Zilla, who appears as an emasculating figure of vengeance in a similar mode to the scissor-wielding Kirsty in Welsh's second novel.[114] *Psychoraag* and *Trainspotting* also share a common linguistic politics that finds its anteced-ent in Kelman, in works such as *The Busconductor Hines*, *A Disaffection* and *How Late It Was, How Late*. The novel's use of interrupted interior monologue establishes a clear debt to Kelman's narrators, such as Rab Hines, Patrick Doyle or Sammy Samuels:

> You didn't remember destinations – it wis the journey . . . argh!
> Self help rubbish. What nonsense all that stuff wis![115]

This is not only realised in the use of non-standard Scottish English, which forms the bulk of the narrative, but also in a keen focus on speaking voice, emblematised in the requirements of radio broadcasting, its free indirect discourse and transgressions against orthographic narration, and in the disintegration of codified representational acts symbolised by the playlist itself.[116]

The dialectal or vernacular qualities of the narrative combine the typographical and expressive practices of Kelman and Welsh with elements of Scots, Gaelic, Arabic, Sanskrit, Farsi, Hindi, Urdu, Punjabi and other useful fragments. Zaf asserts that 'wu're multilingual oan this station. Polyethelene ethnic. The United Nations ae the bin lane'; this back street or 'bin lane' pluralism, the 'plasticity' suggested by 'polyethelene', wheelie bins and bags, is a kind of discrepant *bricolage* that incorporates diverse linguistic influences into a new 'creolised' literary language.[117] Writers such as David Dabydeen, Sam Selvon, E. K. Brathwaite and Linton Kwesi Johnson have been exponents and practitioners of creole literature in Britain, both as a postcolonially informed response to the ideological power of Standard English, and as a validation of migrant experience in a hostile post-war British context, particularly from the Caribbean.[118] An assault on European languages understood as unifying, pure and assimilative is a staple of Caribbean critical thought, expressed by Édouard Glissant: '[a]s opposed to the unilateral relationship with the Metropolis, the multidimensional nature of the diverse Caribbean. As opposed to the constraints of one language, the creation of self-expression'.[119] Glissant's emphasis on multidimensionality over unilateralism, and the critique of rigid 'one language' imperialism, still applies to a post-millennial Britain dominated by 'correct' English and axial relationships between a highly centralised government and its margins. Such a literary language has a political resonance in terms of its drawing together of linguistic formations that have fallen foul of '[writing] good English', the British imperial mantra that Angus Calder translates to 'you tinks and keelies, you Paddies, Taffs and Jocks, you Nigs and Pakis, into line there!'[120] Calder's caustic observation is a reminder that racism and the obsessive prosecution of English 'standards' go hand in hand. The key difference between his Celtic categories and the racialised ones, however, is that the former are white aside from the 'colour of their vowels' in Cairns Craig's formulation. The latter, as Fanon makes clear, can speak the language of the colonial centre perfectly and still remain judged by the colour of their skin – except, as David Starkey's example of David Lammy makes clear – on the radio.[121]

The protected status of English in contemporary Britain extends beyond the threat of contamination from irregular 'others' to the threat of dilution by whole languages. Zaf's literary language is marked by a high degree of lexical importation, but he stresses the 'multilingual' quality of the station; he greets his audience with 'Hiya in fifty thoosand tongues!' and identifies himself as 'the man ae a thoosand tongues'.[122] A commitment to multilingualism has particular purchase in the context of British state multiculturalist discourse and the citizenship test, where English is held up 'as the common language of the British' while multilingualism, normally specifying or implying precisely the South Asian languages incorporated into *Psychoraag*, constitutes 'a barrier to cohesion and integration'.[123] Media and legislative focus on the issue of English proficiency sharpened in the aftermath of the 2001 Oldham riots, which were cited in the House of Commons as resulting from a failure to integrate caused by low academic attainment and lack of English skills, and led to the establishment of the Life in the United Kingdom Advisory Group for the purpose of developing a new citizenship test. Their subsequent report, *The New and the Old*, re-emphasised a commitment to multicultural citizenship, but without any concurrent commitment to multilingual citizenship.[124] Language is a red line in the vision of an ordered anglophone multicultural society, where the enforcement of competent English both provides the guarantee of enfranchisement and suggests the system of values integral to 'Britishness' that are more commonly associated with 'good English' in literary terms. The speaking of other languages lacks an interface with the linguistics operations of official multicultural Britain, and remains a possibility only in the out-of-sight, street-level interactions of the bin lane.

The inscrutable 'enemy within' shrouded in incomprehensible language is already familiar in a Scottish and Welsh context, both historically and in the contemporaneous condescension towards Welsh and Gaelic language provisions in the devolved nations. Scotland's politics of language has generally cohered around a dominant structure of 'three languages': English, including non-standard Scottish forms, Scots and Gaelic. While the contemporary British state's ideology of linguistic standardisation has legislative as well as literary implications, Scotland's national language has been described as a 'generalised will to undo Standard English'.[125] However, the 'three language' schema struggles to admit new linguistic influences in Scotland through migration: as Michael Gardiner asks, '[w]hich of Scotland's "three languages" is attributed to your neighbour in Pollokshields whose native language is Arabic?'[126] This is one of the questions advanced in *Psychoraag*. Zaf's polyphony makes fresh demands of

Scottish literature in its 'minority' form, as described by Robert Crawford, wherein Scottish writing is the literature 'a minority constructs within a major language' of English.[127] *Psychoraag* constitutes a secondary tendency within that minority status, a moment of 'becoming majority' for Scottish writing where an increasingly 'healthy' Scottish 'three language' national tradition becomes the site for new minority interventions with a reformative political charge.

Quantum remapping Glasgow

As the sun comes up on Zaf's night shift, the deranging acoustic and visual effects of the claustrophobic studio produce a narrative bifurcation, as Zaf becomes two concurrent people, simultaneously broadcasting from the DJ chair and wandering the deserted streets of early-morning Glasgow, part psychic projection and part physical experience. Zaf acts out the duality of 'two warulds', simultaneous existence in different spaces: 'OK, so here Ah am,' he announces, 'here, in the cubicle ae *The Junnune Show*, [. . .] And, yet, at the same time, Ah'm roamin aroon the streets ae this magnificent city. How d'ye figure that wan?'[128] This somnambulatory cityscape returns to Alasdair Gray's *Lanark* in its extension of a 'Glasgow imaginary', the act of urban imagination that is mourned as absent in the famous exchange between McAlpin and Thaw in *Lanark*, that 'if a city hasn't been used by an artist not even the inhabitants live there imaginatively'.[129] One of the key contributions of *Lanark*, Randall Stevenson argues, is its suggestion that contemporaneous temporal (and by implication, spatial) systems of control imposed over experience 'can still be escaped or reordered in narrative and imagination'.[130] Playing with these spatial and temporal disjunctions, the rapidly changing faces of Zaf's Glasgow, framed by the novel's staging of a loss of control, hint at a return to *Lanark*'s fantastical Unthank: 'That wis the thing about this city – the time wis always out of joint'; 'the city seemed to be shiftin constantly – not just in that sense of the frenetic automobile turbulence which confers to a place the illusion of excitement but in the slippin of time through brickwork and concrete'.[131] The space of the unsettled city corresponds to the quantum uncertainty of Zaf's position, both inside and outside, static and mobile, and to the disruptions to narrative sequencing and logic introduced by the novel's frequent analeptic passages and final moment of prolepsis.

If *Lanark* demands a reckoning with Glasgow as erasure, as a metonymic space of Scottish national 'obliteration' expressed in the unsettled and unsettling Unthank, then *Psychoraag*'s fictional Glasgow works towards unpacking Scotland's ethnic demarcations previously absent from the literary imagination, a remapping of the city's zones stretch-ing from Pollokshields to the West End.[132] The idea of self-segregating 'minority ghettoes' acting as a barrier to British national identity and social cohesion was a significant part of governmental policy commit-ments to 'break down segregation', seen in reports from the Community Cohesion Panel in 2004.[133] In *Psychoraag*, the suggestion of a racialised ghetto exists, though its causality is less clear. Zaf's semi-ironic description of Pollokshields, its 'buzz', '*joie*' and 'Asian vibe',[134] recalls Kundnani's critique of the 'vibrancy' label attached to Britain's multicultural others. That celebration is contrasted with its insular, 'purgatorial' character, the responsibility of municipal authorities rather than 'refusers of integration', where all the houses 'faced inwards' on streets 'which the city fathers had built to be blocked off'.[135] This ambiguity is foregrounded in the novel: in Pollokshields, there was 'no ease, no sense of plurality. It was not like Woodlands or even Kinnin Park. The Shiels wis a ghetto of sorts, a mental ghetto, and, yet, there was succour and a certain type of strength in that'.[136] As Zaf hits the signal booster that carries his broadcast into unbounded space, his corporeal avatar leaves Pollokshields, '[w]alkin an wakin [. . .] pacin oot the cartogram ae this toon', moving from the acutely delimited space of the studio cubicle to a transhistorical exploration unbound even by physical laws.[137] The idea of the 'cartogram' is itself significant, given its defining quality of delineation or mapping according to variables. Zaf has already announced his ambition to 'redraw all the maps' so that 'whun we come oot ae here in the morning, we willnae recognise the waruld, we will-nae know oorsels', urging a redrawing of the imaginary maps of Glasgow away from the cartogram, the racial demarcations that separate Kinning Park, Pollokshields, the West End and other parts of Glasgow, towards a new civic horizon.[138]

Zaf's circumnavigation reproduces the appropriation of Situationist psychogeography as a literary-political practice in Britain, a French activ-ist and intellectual tradition most strongly associated with the writing of Guy Debord that sought to disrupt habituated urban movement in order to provoke breaks with habituated thought, instigating political change.[139] Psychogeography as a literary practice in Britain had already been pio-neered by the work of Iain Sinclair, with *Psychoraag* immediately preceded by *London Orbital* (2002). Expanding on earlier work such as *Lights Out for the Territory* (1997), Sinclair's travelogue relentlessly critiques the forced Britishing of New Labour epitomised by the Millennium Dome, through a politics of place, an attention to forgotten histories and a reconnection with territory, in a nationally English gesture that rebelled against a British state imaginary.[140] *Psychoraag*'s walking politics presents a similarly national chal-lenge in fiction, a perambulatory *dérive* or form of experimental wandering around deterritorialised Glasgow, a psychogeographic process of active 'drifting' through the city that runs counter to the streamlined movement of life in a late capitalist metropolis, experienced sensorily.

While Zaf channels the spirit of spontaneity that characterises the role of the DJ in the novel, moving 'in the direction that his legs took him' with 'no logic to his direction',[141] the narrative enacts in microcosm his parents' journey to Scotland, travelling north and west through Glasgow, from Pollokshields – Pakistan suggested metonymically in the 'migrant ghetto' of 'Wee Faisalabad' – to the Botanic Gardens and the West End – the symbolic space of white, cosmopolitan Scotland – and back. Debord's description of 'wandering in subterranean catacombs forbidden to the public',[142] part of the general transgression of propriety and authority characteristic of the *dérive*, is precisely replicated in *Psychoraag* in the exploration of an access tunnel lying beneath Kirklee Bridge, spanning 'North Kelvinside or South Maryhill, dependin on which social class you wanted to impress'.[143] Beyond the cartographic project of 'redrawing maps', the physicality of Zaf's descent literally into Glasgow, on all fours, in darkness, 'crawlin over more than mud',[144] echoes Sinclair's national project which emphasises embodied activity and participation over the 'mere representational'. In his breaching of demographic 'territories', his staking of a claim to Glaswegian histories encoded in the cityscape itself and his transgressions against urban and even physical laws – at one point literally jumping over the River Clyde – Zaf's *dérive* is a response to a culturalist logic of space expressed in anxieties over 'no go' areas of migrant settlement which continue to the present day. Zaf's 'walkin', 'roamin' and 'wanderin' across Glasgow, unbounded by social mores, physical laws and, crucially, his own habituated movements, can be read as a political act that responds to the ethnic 'cartogram' of his Glasgow.

Building on his imperative to 'redraw the maps', Zaf imagines a moment of transformation, a demand for change under the whimsical label of 'piscanthropy', a 'move back up the evolutionary scale' that involves a return to the primordial life of the fish.[145] The play on words implied by moving back up the evolutionary scale, a move down the devolutionary scale, situates the novel in a Scottish political-historical moment at the last. In keeping with the novel's multilingual propagation, '[s]uch a change demands anither language'.[146] Piscanthropy is a radical transformation, a life of pure instinct with its own phenotypical character, in which the skin of all people will stretch and become '*siller*' (silver) to accommodate their new form.[147] Transforming his listeners into fish is typical of Zaf's anarchic play, but the return to the primordial is not his first identification of a radical genetic commonality as a progressive 'devolutionary' idea. He notes that, as per the human race's originary migration out of 'the same wee green hollow in East Africa', that '[d]eep down, we were all black'.[148] While such an assertion misses the fact that blackness is a historical discourse with the thinnest of threads to prehistory, it conjoins an idea of racial justice – the taxonomic equalisation of all people – to his thinking on (d)evolution. Devolution as reverse evolution is associated with the 'social' Darwinism of Herbert Spencer, who called it 'dissolution' and applied the idea to human populations as a way of evidencing his idea of the 'survival of the fittest' understood as a social phenomenon.[149] Zaf's call for devolution is concomitantly a call to resist principles associated with Spencerian rational thought: the imperial teleology of civilisational progress, and the racial-biological determinism inherent in 'clearing the earth of inferior races of men'.[150] That resistance doesn't have much to do with the ambitions of the Kilbrandon Report, but it puts forward a radical demand of Scotland's new political conditions which are delicately balanced, 'poised on the brink of a stillness'.[151]

Notes

1. Asian Dub Foundation, 'Black White', *Rafi's Revenge* (Polygram, 1998).
2. Saadi, Suhayl, *Psychoraag* (Edinburgh: Chroma, 2005 [2004]), p. 22.
3. Asian Dub Foundation, 'Black White'; Gilroy, *There Ain't No Black in the Union Jack*, p. 148.
4. Eldridge, 'Rise and Fall', p. 37.
5. Huggan, *The Postcolonial Exotic*, p. 136.
6. Hall, Stuart, *The Multicultural Question 2001* (Milton Keynes: Pavis Papers, 2001), p. 3.
7. Huggan, *The Postcolonial Exotic*, p. xii.
8. See Gardiner, *From Trocchi to Trainspotting*, p. 5.
9. Saadi, *Psychoraag*, p. 302.
10. Lentin and Titley, *Crises of Multiculturalism*, p. 49.
11. Hage, Ghassan, 'Intercultural Relations at the Limits of Multiculturalism' in Duncan Ivison (ed.), *The Ashgate Research Companion to Multiculturalism* (London: Ashgate, 2010), pp. 235–54: 235.
12. Hall, *Multicultural Question 2001*, p. 3, emphasis added.
13. Lentin and Titley, *Crises of Multiculturalism*, p. 11.
14. See Gardiner, Michael, *The Constitution of English Literature: The State, the Nation and the Canon* (London: Bloomsbury Academic, 2013), p. 2.
15. Barker, *The New Racism*, p. 23.
16. Hall, 'New Ethnicities', p. 272.
17. Balibar, Étienne, 'Is there a "Neo-Racism"?' in Étienne Balibar and Immanuel Wallerstein (eds), *Race, Nation, Class: Ambiguous Identities* (London: Verso, 1991), pp. 17–28: 26.
18. Hall, 'New Ethnicities', p. 272.
19. Saadi, *Psychoraag*, p. 23.
20. See Back et al., 'New Labour's White Heart', p. 452.
21. Back et al., 'New Labour's White Heart', p. 452; Kundnani, 'Rise and Fall', p. 107; Pitcher, *Politics of Multiculturalism*, p. 27.

22. Hopkins, 'Politics, Race and Nation', pp. 119–20.
23. See for example the pamphlet 'New Laws for Race Equality in Scotland', published by the Scottish Executive in 2001.
24. 'Promoting Race Equality in Schools and Pre-School Education Centres', Scottish Executive, 2003.
25. Penrose and Howard, '*One Scotland, Many Cultures*', p. 101. Penrose and Howard also critique certain elements of the racial sorting function of the 'One Scotland' billboard advertising campaign, arguing that it promotes a 'dominant Scottish culture', which 'has the effect of reinforcing the perspective of those Whites who see themselves as "more Scottish" than non-Whites and, in consequence, as having greater rights to determine the future of "their" country' (p. 105).
26. 'Race Equality', *One Scotland* (2016), http://onescotland.org/equality-themes/race/ (last accessed 1 October 2017).
27. The *Scotland Against Racism* website is now obsolete and offline; an archived copy from 2008 is available through the Internet Archive, https://archive.org/.
28. Kundnani, 'Rise and Fall', p. 105.
29. Kundnani, 'Rise and Fall', pp. 105–6.
30. Fowler, 'A Tale of Two Novels', p. 75; Fowler also quotes Saadi himself on the dominance of an Oxbridge–London axis in commissioning and publishing fiction in Britain (p. 79).
31. Fowler, 'A Tale of Two Novels', p. 83.
32. Respectively, quotations from the *Sunday Herald*, *New Statesman* and *The List* from the cover of the paperback edition of *Psychoraag* (Edinburgh: Chroma, 2005).
33. Huggan, *The Postcolonial Exotic*, p. 87.
34. Pittin-Hedon, Marie-Odile, *The Space of Fiction: Voices from Scotland in a Post-Devolution Age* (Glasgow: Scottish Literature International, 2015), p. 88.
35. See Huggan, *The Postcolonial Exotic*, pp. xi–xii.
36. Upstone, Sara, *British Asian Fiction: Twenty-First-Century Voices* (Manchester: Manchester University Press, 2010), p. 196.
37. Upstone, *British Asian Fiction*, p. 205.
38. Pittin-Hedon, *The Space of Fiction*, pp. 81, 88, 89.
39. Rodríguez González, Carla, 'The Rhythms of the City: The Performance of Time and Space in Suhayl Saadi's *Psychoraag*', *The Journal of Commonwealth Literature* 51:1 (2016), pp. 92–109: 92, 94, 97.
40. Innes, Kirstin, 'Renton's Bairns: Identity and Language in the Post-Trainspotting Novel' in Schoene (ed.), *Edinburgh Companion to Contemporary Scottish Literature*, pp. 301–9: 308.
41. Huggan, *The Postcolonial Exotic*, p. 153.
42. Saadi, *Psychoraag*, p. 27.
43. Saadi, *Psychoraag*, p. 134.
44. Fanon, *Black Skin, White Masks*, p. 5.
45. Fanon, *Black Skin, White Masks*, p. 8.
46. Saadi, *Psychoraag*, pp. 134–5; the glossary of *Psychoraag* defines *Burzakhí* as 'purgatory' (p. 422).
47. Fanon, *Black Skin, White Masks*, p. 45, original emphasis.
48. Saadi, Suhayl, *The Burning Mirror* (Edinburgh: Polygon, 2001), p. 21.
49. Saadi, *The Burning Mirror*, pp. 110, 114.
50. Saadi, *Psychoraag*, pp. 200, 229, 312.
51. Fanon, *Black Skin, White Masks*, p. 86.
52. Saadi, *Psychoraag*, pp. 164, 201, 229.
53. Fanon, *Black Skin, White Masks*, p. 30.
54. Fanon, *Black Skin, White Masks*, p. 45.
55. Saadi, *Psychoraag*, p. 25.
56. Fortier, *Multicultural Horizons*, p. 51.

57. *Ae Fond Kiss*, dir. Ken Loach (Icon Film Distribution, 2004).
58. Saadi, *Psychoraag*, p. 76
59. Fanon, *Black Skin, White Masks*, p. 45.
60. Saadi, *The Burning Mirror*, p. 5.
61. Saadi, *Psychoraag*, pp. 27, 410, 68.
62. Saadi, *Psychoraag*, p. 141.
63. Saadi, *Psychoraag*, pp. 25–6.
64. Sulter, *As a Black Woman*, p. 23.
65. Modood, Tariq, 'Political Blackness and British Asians', *Sociology* 28:4 (1994), pp. 859–76: 859.
66. Saadi, *Psychoraag*, p. 46.
67. Saadi, *Psychoraag*, p. 90.
68. Saadi, *Psychoraag*, p. 91.
69. Saadi, *Psychoraag*, p. 90.
70. Saadi, *Psychoraag*, p. 59.
71. Wester, Maisha L., *African American Gothic: Screams from Shadowed Places* (New York: Palgrave Macmillan, 2012), pp. 1–2.
72. Wester, *African American Gothic*, p. 25.
73. Foucault, Michel, *History of Madness*, trans. Jonathan Murphy and Jean Khalfa (London: Routledge, 2006), p. 156.
74. Saadi, *Psychoraag*, pp. 180, 183, 300–3.
75. Deleuze, Gilles, and Félix Guattari, *A Thousand Plateaus*, trans. Brian Massumi (London: Athlone, 1999), p. 249, original emphasis.
76. Saadi, *Psychoraag*, pp. 180, 303, 306.
77. Saadi, *Psychoraag*, pp. 300–1.
78. Saadi, *Psychoraag*, pp. 209, 339–40.
79. Duncan, Ian, 'Walter Scott, James Hogg, and Scottish Gothic' in David Punter (ed.), *A New Companion to the Gothic* (London: Blackwell, 2012), pp. 123–34: 126.
80. Duncan, 'Scottish Gothic', p. 126.
81. Duncan, 'Scottish Gothic', p. 126.
82. Craig, *Modern Scottish Novel*, p. 165.
83. Saadi, *Psychoraag*, pp. 166, 338.
84. Smith, C. Gregory, *Scottish Literature, Character and Influence* (London: Macmillan, 1919).
85. Duncan, 'Scottish Gothic', p. 131.
86. Saadi, *Psychoraag*, pp. 106, 107.
87. Saadi, *Psychoraag*, pp. 256, 394.
88. Saadi, *Psychoraag*, p. 257.
89. Saadi, *Psychoraag*, p. 134.
90. Saadi, *Psychoraag*, p. 25.
91. Smithies, Bill, Peter Fiddick and John Enoch Powell, *Enoch Powell on Immigration* (London: Sphere, 1969), p. 37.
92. Saadi, *Psychoraag*, pp. 113, 37.
93. Felman, Shoshana, *Writing and Madness* (Ithaca: Cornell University Press, 1985), p. 37.
94. Saadi, *Psychoraag*, pp. 147, 340, 415.
95. Saadi, *Psychoraag*, p. 173; the glossary of *Psychoraag* defines *Paagal* as 'madness' (p. 427).
96. Cooper, David, 'Introduction' in Michel Foucault, *Madness and Civilization: A History of Insanity in the Age of Reason*, trans. Richard Howard (London: Routledge, 2001 [1961]), pp. vii–ix: ix.
97. Miller, Gavin, *R. D. Laing* (Edinburgh: Edinburgh Review, 2004), p. 131.
98. Foucault, *History of Madness*, p. 517.
99. Felman, *Writing and Madness*, p. 254.

100. Mercer, *Welcome to the Jungle*, p. 124; see Paul Gilroy, 'Two Sides of Anti-Racism' in *There Ain't No Black in the Union Jack*, pp. 146–99.
101. Saadi, *Psychoraag*, pp. 344, 368.
102. Gilroy, *Small Acts*, p. 35.
103. Mercer, *Welcome to the Jungle*, p. 29.
104. Saadi, *Psychoraag*, pp. 96, 193, 389.
105. Saadi, *Psychoraag*, pp. 208–9.
106. Hornby, Nick, *High Fidelity* (London: Victor Gollancz, 1995).
107. Scruton, Roger, *England: An Elegy* (London: Continuum, 2001); Paxman, Jeremy, *The English: A Portrait of a People* (London: Penguin, 1999); Barnes, Julian, *England, England* (London: Jonathan Cape, 1998); see Aughey, Arthur, '"England Is the Country and the Country Is England": But What of the Politics?' in Westall and Gardiner (eds), *Literature of an Independent England*, pp. 46–59.
108. Saadi, *Psychoraag*, pp. 126, 173, 251.
109. Saadi, *Psychoraag*, p. 374.
110. Kelly, Aaron, *Irvine Welsh* (Manchester: Manchester University Press, 2005), p. 56.
111. Saadi, *Psychoraag*, p. 396.
112. Kelman, *How Late It Was, How Late*.
113. See Huggan, *The Postcolonial Exotic*, p. 26 for more on the positioning of authors as representative of marginal subject positions and 'communities'.
114. Saadi, *Psychoraag*, pp. 22, 21, 308, 61.
115. Saadi, *Psychoraag*, p. 191.
116. The relationship between 'voice' understood as democratic metonym and the representational politics of speaking interrogated by Scottish writers is expanded on by Scott Hames in 'On Vernacular Scottishness and its Limits'.
117. Saadi, *Psychoraag*, p. 384.
118. See Dabydeen, David, 'On Not Being Milton: Nigger Talk in England Today' in Christopher Ricks and Leonard Michaels (eds), *The State of the Language* (Oxford: University of California Press, 1990), pp. 3–14: 11–12.
119. Glissant, Édouard, *Caribbean Discourse: Selected Essays* (Charlottesville: University of Virginia Press, 1999), p. 165.
120. Calder, *Revolving Culture*, p. 2.
121. 'David Starkey Claims "the Whites Have Become Black"', *The Guardian*, 13 August 2011, www.theguardian.com/uk/2011/aug/13/david-starkey-claims-whites-black (last accessed 25 July 2019).
122. Saadi, *Psychoraag*, pp. 66, 173.
123. Cooke, Melanie, 'Barrier or Entitlement? The Language and Citizenship Agenda in the United Kingdom', *Language Assessment Quarterly* 6:1 (2009), pp. 71–7: 72.
124. See Blackledge, Adrian, 'The Racialization of Language in British Political Discourse', *Critical Discourse Studies* 3:1 (2006), pp. 61–79; and Cooke, 'Barrier or Entitlement?'.
125. Gardiner, *Cultural Roots*, p. 157.
126. Gardiner, *From Trocchi to Trainspotting*, p. 34.
127. Gilles Deleuze and Félix Guattari, quoted in Crawford, *Devolving English Literature*, p. 6.
128. Saadi, *Psychoraag*, pp. 377–8.
129. Gray, *Lanark*, p. 243.
130. Stevenson, Randall, 'A Postmodern Scotland?' in Gerald Carruthers, David Goldie and Alastair Renfrew (eds), *Beyond Scotland: New Contexts for Twentieth-Century Scottish Literature* (Amsterdam: Rodopi, 2004), pp. 209–28: 215.
131. Saadi, *Psychoraag*, pp. 8, 372.
132. See Craig, *Modern Scottish Novel*, pp. 33–4.
133. Phillips, Deborah, Cathy Davis and Peter Ratcliffe, 'British Asian Narratives of Urban Space', *Transactions of the Institute of British Geographers* 32:2 (2007), pp. 217–34: 218.

134. Saadi, *Psychoraag*, pp. 377–8.
135. Saadi, *Psychoraag*, pp. 376, 377.
136. Saadi, *Psychoraag*, p. 383.
137. Saadi, *Psychoraag*, p. 331.
138. Saadi, *Psychoraag*, p. 208.
139. Debord, Guy, 'Introduction to the Critique of Urban Geography' in Knabb, Ken (ed. and trans.), *Situationist International Anthology*, 2nd edn (Berkeley: Bureau of Public Secrets, 2006), pp. 8–11.
140. See Gardiner, *Return of England*, p. 149.
141. Saadi, *Psychoraag*, pp. 338, 366.
142. Debord, 'Theory of the Dérive', in Knabb (ed. and trans.), *Situationist International Anthology*, pp. 62–6: 65.
143. Saadi, *Psychoraag*, p. 338.
144. Saadi, *Psychoraag*, p. 347.
145. Saadi, *Psychoraag*, p. 405.
146. Saadi, *Psychoraag*, p. 405.
147. Saadi, *Psychoraag*, p. 405, original emphasis.
148. Saadi, *Psychoraag*, p. 360.
149. See Allend, Alexander, Jr, 'Why Not Spencer?' in John Offer (ed.), *Herbert Spencer: Critical Assessments Vol. II* (London: Routledge, 2000), pp. 460–9.
150. Allend, 'Why Not Spencer?', pp. 462–3.
151. Saadi, *Psychoraag*, p. 419.

Conclusion:
Anchoring in 2020

Hannah Lavery's *The Drift* (2019), a spoken word poetry performance produced by the National Theatre of Scotland and published in the pamphlet *Finding Sea Glass*, relates a wholly ambiguous racialised experience of Scotland at the end of the 2010s.[1] In 'You Were Mine to Carry', the poetic voice is that of a daughter whose white 'passing' means 'a limbo / under the colour bar for me / an almost slip into nationhood', in contradistinction to her father, 'kidding yourself / in your Scotland top' while 'this mother country made you fucking / exotic'; like Zaf in *Psychoraag*, the father has his own white fantasies, asking her to 'pass as white for me' vicariously.[2] Taken as a whole, the collection represents an experience of racism and the white assumptions of national Scotland, which seem more or less unchanged since they were chronicled by Maud Sulter thirty years before: '*Are you a Paki? / A half caste? English?*'; '*ya black bastard*'; '*You're dirty brown! You look like / you have rolled in mud*'.[3] The most explicit engagement with Scotland as a national formation is in 'Scotland, You're No Mine'. The poem's tidal rhythms and imagery complement the motif of Atlantic plantation economics and the 'swept away' history of 'sugar for your tablet', riffing on Stuart Hall's observation that Caribbean migrants, and colonial history, are represented in the 'sugar at the bottom of the English cup of tea'.[4] The injunction to 'courie in' serves only to establish a precipitous drop from sentimental Scots to the 'broken bones', 'whips and chains' and 'blood' of slavery.[5] The ebbing and building of a fraught relationship with nation, a 'limpet stuck on you', is secured with the kind of fricative-plosive emphasis familiar from Kelman and Welsh, one that reminds us that 'expletives' are both intensifying swear words and a metrical measure to round out poetic lines: 'fuck you, my sweet forgetful Caledonia / with love, fuck you'.[6] Twenty years after devolution, the precariousness of Scots of colour (Lavery's formulation) in the national order, and a lack of purchase on Scotland's imperial and slave-holding past, remains.

Finding Sea Glass also speaks to something not so much unbegun, or unfinished, but stuck in a lower gear. One reason why *Writing Black Scotland* focuses on *Trumpet*, *Jelly Roll* and *Psychoraag* is because, as longer-form fictions that actively represent black lives and racism in contemporary Scotland, they seem to stand as larger and more salient remnants of a phase in publishing and book-buying taste in Scotland. Bernardine Evaristo has written about a specific 'breakthrough' moment in the British literary world, from the 1990s to the middle of the 2000s, for young black novelists.[7] In the light of their limited longevity, Evaristo points out that many have fallen foul of patterns of literary fashion and promotion, as publishers seek out the 'next big thing after the last big thing'.[8] This is precisely the kind of literary economy, inseparable from broader political culture, that Corinne Fowler details in 'A Tale of Two Novels'. The fortunes of individual texts are bound up with their relationship with the tenor of national 'cultural associations'; the relative prosperity of the late 1990s and early 2000s in terms of publishing opportunities for black writers is bound up with the wider fortunes of New Labour, 'Cool Britannia' and elaborated Britishness.[9] Similarly, the moment of the 'black Scottish' or 'Scottish multicultural' novel transpired against the backdrop of the early New Labour years of the devolved Parliament and the muted efforts to celebrate a 'Cool Caledonia', which may have oriented those 'cultural associations' in publishing towards a diversity agenda both complementing and in competition with that of the British state itself.

Jackie Kay's movement towards the official centre of Scotland's cultural life has enshrined this moment in perpetuity, but the broader picture for writers of a certain 'history', in Suhayl Saadi's euphemistic phrasing, is decidedly mixed. While Saadi's description of the 'infinite diversity' available as the raw stuff of literary creativity in Scotland still rings true, the publishing landscape for longer fiction seems denuded.[10] Saadi has published almost nothing since the critical and commercial difficulties of his ambitious and experimental *Joseph's Box*. Shortly before that novel's publication, Saadi observed a British 'liberal censorship' on behalf of 'saturnine, suffocating purple togas of Oxbridge', and argued that his politics, his geography and his history had 'excluded [his] work from the sources of capital in the corporate publishing industry and, outside Scotland, from the media-literary complex which services this industry'.[11] Luke Sutherland has returned to music with a series of bands after two further short novels, *Sweetmeat* (2002) and *Venus as a Boy* (2004). Since *Trumpet*, Kay has focused on poetry, as well as writing new screenplays, short stories and memoirs. The 'sample size' of black and Asian novelists active in Scotland during the period is small, but is in parallel with the dramatic emergence and sudden attenuation of black novelists in England described by Evaristo; a window seemingly opened for a certain kind of novel during a period in the late 1990s and 2000s in Scotland, before easing shut again.

Nevertheless, spearheaded by poets and organisers like Hannah Lavery, there continues to be a strong grassroots presence in supporting the writing of people of colour. Lavery herself organises a regular 'Writers of Colour' group through the Scottish Poetry Library, and the group has recently collaborated with *Gutter* to produce a special issue of the magazine.[12] The Scottish BAME Writers Network was formed by a number of writers and academics in 2018, to provide 'advocacy, literary events and development opportunities' for black, Asian and minority ethnic writers in Scotland.[13] The Zanana Project, funded by Creative Scotland and run by Scottish-Mauritian Veronique A. A. Lapeyre, aims to re-centre work by 'Black, Asian and People of Colour (POC)' in Scottish creative industries.[14] The 'Fringe of Colour' promotes black and brown performers at the Edinburgh Festival and aims to diversify audiences by ticket subsidies and distribution, and outreach.[15] These manifold activities suggest that the environment for black writers in Scotland is markedly different at the outset of the 2020s compared to the context for groundbreaking writers like Kay and Maud Sulter in the middle of the 1980s. But in each case, these organisations identify the way that 'quality work by BAME writers is overlooked due to patterns of white dominance, discrimination and other systemic barriers' at work both in Scotland and in Britain more broadly.[16] There is a disparity between the grassroots activity of writers of colour and their visibility in the larger milieu of Scottish cultural life, and in particular 'mainstream' publishing.

Meanwhile, the pattern of white writers exploring the politics of race, traced in Chapter 2, has continued, and would justify further scrutiny. As a significant example, James Kelman's work since the millennium constitutes a considerable ramping up of his aesthetic interrogation of race and racism. After the shift to a larger transnational-geopolitical focus signalled by *Translated Accounts* (2001), novels like *You Have to Be Careful in the Land of the Free* (2004) and *Dirt Road* (2016) have acted to denaturalise and rematerialise whiteness via transposition into spaces of acute racial encounter in the United States: jazz clubs and zydeco festivals; the airport as a space of segregation, mobility and precarious migrant labour; the everyday segregation of American life. Both Jeremiah Brown, an 'Inkliz-spaking pink-faced caucasian frae a blood-and-soil motherland', and Murdo, 'white and a stranger' in the American South, are Scottish protagonists whose experiences encode the tension between shared humanity and the enduring social power of racial demarcation.[17] Murdo, a teen-age boy moving across the United States from Memphis, Tennessee to Lafayette, Louisiana, is a naïf whose accordion-playing carries him across strictly prosecuted racial divides between black and white; the gradual, unfolding realisation of race at the social-interpersonal level speaks to a larger national-political realisation. Brown, a white 'security operative' in an American airport, has a black girlfriend and an acute sense of his own white privilege, but finds himself unable to get purchase on the racialised politics of the US: 'could never get to grips with that yin, how come bodies like [him] were excluded from the debate'.[18] There are textual clues as to why this 'exclusion' takes place. After a word out of turn at his child's christening, Brown remarks that 'I thought I was gauny get fuck-ing lynched' by his girlfriend's extended family, a playful-serious faux pas that intimates the depth of black history in America to which even the sympathetic, and politically minded, white Scot has only partial access.[19] Kelman's works seem to stick close to the awkwardness and difficulty of representing race from a white authorial and subject position. But these texts also cast beyond territorial Scotland for the kind of 'grip' on the slippery discourse of contemporary race for which Jeremiah Brown is searching. Even Mohammed, the eponymous Asian boyfriend of narrator Helen in Kelman's *Mo Said She Was Quirky* (2012), is from London; they meet when he is in Scotland only temporarily, as a precariously employed worker. The imagination of black Scots remains a challenge even into the twenty-first century, and the working-through of the political questions attached to literary representations of race are more securely conducted in geographies where there are greater precedents.

There are other, cognate areas of enquiry that would naturally follow some of the work done in *Writing Black Scotland*. More could be said about the representation of blackness in writing that lies outside the secured cultural nationalist taxonomy of Scottish literature, writers with a military-colonial background and works that remain in closer proximity to the imperial imagination. One example would be George MacDonald Fraser's *Flashman* chronicles, peppered with terms of racial abuse, or his later fiction representing Scottish regiments in the immediate aftermath of the Second World War, such as the iconic regimental piper Crombie, a picture of Highland military pomp and proficiency with the fatal caveat that he is a black man and hence does not 'fit'.[20] Another would be William Boyd's novels, such as *A Good Man in Africa* (1981) or *An Ice-Cream War* (1982), which offer parodic representations of the racial politics of the declining Empire. Even Alexander McCall Smith's *The No. 1 Ladies' Detective Agency* series shows the way that Scottish writers have apprehended and re-presented black characters. The popularity of McCall

Smith's franchise says something about the ongoing need to translate the complexity of black life in Africa into recognisable tropes for the UK literary marketplace. While they have less to do with the literary representation of Scotland itself, the elements of postcolonial melancholia perceptible in these texts, in combination with the rehabilitative history-making going on in Michael Fry's *The Scottish Empire*, are part of an economy of racial representation within Scottish literature. Much remains to be written about these fictions from the standpoint of Scottish postcolonial thought and critical black studies.

In a wider frame, any more comprehensive approach to 'writing racism' in Scotland would demand greater engagement with the 'key political minority identity' of the twenty-first century: the culturalist formation of the Muslim.[21] Tariq Modood has long argued that 'Britain [cannot] be understood in terms of a racial-dualist framework', and that '[e]ven before September 11, it was becoming evident that Muslims, not blacks, were being perceived as "the Other" most threatening to British society'.[22] Modood's observations have been borne out by recent history, where the construction of Islam as a radical alterity has underpinned much of the racial politics of the British state and the wider 'developed world', although the categories of black and Muslim are of course not mutually exclusive. This has certainly applied in Scotland, where Bashir Maan dubbed Scottish-Pakistani Muslims the 'New Scots'; they form the largest minority census group, and Islamophobia is a persistent and under-recognised problem in Scotland.[23] While I have briefly touched on Islam in Scotland in my analysis of *Psychoraag*, much more remains to be done in analysing the literary representation of Scottish Muslims and their imagination as a 'culturalist' category. A more author-defined approach to black writing might have included Scottish-Sudanese writer Leila Aboulela, whose novel *The Translator* (1999) and short fiction such as the collection *Coloured Lights* (2001) have engaged more directly with the neo-racist creation of Muslim alterity with a particular focus on Scotland.[24]

Britain's Black Lives Matter

The need for a continued critical approach to blackness in Scotland, and in Britain more broadly, remains urgent. The decade to 2020 has continued to throw up examples of the gap between a celebratory rhetoric of achieved multiculturalism and the lifeworlds of Britain's racialised people. In his analysis of the British manifestation of the Black Lives Matter movement, Kehinde Andrews lists the ways that the lives of black people in Britain have remained subject to structural racism despite reforms to policing, citizenship and equality laws. Black people are far more likely to be stopped and searched by the police, to be charged after arrest and to be given a longer prison sentence if found guilty of a crime; black people are even more disproportionately represented in the criminal justice system and in prison in Britain than within the racial-carceral complex of the United States; and black people are more likely to die in police custody.[25] This structural-institutional racism has its own correlates in Scotland too: Neil Davidson and Satnam Virdee point to the death of Sheku Bayoh, 'restrained by 15 police officers' in Kirkcaldy in 2015, as evidence of the 'deeply structuring force' of racism for black and brown Scots.[26] The most startling implosion of a celebratory account of black Britishness has likely come in revelations around the 2018 'Windrush scandal' amidst the Home Office 'hostile environment' policy, in which the British government proactively sought to deport Caribbean migrants without official citizenship status as part of a larger, target-driven immigration 'removals' policy.[27] In some cases those targeted had been resident in Britain for their entire adult lives, part of a 'Windrush Generation' that was itself a coinage designed as part of a celebratory recognition of migrant contribution to British life.[28] The Windrush scandal stands as evidence that hard-won rights for racialised people in Britain remain contingent and in need of constant re-evaluation and defence; the governing party responsible for deporting people who had raised two generations of children back to the Caribbean under the 'hostile environment' policy was, in 2019, returned as the largest in Parliament for the fourth successive general election.

Despite these stubbornly material features of racism in contemporary Britain, the mediascape of recent 'race representation' has continued to underline a narrative of progress and national unity via the celebration of symbolic figures, events and achievements as tangible, or even 'radical', political progress: the Britishness of black Britain. Nowhere is this tendency more starkly illustrated, and debunked, than in the marriage of Henry 'Harry' Windsor and Meghan Markle. The Markle–Windsor wedding was, according to Afua Hirsch, both a 'pageant of tradition' and a 'celebration of blackness'.[29] It does seem likely that the wedding offered some form of empowering narrative to black people in Britain. Bishop Michael Curry's 'The Power of Love' speech had political moments, quoting Martin Luther King Jr and briefly referencing the faith of enslaved people, manifested in spirituals.[30] However, it is easy to overstate the subversive quality of the ceremony and the marriage itself. The British royal family, for the best part of three centuries, has been no stranger to 'race relations'-style management in a larger imperial and neo-imperial capacity, and contemporaneously has had no problem dealing with significant black figures across the political spectrum. In the course of her reign,

Queen Elizabeth has visited Africa and the Caribbean countless times. She has met Nelson Mandela and Haile Selassie. She has knighted Robert Mugabe and greeted Idi Amin, the last King of Scotland. Domestically, the performance of racial tolerance, adopting a 'race-friendly face', is the baseline requirement not just for the monarchy but for virtually all people operating in the public political culture of Britain.

The real usefulness of the Markle–Windsor wedding to the ongoing reconfiguration of Britain is shown in Irenosen Okojie's article, published on the same day as Hirsch's. Okojie strikingly describes the wedding, an orgy of state-sanctioned and sanctifying culture, as a 'radical act' which symbolises the way that black people can now imagine themselves part of the 'upper social echelons' and 'gain [the] privileges' entailed therein.[31] It should immediately be obvious that there is little that is 'radical', in the language of C. L. R. James or Cedric Robinson, about aspiring towards the extremely individuated anointment of princesshood. It would be more fitting to see an adaptation of the status quo in the laundering of the reputation of the monarchy, the zenith of the oppressive British class structure, through a wealthy and glamorous American actress, even with the caveat of her status as a person of colour. The title of Okojie's article hints at another way the wedding might be read. In 'revitalising our divided nation', the wedding ostensibly offered a bridge between the political polarities of the 'Leave' and 'Remain' camps of the European Union referendum. But it also stands as another example of how useful blackness is for national Britishness. To return to Anne-Marie Fortier's identification of the mixed-race marriage as the definitive illustration of achieved multiculturalism, the Markle–Windsor union is also a refurbishment of the bigger Union, the awkward match of a deeply conservative 'pageant' and a multicultural 'celebration' that epitomises the way that elaborated Britishness has re-engineered the post-imperial British national fabric. Meanwhile, it has not taken long for history to show exactly how contingent that symbolic victory was, as the press and the monarchy have veered from hagiography to the vilification of Markle in the space of two short years.

The urge to celebrate black British representative gains remains strong but also flags up a more fundamental political stasis in the battle against structural racism. When Stormzy wore a Union-flag-emblazoned stab-proof vest during his set at the Glastonbury Festival in 2019, it suggested a literal 'puncturing' of British post-racial myths. As he celebrated being the first black British artist to headline Glastonbury, he implied a new political condition: a protected sphere of white-dominated culture had been breached and a new-found visibility for black expressive culture had been achieved. When Skin from Skunk Anansie observed that she, some twenty years before, had in fact been the first black artist to headline Glastonbury, she not only invalidated Stormzy's personal claim to path-breaking representation, but the whole premise of symbolic artistic representation of that sort constituting decisive political progress.[32] The first, symbolic black headlining of Glastonbury did not have the significance Stormzy attached to it because it had in fact taken place two decades previously and had already been forgotten, a forgetting spectacularly illustrated by his claim. Indeed, Skin went on to suggest that Maxim, vocalist in The Prodigy, had his own claim as the trailblazer, having been part of the headline set from the 1997 festival. Stormzy takes his place in a continuum of Glastonbury stage sets that accord with Paul Gilroy's argument that there have always been spaces in which black existence is permitted: in Britain, '[w]e certainly get to see more black people in the dreamscape of advertising, on television, and on the sports field, though not in Parliament, the police service, or the judge's bench'.[33]

Greater prominence for this activated and disruptive black expressive culture is valuable in anti-racist politics, and Stormzy himself has pioneered local and national projects to address racism in Britain. His Glastonbury performance certainly went beyond a 'safe' mediatised visibility. The stab-proof vest sews together, and 'exposes', the stark contrast between flag-waving British pageantry and urban English knife crime, particularly among young black men in London. Symbolically, the vest offered protection not only from physical attack in its material resistance, but criticism in its demonstrative national loyalty. Stormzy's set featured explicit references to the politics of race in contemporary Britain, replaying a speech by the Labour MP David Lammy on racism in the criminal justice system.[34] Meanwhile, the creation of the Stormzy Scholarship for Black UK Students at the University of Cambridge is a form of direct action to address structural inequalities.[35] The force of Stormzy's anti-racist critique is not in question; it is instead the claim of 'firstness' that signifies something here. The discursive mode of pluralist iconicity entailed by the notability of Stormzy's performance, and before that, of Skin's performance, and before that, of Maxim's performance, all seem to aggregate into a kind of multicultural symbolic order that reaffirms British unity even while critiquing its racism, exclusions and inequities. The 'Union' element of the Union flag is suppressed; the 'British' component of Stormzy's pioneering black British performance remains integrated; and the unspoken and unrecognised *telos* of black Britain is the refashioning of the Union state-nation itself.

At time of writing, the death of George Floyd in police custody in Minneapolis has impelled new street-level activism in the global Black Lives Matter movement, forcing a dramatic engagement with imperial history and contemporary racism in Britain too. This has manifested in a renewed attention to racist violence, both at the hands of the police and in wider society, and in a new critical focus on the dynamics of commemoration. Following a decision by Oriel College, Oxford, it now seems possible that their statue of Cecil Rhodes will finally be removed, but the most dramatic illustration of direct action came in the toppling of the Edward Colston statue by protestors in Bristol due to his significant involvement in the transatlantic slave trade. In combination with the recognised serious impact of Covid-19 on black and minority ethnic people in Britain, racial justice seems to be established more firmly in the public consciousness than at any time since Stephen Lawrence. In governmental terms, however, all that has been promised is a reheated 'cross-governmental commission to look at all aspects of inequality'.[36] The contrast between the moral outrage that saw Colston cast into Bristol Harbour and the postponement and diffusion of BLM demands in the Prime Minister's response suggests that racial justice can only be achieved through direct and grassroots organisation rather than the status quo of British state multicultural governmentality.

Breaking up is hard to do

The prospect of post-British nationhood has become more pressing since the referendums of 2014 and 2016. The early successes of devolution, in remodelling Britain and stifling any movement towards Scottish independence, have been transformed in the last few years into something more unpredictable. Tom Devine suggested in 2005 that Tom Nairn's prognostications on the break-up of Britain looked shaky on the basis of the continuing health of the Union and the relative weakness of the Scottish National Party in the new Scottish Parliament.[37] Now the wheel has turned again, and Devine's stable Union has moved into a new phase of dislocation and uncertainty. The referendum on independence came closer to ending the Union than had seemed possible even a year before. The margin for 'No' over 'Yes' was much narrower than had seemed likely, and polling immediately before the referendum suggested such a close result that the main political players were spooked, leading to the notorious cross-party 'Vow', a last-gasp concession that may have swung the referendum decisively. 'The Vow' was effectively another promise of devolutionary adaptation, in the form of the Smith Commission to recommend further powers for the devolved Parliament. The outcome of 2014, while encouraging to independence-oriented Scottish nationalists, was thus ultimately something of a victory for the 'containment logic' of devolution. Instead, the radical referendum outcome that would threaten to destroy the status quo was coming only slightly further down the road, in the 2016 vote on membership of the European Union. Polling in 2019 has indicated that, among the membership of the Conservative and Unionist Party, some 63 per cent would prefer to have Scotland leave the United Kingdom than for Britain to remain within the European Union.[38] This shift seems to manifest the gradual realisation of Tom Nairn's prognosis that English national distinctiveness cannot be submerged forever under Britishness: 'Brexit' might be the street-corner where England will be reborn, rather than in the 'maternity ward' of, say, a constitutional convention.[39]

The relationship between Scottish nationalism and anti-racist politics has also developed more definition in the last two decades of devolution and during the campaign for independence. The national government's approach has been conservative. The white paper *Scotland's Future* (2013) has a great deal to say about immigration, but aside from interposing strategic distance between a prospective independent Scotland and the 'inhumane' treatment of asylum seekers in Britain's detention centres, the stress is significantly on benefits to be reaped in terms of economic contribution and skills. The white paper does not mention racism; it merely suggests, in language redolent of British state discourse, that new powers 'including race equality and anti-discrimination will be important in supporting Scotland's ambition to be a progressive, welcoming and inclusive state'.[40] As Jan Penrose and David Howard point out, the Scottish Government's 'One Scotland, Many Cultures' campaign subtly shifted emphasis and is now solely 'One Scotland', although a case could be made that rather than a crude assimilative gesture towards national unity, the truncation of 'Many Cultures' could be about scepticism towards an orthodoxy of 'countable cultures' that underpins multicultural governmentality.[41] Meanwhile, as Minna Liinpää points out, the Scottish National Party 'focuses on very specific strands of history at the expense of some of the more uncomfortable episodes' in Scotland's imperial past.[42]

The Scottish National Party and the Scottish Government are not the only nationalist game in town, and race has also been mobilised to evidence the progressive credentials of the Scottish independence movement. The existence of organisations like Scots Asians for Yes is often cited as evidence that the radical independence movement was swimming against the tide of ethno-exclusive nationalism. Responding to Sadiq Khan's speech on the 'divisions' presented by Scottish nationalism, Robert Somynne has commented that it was 'the independence movement that, unlike many other groups in Scotland, was the most self-reflective about racism today, representation and historical racial injustice'.[43] However, Somynne was responding to an article by Claire Heuchan supporting Sadiq Khan, for which she was targeted by racist abuse online, including comments that discredited her for being 'an African who had no right to discuss ethnic white Scottish affairs'.[44] The Radical Independence Campaign constitution offers as one of its five pillars the commitment 'to equality and opposition to discrimination', including on the grounds of race, though such a commitment would not be out of place in a corporate press release.[45] The progressivist orientation of the movement, however, certainly challenges the common arguments deployed around the 2014 referendum, framed as 'maintaining unity' within the British Union versus 'erecting borders' brought about by Scottish independence; the tenor of discourse within the independence movement is more internationalist and anti-racist than anything on offer at a British state level, in which the preservation of borders has been the defining political rallying cry of at least the past decade.

The aftershocks of the European Union referendum on just that political terrain have triggered a period of far greater engagement with questions of explicitly English national politics, but the recognition of England as a neglected national formation with revolutionary potential has a longer history elsewhere. In 'Black British Writing and Post-British England', John McLeod has linked the unfinished project of black equality to this opaque Englishness, arguing for the scrutiny of some of the national assumptions of black British literary studies, and observing the possibility of a black studies approach to post-British England.[46] As I have tried to show in my reading of Paul Gilroy, the possibility of a more fundamental critique of contemporary Britishness and its racisms can be found in a redoubled focus on the peculiarities of Englishness. It may be that such a path to post-Britishness will not involve overcoming, in Hall's formulation, the 'resistance to radical appropriation' presented by an English nationalism, but instead take a larger step towards decentralisation and federalist organisation. Echoing the vision of a desiccated 'national' body and the demand for a convivial localism in Gilroy's *After Empire*, Alex Niven has argued that the 'hollowness of English dreaming', its 'sullen and soulless state of unbeing', are insurmountable imaginative and political obstacles to the restoration of the English nation.[47] Niven, channelling Édouard Glissant's 'archipelagic thinking', calls for a 'dream archipelago' that would offer 'a renewed programme for regional government, based on a fundamental, radical and imaginative overhaul of our civic architecture'.[48] There has always been Scottish writing at the forefront of such a 'post-British' civic imagination. My hope is that the preliminary work done in *Writing Black Scotland* can contribute to a larger project of developing the substance and significance of Britain's sub-national formations, and its constitutional integrity, within the cultural politics and critical examination of blackness.

Are white men black men?

Where Lavery's *The Drift* is more conventionally post-colonial and anti-racist, seeking to hold Scotland to account for an imperial past and a racist present, the Edinburgh band Young Fathers represent a different take on blackness coming out of contemporary Scotland. The title of Young Fathers' second album, *White Men Are Black Men Too* (2015), would not be out of place in a discourse of race-relativism centred on the 'black' Irish or the Highland Scots. The argument that white Scotland has its own black characteristics is one that *Writing Black Scotland* has tracked through the 'inferiorisation' thesis of certain critics. It is also recognisable from Irvine Welsh: the contention that 'white men are black men too' is familiar from the examples of both Roy Strang in *Marabou Stork Nightmares* and Bruce Robertson in *Filth*, a manoeuvre that, as Carole Jones says, 'puts the white man back at the centre of discourses of power as a victim'.[49] But just as Welsh's representations of blackness are an ontological provocation rather than advocacy for a crass acquisition of persecution, Young Fathers also refuse a clean narrative of racial definition and hierarchy in favour of something more troubling. The actual track that carries the titular lyric, 'Old Rock and Roll', stays close to the more philosophical racial problematic inherent in blackness, the fundamental conflictual or deliberative character of that formation:[50]

> I'm tired of playing the good black / I said I'm tired of playing the good black
> I'm tired of having to hold back / I'm tired of wearing this hallmark for some evils that happened way back
> I'm tired of blaming the white man / His indiscretion don't betray him
> A black man can play him / Some white men are black men too
> Niggah to them / A gentleman to you
> Some white men are black men too[51]

The lyrics are contradictory. The song points to a truncated lifeworld of 'good behaviours' and the inescapability of the 'hallmark' of racial history, and simultaneously repudiates the easy equivalence between the 'white man' and these oppressions. Strict taxonomy fails: the black man can both play – 'act' – and play – 'con' – the white man. The classification of 'niggah' and 'gentleman' apply ambiguously, where both 'them' and 'you' are indistinct. Among this inchoate politics, the lyrics express a desire to move beyond the impasse of contemporary race, but equally register the subtle operations, enduring legacies, and recalcitrant fixedness of race taxonomies. Lavery's work points to the local dimensions of Scotland, to the need for a national consciousness of racism and the legacy of imperialism.

Young Fathers gesture outwards, towards a global manifestation of blackness, towards its elusive, unmanageable and paradoxical qualities. Both constitute frontiers in which the future work on a black Scotland might be conducted.

Notes

1. Lavery, Hannah, *Finding Sea Glass: Poems from The Drift* (Edinburgh: Stewed Rhubarb Press, 2019).
2. Lavery, *Finding Sea Glass*, p. 4.
3. Lavery, *Finding Sea Glass*, pp. 16, 20, 21.
4. Lavery, *Finding Sea Glass*, p. 10; Hall, Stuart, 'Old and New Identities, Old and New Ethnicities' in Anthony D. King (ed.), *Culture, Globalization, and the World-System: Contemporary Conditions for the Representation of Identity* (Minneapolis: University of Minnesota Press, 1997), pp. 41–68: 48.
5. Lavery, *Finding Sea Glass*, p. 10.
6. Lavery, *Finding Sea Glass*, pp. 10–11.
7. Evaristo, Bernardine, 'The Illusion of Inclusion', *Wasafiri* 25:4 (2010) pp. 1–6: 4.
8. Evaristo, 'Illusion of Inclusion', p. 4.
9. Fowler, 'A Tale of Two Novels', p. 80.
10. Saadi, Suhayl, 'Infinite Diversity in New Scottish Writing', Association for Scottish Literary Studies (2000), https://asls.arts.gla.ac.uk/SSaadi.html (last accessed 30 March 2020).
11. Fowler, 'A Tale of Two Novels', p. 79; Saadi, Suhayl, 'In Tom Paine's Kitchen: Days of Rage and Fire' in Schoene (ed.), *Edinburgh Companion to Contemporary Scottish Literature*, pp. 28–33: 30.
12. 'Issue 21: Gutter Magazine × Scottish BAME Writers' Network', *Gutter Magazine*, www.guttermag.co.uk/blog/issue21editorial (last accessed 30 March 2020).
13. 'Mission and Values', Scottish BAME Writers Network, https://scottishbamewriter snetwork.wordpress.com/ (last accessed 04 March 2020).
14. www.projectzanana.com/about (last accessed 30 March 2020).
15. https://fringeofcolour.weebly.com/ (last accessed 30 March 2020).
16. 'Mission and Values', Scottish BAME Writers Network, https://scottishbamewriter snetwork.wordpress.com/ (last accessed 4 March 2020).
17. James Kelman, *You Have to Be Careful in the Land of the Free* (London: Penguin, 2005 [2004]), p. 328; *Dirt Road* (Edinburgh: Canongate, 2016), p. 25.
18. Kelman, *You Have to be Careful*, p. 76.
19. Kelman, *You Have to be Careful*, p. 100.
20. MacDonald Fraser, George, *McAuslan in the Rough* (New York: Alfred Knopf, 1974), p. 50.
21. Modood, Tariq, *Multicultural Politics: Racism, Ethnicity and Muslims in Britain* (Edinburgh: Edinburgh University Press, 2005), p. 160.
22. Modood, *Multicultural Politics*, pp. 6, 186.
23. Maan, Bashir, *The New Scots: The Story of Asians in Scotland* (Edinburgh: John Donald, 1992); see Bonino, Stefano, *Muslims in Scotland: The Making of Community in a Post-9/11 World* (Edinburgh: Edinburgh University Press, 2017) and Goldie, Paul, 'Cultural Racism and Islamophobia in Glasgow' in Davidson et al. (eds), *No Problem Here*, pp. 128–44.
24. A special edition of *Scottish Literary Review* addressing Scotland and Islam, entitled 'The Thistle and the Crescent', edited by Silke Stroh and Manfred Malzahn, and due for publication in 2021, is likely to contribute greatly to advancing this field.

25. Andrews, *Back to Black*, p. xiv.
26. Davidson and Virdee, 'Understanding Racism', n. pag; the story of Sheku Bayoh formed the basis of a series of performances, *Call and Response: Lament for Sheku Bayoh* written and organised by Hannah Lavery at the Edinburgh International Festival in 2019.
27. Wardle, Huon and Laura Obermuller, '"Windrush Generation" and "Hostile Environment": Symbols and Lived Experience in Caribbean Migration to the UK', *Migration and Society* 2:1 (2019), pp. 81–9.
28. Wardle and Obermuller, 'Windrush Generation', p. 81.
29. Hirsch, Afua, 'Meghan Markle's Wedding Was a Rousing Celebration of Blackness', *The Guardian*, 20 May 2018, www.theguardian.com/uk-news/2018/may/19/meghan-markles-wedding-was-a-celebration-of-blackness (last accessed 4 March 2020).
30. 'Bishop Michael Curry's Royal Wedding Sermon: Full Text of "The Power of Love"', *National Public Radio*, www.npr.org/sections/thetwo-way/2018/05/20/612798691/-bishop-michael-currys-royal-wedding-sermon-full-text-of-the-power-of-love?t=1588012604027 (last accessed 30 March 2020).
31. Okojie, Irenosen, 'The Spirit of Harry and Meghan Can Revitalise Our Divided Nation', *The Guardian*, 20 May 2018, www.theguardian.com/uk-news/2018/may/19/markle-harry-royal-wedding-race-curry-family-britain-society (last accessed 4 March 2020).
32. Chalk, Will, 'Stormzy: Skunk Anansie Don't Want to "Throw Shade"', BBC News, July 2019, www.bbc.co.uk/news/newsbeat-48852960 (last accessed 4 March 2020).
33. Gilroy, *After Empire*, p. 136.
34. Walker, Amy, 'All Hail Stormzy for Historic Glastonbury Performance', *The Guardian*, 29 June 2019, www.theguardian.com/music/2019/jun/29/stormzy-historic-glastonbury-performance (last accessed 30 March 2020).
35. www.undergraduate.study.cam.ac.uk/stormzy-scholarship (last accessed 30 March 2020).
36. 'Prime Minister's Article in the Telegraph: 15 June 2020', www.gov.uk/government/speeches/prime-ministers-article-in-the-telegraph-15-june-2020 (last accessed 21 July 2020).
37. Devine, 'Break-Up', p. 165.
38. Smith, Matthew, 'Most Conservative Members Would See Party Destroyed to Achieve Brexit', *YouGov*, https://yougov.co.uk/topics/politics/articles-reports/2019/06/18/most-conservative-members-would-see-party-destroye (last accessed 30 March 2020).
39. The analogy is from Tom Nairn, *After Britain*, p. 88.
40. The Scottish Government, *Scotland's Future* (Edinburgh: Scottish Government, 2013), p. 494.
41. Penrose and Howard, '*One Scotland, Many Cultures*', p. 109.
42. Liinpää, Minna, 'Nationalism and Scotland's Imperial Past' in Davidson et al., *No Problem Here*, pp. 14–31.
43. Somynne, Robert, 'Scottish Nationalists Aren't Racists – They're Reacting against the UK's Bigotry', *The Guardian*, 1 March 2017, www.theguardian.com/commentisfree/2017/mar/01/scottish-nationalists-racist-uk-bigotry-sadiq-khan (last accessed 4 March 2020).
44. Carrell, Severin, 'Woman Who Linked Racism with Scottish Nationalism Quits Twitter over Safety Fears', *The Guardian*, 28 February 2017, www.theguardian.com-uk-news/2017/feb/28/woman-who-linked-racism-with-scottish-nationalism-sadiq-khan-quits-twitter-over-safety-fears (last accessed 30 March 2020).
45. 'RIC Constitution', *Radical Independence Campaign*, http://radical.scot/ric-constitution/ (last accessed 30 March 2020).
46. McLeod, 'Black British Writing and Post-British England', pp. 175–87.

47. Niven, Alex, *New Model Island: How to Build a Radical Culture Beyond the Idea of England* (London: Repeater Books, 2019), pp. 20–1.
48. Niven, *New Model Island*, p. 108.
49. Jones, 'White Men on Their Backs', n. pag.
50. Mbembe, *Critique of Black Reason*, p. 43.
51. Young Fathers, 'Old Rock and Roll', *Some White Men Are Black Men Too* (Big Dada Recordings, 2015).

Bibliography

'Bishop Michael Curry's Royal Wedding Sermon: Full Text of "The Power of Love"', National Public Radio, www.npr.org/sections/thetwo-way/2018/05/20/612798691/-bishop-michael-currys-royal-wedding-sermon-full-text-of-the-power-of-love?t=1588012604027 (last accessed 30 March 2020).

'Black History Month Row over Zayn Malik Image', BBC News, www.bbc.co.uk/news/-uk-england-37772968, 26 October 2016 (last accessed 1 October 2017).

'David Starkey Claims "the Whites Have Become Black"', *The Guardian*, 13 August 2011, www.theguardian.com/uk/2011/aug/13/david-starkey-claims-whites-black (last accessed 25 July 2019).

'European Election Database', Norwegian Centre for Research Data, www.nsd.uib.no/ (last accessed 01 November 2017).

'Fringe of Colour', https://fringeofcolour.weebly.com/ (last accessed 30 March 2020).

'IndyRef: Culture and Politics Five Years On', Stirling Centre for Scottish Studies (2019); https://stirlingcentrescottishstudies.wordpress.com/2019/09/24/indyref-culture-and-politics-five-years-on-summary/ (last accessed 01 March 2020).

'Issue 21: Gutter Magazine × Scottish BAME Writers' Network', Gutter Magazine, www.guttermag.co.uk/blog/issue21editorial (last accessed 30 March 2020).

'The Jeely Piece Song', Scottish Book Trust, www.scottishbooktrust.com/songs-and-rhymes/the-jeely-piece-song (last accessed 24 February 2020).

'Liam Neeson in Racism Storm after Admitting He Wanted to Kill Black Man', BBC News, www.bbc.co.uk/news/entertainment-arts-47117177 (last accessed 27 September 2019).

'Mission and Values', Scottish BAME Writers Network, https://scottishbamewritersnetwork.wordpress.com/ (last accessed 4 March 2020).

'New Laws for Race Equality in Scotland', Scottish Executive (2001).

'Prime Minister's Article in the Telegraph: 15 June 2020', www.gov.uk/government/speeches/prime-ministers-article-in-the-telegraph-15-june-2020 (last accessed 21 July 2020).

'Promoting Race Equality in Schools and Pre-School Education Centres', Scottish Executive (2003).

'Race Equality', One Scotland (2016), http://onescotland.org/equality-themes/race/ (last accessed 1 October 2017).

'RIC Constitution', Radical Independence Campaign, http://radical.scot/ric-constitution/ (last accessed 30 March 2020).

'Sadiq Khan: Scottish Labour's Best Days Still Lie Ahead with Kezia at the Helm', Labour List (2017), http://labourlist.org/2017/02/sadiq-khan-scottish-labours-best-days-still-lie-ahead/ (last accessed 1 September 2019).

'Scottish Independence: Salmond in Darling Interview Apology Call', BBC News (2014), www.bbc.co.uk/news/uk-scotland-scotland-politics-27793285 (last accessed 1 September 2019).

'Stormzy Scholarship for Black Students', University of Cambridge, www.undergraduate. study.cam.ac.uk/stormzy-scholarship (last accessed 30 March 2020).

'Tony Blair's Britain Speech', *The Guardian*, 28 March 2000, www.theguardian.com/uk/-2000/mar/28/britishidentity.tonyblair (last accessed 1 September 2019).

'Zanana Project', www.projectzanana.com/about (last accessed 30 March 2020)

Alexander, Claire (ed.), *Stuart Hall and 'Race'* (London: Routledge, 2011).

Allend, Alexander, Jr, 'Why Not Spencer?' in John Offer (ed.), *Herbert Spencer: Critical Assessments Vol. II* (London: Routledge, 2000), pp. 460–9.

Anderson, Benedict, *Imagined Communities: Reflections on the Origin and Spread of Nationalism* (London: Verso, 1991[1983]).

Andrews, Kehinde, *Back to Black: Black Radicalism for the 21st Century* (London: Zed Books, 2018).

Arana, R. Victoria, 'Aesthetics as Deliberate Design: Giving Form to Tigritude and Nommo' in R. Victoria Arana (ed.), *Black British Aesthetics Today* (Newcastle upon Tyne: Cambridge Scholars Publishing, 2007), pp. 1–13.

Arana, R. Victoria and Lauri Ramey, *Black British Writing* (Basingstoke: Palgrave Macmillan, 2004).

Arday, Jason, *Cool Britannia and Multi-Ethnic Britain: Uncorking the Champagne Supernova* (London: Routledge, 2020).

Arnold, Matthew, *On the Study of Celtic Literature* (London: Smith, Elder and Co., 1864).

Ashton, C. Heather, 'Benzodiazepine Abuse' in Woody Caan and Jackie de Belleroche (eds), *Drink, Drugs and Dependence: From Science to Clinical Practice* (London: Routledge, 2002), pp. 197–212.

Asian Dub Foundation, *Rafi's Revenge* (Polygram, 1998).

Aughey, Arthur, '"England Is the Country and the Country Is England": But What of the Politics?' in Westall and Gardiner (eds), *Literature of an Independent England*, pp. 46–59.

Back, Les, Michael Keith, Azra Khan, Kalbir Shukra and John Solomos, 'New Labour's White Heart: Politics, Multiculturalism and the Return of Assimilation', *Political Quarterly* 73:4 (2002), pp. 445–54.

Baker, Houston A., Jr, Manthia Diawara and Ruth H. Lindeborg (eds), *Black British Cultural Studies* (Chicago: University of Chicago Press, 1996).

Balibar, Étienne, 'Is there a "Neo-Racism?"' in Étienne Balibar and Immanuel Wallerstein (eds), *Race, Nation, Class: Ambiguous Identities* (London: Verso, 1991), pp. 17–28.

Barker, Martin, *The New Racism: Conservatives and the Ideology of the Tribe* (London: Junction, 1981).

Barnes, Julian, *England, England* (London: Jonathan Cape, 1998).

Barzun, Jacques, *Race: A Study in Modern Superstition* (London: Methuen, 1938).

Baucom, Ian, *Out of Place: Englishness, Empire and the Locations of Identity* (Princeton: Princeton University Press, 1999).

Benston, Kimberly, 'I Yam What I Am: The Topos of (Un)naming in Afro-American Literature', *Black American Literature Forum* 16:1 (1982), pp. 3–11.

Beveridge, Craig and Ronald Turnbull, *The Eclipse of Scottish Culture* (Edinburgh: Polygon, 1989).

Billig, Michael, *Banal Nationalism* (London: Sage, 1995).

Blackledge, Adrian, 'The Racialization of Language in British Political Discourse', *Critical Discourse Studies* 3:1 (2006), pp. 61–79.

Blevins, Steven, *Living Cargo: How Black Britain Performs Its Past* (Minneapolis: University of Minnesota Press, 2016).

Body-Gendrot, Sophie, 'Race: A Word Too Much? The French Dilemma' in Martin Bulmer and John Solomos (eds), *Researching Race and Racism* (London: Routledge, 2004), pp. 150–61.

Bogdanor, Vernon, *The New British Constitution* (London: Hart Publishing, 2009).

Bonino, Stefano, *Muslims in Scotland: The Making of Community in a Post-9/11 World* (Edinburgh: Edinburgh University Press, 2017).

Bourne, Jenny, '"May We Bring Harmony"? Thatcher's Legacy on "Race"', *Race and Class* 55:1 (2013), pp. 87–91.

Boyle, Danny dir., *Trainspotting* (Film4 Productions, 1996).

Brooks, Libby, 'Don't Tell Me Who I Am', *The Guardian*, 12 January 2002, www.theguardian.com/books/2002/jan/12/fiction.features (last accessed 30 June 2019).

Brown, Matthew, 'In/Outside Scotland: Race and Citizenship in the Work of Jackie Kay', in Schoene (ed.), *Edinburgh Companion to Contemporary Scottish Literature*, pp. 219–26.

Brown, Wendy, *Edgeworks: Critical Essays on Knowledge and Politics* (Princeton: Princeton University Press, 2005).

Burnett, James, *Sketches of the History of Man*, ed. James Harris (Indianapolis: Liberty Fund, 2007 [1788]).

Byrne, John, *Tutti Frutti*, dir. Tony Smith (BBC Scotland, 1987).

Calder, Angus, *Revolving Culture: Notes from the Scottish Republic* (London: I. B. Tauris, 1994).

Carrell, Severin, 'Woman Who Linked Racism with Scottish Nationalism Quits Twitter over Safety Fears', *The Guardian*, 28 February 2017, www.theguardian.com/uk-news/2017/feb/28/woman-who-linked-racism-with-scottish-nationalism-sadiq-khan-quits-twitter-over-safety-fears (last accessed 30 March 2020).

Centre for Contemporary Cultural Studies, *The Empire Strikes Back: Race and Racism in 70s Britain* (London: Routledge, 1982).

Centre on Dynamics of Ethnicity, 'Who Feels Scottish? National Identities and Ethnicity in Scotland', *The Dynamics of Diversity* (Joseph Rowntree Foundation/Manchester University Press, August 2014).

Chalk, Will, 'Stormzy: Skunk Anansie Don't Want to "Throw Shade"', BBC News, July 2019, www.bbc.co.uk/news/newsbeat-48852960 (last accessed 4 March 2020).

Chrisman, Laura, 'The Vanishing Body of Frantz Fanon in Paul Gilroy's *Against Race* and *After Empire*', *The Black Scholar* 41:4 (2011), pp. 18–30.

Clandfield, Peter, '"What is in My Blood?" Contemporary Black Scottishness and the Work of Jackie Kay' in Teresa Hubel and Neil Brooks (eds), *Literature and Racial Ambiguity* (Amsterdam: Rodopi, 2002), pp. 1–25.

Connell, Liam, 'Modes of Marginality: Scottish Literature and the Uses of Postcolonial Theory', *Comparative Studies of South Asia, Africa and the Middle East* 23:1&2 (2003), pp. 41–53.

Cooke, Melanie, 'Barrier or Entitlement? The Language and Citizenship Agenda in the United Kingdom', *Language Assessment Quarterly* 6:1 (2009), pp. 71–7.

Cooper, David, 'Introduction' in Michel Foucault, *Madness and Civilization: A History of Insanity in the Age of Reason*, trans. Richard Howard (London: Routledge, 2001 [1961]), pp. vii–ix.

Cottle, Simon, 'Mediatized Public Crisis and Civil Society Renewal: The Racist Murder of Stephen Lawrence', *Crime, Media, Culture* 1:1 (2005), pp. 49–71.

Craig, Cairns, *The Modern Scottish Novel: Narration and the National Imagination* (Edinburgh: Edinburgh University Press, 1999).

Craig, Cairns, *The Wealth of the Nation: Scotland, Culture and Independence* (Edinburgh: Edinburgh University Press, 2018).

Crawford, Robert, *Devolving English Literature*, 2nd edn (Oxford: Oxford University Press, 2000).

Dabydeen, David (ed.), *The Black Presence in English Literature* (Manchester: Manchester University Press, 1985).

Dabydeen, David, *A Harlot's Progress* (London: Jonathan Cape, 1999).

Dabydeen, David, 'On Not Being Milton: Nigger Talk in England Today' in Christopher Ricks and Leonard Michaels (eds), *The State of the Language* (Oxford: University of California Press, 1990), pp. 3–14.

Dabydeen, David, John Gilmore and Cecily Jones (eds), *The Oxford Companion to Black British History* (Oxford: Oxford University Press, 2007).

D'Aguiar, Fred, 'Against Black British Literature' in Maggie Butcher (ed.), *Tibisiri: Caribbean Writers and Critics* (Sydney: Dangaroo Press, 1989), pp. 106–14.

Daly, Mark, 'Sheku Bayoh Custody Death Officer "Hates Black People"', BBC News, www.bbc.co.uk/news/uk-scotland-34529611 (last accessed 30 March 2020).

Davidson, Neil and Satnam Virdee, 'Understanding Racism in Scotland' in Davidson et al. (eds), *No Problem Here*, pp. 9–12.

Davidson, Neil, Minna Liinpää, Maureen McBride and Satnam Virdee (eds), *No Problem Here: Understanding Racism in Scotland* (Edinburgh: Luath Press, 2018).

Dawson, Ashley, *Mongrel Nation: Diasporic Culture and the Making of Postcolonial Britain* (Ann Arbor: University of Michigan Press, 2007).

Debord, Guy, 'Introduction to the Critique of Urban Geography' in Knabb (ed. and trans.), *Situationist International Anthology*, pp. 8–11.

Debord, Guy, 'Theory of the Dérive' in Knabb (ed. and trans.), *Situationist International Anthology*, pp. 62–6.

Defoe, Daniel, *The True-Born Englishman* in *The Earlier Life and the Chief Earlier Works of Daniel Defoe*, ed. Henry Morley (London: Routledge, 1889), pp. 175–218.

Deleuze, Gilles and Félix Guattari, *Kafka: Towards a Minor Literature*, trans. Dana Polan (Minneapolis: University of Minnesota Press, 1986 [1975]).

Deleuze, Gilles and Félix Guattari, *A Thousand Plateaus*, trans. Brian Massumi (London: Athlone, 1999).

Derbyshire, Jonathan, 'Stuart Hall: We Need to Talk about Englishness', *The New Statesman*, 23 August 2012 (last accessed 3 April 2018), n. pag.

Devine, Tom, 'The Break-Up of Britain? Scotland and the End of Empire', *Transactions of the Royal Historical Society* 16 (2006) pp. 163–80.

Devine, Tom (ed.), *Recovering Scotland's Slavery Past: The Caribbean Connection* (Edinburgh: Edinburgh University Press, 2015).

Devine, Tom, *Scotland's Empire* (London: Penguin, 2012).

Dewdney, Richard, 'Commons Research Briefing RP97-113: Results of Devolution Referendums 1979 & 1997', House of Commons Library, p. 12, https://-commonslibrary.parliament.uk/research-briefings/rp97-113/ (last accessed 30 March 2020).

Dimeo, Paul and Gerry P. T. Finn, 'Racism, National Identity and Scottish Football' in Ben Carrington and Ian McDonald (eds), *'Race', Sport and British Society* (London: Routledge, 2001), pp. 29–48.

Donnell, Alison (ed.), *Companion to Contemporary Black British Culture* (London: Routledge, 2001).

Donnell, Alison, 'In Praise of a Black British Canon and the Possibilities of Representing the Nation "Otherwise"' in Low and Wynne-Davies (eds), *A Black British Canon?*, pp. 189–204.

Donnell, Alison, 'Nation and Contestation: Black British Writing', *Wasafiri* 17:36 (2002), pp. 11–17.

Dunbar, Paul Laurence, *The Collected Poetry of Paul Laurence Dunbar*, ed. Joanne M. Braxton (Charlottesville: University of Virginia Press, 1993 [1913]).

Dunbar, William, 'Of Ane Blak-Moir' in Louise Olga Fradenburg, *City, Marriage,*

Tournament: Arts of Rule in Late Medieval Scotland (Madison: University of Wisconsin Press, 1991), pp. 255–6.

Duncan, Ian, *Scott's Shadow: The Novel in Romantic Edinburgh* (Princeton: Princeton University Press, 2007).

Duncan, Ian, 'Walter Scott, James Hogg, and Scottish Gothic' in David Punter (ed.), *A New Companion to the Gothic* (London: Blackwell, 2012), pp. 123–34.

Dwyer, Claire and Caroline Bressey (eds), *New Geographies of Race and Racism* (London: Routledge, 2008).

Edwards, Paul, 'Black Writers of the Eighteenth and Nineteenth Centuries' in Dabydeen (ed.), *The Black Presence in English Literature*, pp. 50–67.

Eldridge, Michael, 'The Rise and Fall of Black Britain', *Transition* 74 (1997), pp. 32–43.

Evaristo, Bernardine, 'The Illusion of Inclusion', *Wasafiri* 25:4 (2010), pp. 1–6.

Fanon, Frantz, *Black Skin, White Masks*, trans. Charles Lam Markmann (London: Pluto Press, 2008 [1952]).

Fanon, Frantz, *The Wretched of the Earth* (New York: Grove Press, 2004 [1961]).

Farris, Sara and Catherine Rottenberg, 'Righting Feminism', *New Formations* 91 (2017), pp. 5–15.

Felman, Shoshana, *Writing and Madness* (Ithaca: Cornell University Press, 1985).

Ferrebe, Alice, 'Between Camps: Masculinity, Race and Nation in Post-Devolution Scotland' in Schoene (ed.), *Edinburgh Companion to Contemporary Scottish Literature*, pp. 275–82.

Folorunso, Femi, Gail Low and Marion Wynne-Davies, 'In the Eyes of the Beholder: Diversity and Cultural Politics of Canon Reformation in Britain – Femi Folorunso in Conversation with Gail Low and Marion Wynne-Davies (9 December 2004)' in Low and Wynne-Davies (eds), *A Black British Canon?*, pp. 74–90.

Fortier, Anne-Marie, *Multicultural Horizons: Diversity and the Limits of the Civil Nation* (London: Routledge, 2008).

Foucault, Michel, *History of Madness*, trans. Jonathan Murphy and Jean Khalfa (London: Routledge, 2006).

Fowler, Corinne, 'A Tale of Two Novels: Developing a Devolved Approach to Black British Writing', *Journal of Commonwealth Literature* 43:4 (2008), pp. 75–94.

Fry, Michael, *The Scottish Empire* (Edinburgh: Birlinn, 2002).

Gardiner, Michael, *The Constitution of English Literature: The State, the Nation and the Canon* (London: Bloomsbury Academic, 2013).

Gardiner, Michael, *The Cultural Roots of British Devolution* (Edinburgh: Edinburgh University Press, 2004).

Gardiner, Michael, *From Trocchi to Trainspotting: Scottish Critical Theory since 1960* (Edinburgh: Edinburgh University Press, 2006).

Gardiner, Michael, *The Return of England in English Literature* (Basingstoke: Palgrave Macmillan, 2012).

Gardiner, Michael, Graeme Macdonald and Niall O'Gallagher (eds), *Scottish Literature and Postcolonial Literature: Comparative Texts and Critical Perspectives* (Edinburgh: Edinburgh University Press, 2011).

Garrett, Aaron and Silvia Sebastiani, 'David Hume on Race' in Naomi Zack (ed.), *The Oxford Handbook to Philosophy and Race* (Oxford: Oxford University Press, 2017), pp. 31–43.

Gates, Henry Louis, Jr, *Figures in Black: Words, Signs and the 'Racial' Self* (Oxford: Oxford University Press, 1989).

Gibb, Eddie, 'Kelman and LKJ Speak Out for Black Writers', *The List*, 24 March 1995, https://archive.list.co.uk/the-list/1995-03-24/6/ (last accessed 30 March 2020).

Giddens, Anthony, *The Consequences of Modernity* (Cambridge: Polity, 1990).

Gilkes, Michael, *The Literate Imagination: Essays on the Novels of Wilson Harris* (London: Macmillan, 1989).

Gilroy, Paul, *After Empire: Melancholia or Convivial Culture?* (Abingdon: Routledge, 2004).

Gilroy, Paul, *Against Race: Imagining Political Culture Beyond the Color Line* (London: Harvard University Press, 2002).

Gilroy, Paul, *The Black Atlantic: Modernity and Double Consciousness* (London: Verso, 1993).

Gilroy, Paul, *Small Acts: Thoughts on the Politics of Black Cultures* (London: Serpent's Tail, 1993).

Gilroy, Paul, *There Ain't No Black in the Union Jack* (London: Routledge, 2002 [1987]).

Glissant, Édouard, *Caribbean Discourse: Selected Essays* (Charlottesville: University of Virginia Press, 1999).

Goddard, Lynette (ed.), *The Methuen Drama Book of Plays by Black British Writers* (London: Bloomsbury, 2011).

Goldie, Paul, 'Cultural Racism and Islamophobia in Glasgow' in Davidson et al. (eds), *No Problem Here*, pp. 128–44.

Gray, Alasdair, *1982, Janine* (Edinburgh: Canongate, 2003 [1984]).

Gray, Alasdair, *Lanark: A Life in Four Books* (Edinburgh: Canongate, 2002 [1981]).

Gray, Alasdair, *Poor Things* (New York: Harcourt, 1992).

Griffith, Phoebe and Mark Leonard (eds), *Reclaiming Britishness* (London: The Foreign Policy Centre, 2002).

Gunning, Dave, 'Anti-Racism, the Nation-State, and Contemporary Black British Literature', *Journal of Commonwealth Literature* 39:2 (2004), pp. 29–43.

Guptara, Prabhu, *Black British Literature: An Annotated Bibliography* (Hebden Bridge: Dangaroo Press, 1986).

Hage, Ghassan, 'Intercultural Relations at the Limits of Multiculturalism' in Duncan Ivison (ed.), *The Ashgate Research Companion to Multiculturalism* (London: Ashgate, 2010), pp. 235–54.

Hague, Euan, Benito Giordano and Edward H. Sebesta, 'Whiteness, Multiculturalism and Nationalist Appropriation of Celtic Culture: The Case of the League of the South and the Lega Nord', *Cultural Geographies* 12 (2005), pp. 151–73.

Hall, Stuart, 'Life and Times of the First New Left', *New Left Review* 61:1 (2010), pp. 177–96.

Hall, Stuart, 'Minimal Selves' in Baker, Diawara and Lindeborg (eds), *Black British Cultural Studies*, pp. 114–19.

Hall, Stuart, *The Multicultural Question 2001* (Milton Keynes: Pavis Papers, 2001).

Hall, Stuart, 'New Ethnicities' [1988] in James Procter (ed.), *Writing Black Britain 1948–1998: An Interdisciplinary Anthology* (Manchester: Manchester University Press, 2000), pp. 265–75.

Hall, Stuart, 'Old and New Identities, Old and New Ethnicities' in Anthony D. King (ed.), *Culture, Globalization, and the World-System: Contemporary Conditions for the Representation of Identity* (Minneapolis: University of Minnesota Press, 1997), pp. 41–68.

Hall, Stuart, 'Racism and Reaction', *Five Views of Multi-Racial Britain* (London: Commission for Racial Equality, 1978), pp. 23–35.

Hall, Stuart, Chas Critcher, Tony Jefferson, John Clarke and Brian Roberts, *Policing the Crisis: 'Mugging', the State, and Law and Order* (London: Macmillan, 1978).

Hames, Scott, *The Literary Politics of Scottish Devolution: Voice, Class, Nation* (Edinburgh: Edinburgh University Press, 2019).

Hames, Scott, 'Narrating Devolution: Politics and/as Scottish Fiction', *C21 Literature* 5:2 (2017), pp. 1–25.

Hames, Scott, 'On Vernacular Scottishness and its Limits: Devolution and the Spectacle of "Voice"', *Studies in Scottish Literature* 39:1 (2013), pp. 201–22.

Hamilton, Douglas, *Scotland, the Caribbean and the Atlantic World 1750–1820* (Manchester: Manchester University Press, 2010).

Hansen, Randall, *Citizenship and Immigration in Post-War Britain* (Oxford: Oxford University Press, 2000).

Haria, Jatin, 'Race, Ethnicity and Employment in Scotland' in Davidson et al. (eds), *No Problem Here*, pp. 199–211.

Harris, Wilson, *Black Marsden* (London: Faber and Faber, 1972).

Harris, Wilson, *Palace of the Peacock*, in *The Guyana Quartet* (London: Faber and Faber, 1985 [1960]), pp. 15–117.

Harris, Wilson and Alan Riach, 'Wilson Harris Interview by Alan Riach' in Wilson Harris, *The Radical Imagination: Lectures and Talks*, ed. Alan Riach and Mark Williams (Liège: L3. Liège Lang & Lit, 1992).

Hartman, Saidiya, 'Venus in Two Acts', *Small Axe* 12:2 (2008), pp. 1–14.

HC Deb (21 December 1988), vol. 144, col. 428, https://api.parliament.uk/historic-hansard/sittings/1988/dec/21 (last accessed 18 August 2019).

Head, Dominic, 'Multiculturalism of the Millennium: Zadie Smith's *White Teeth*' in Richard J. Lane, Rod Mengham and Phillip Tew, *Contemporary British Fiction* (Cambridge: Polity Press, 2002), pp. 106–19.

Hewison, Robert, *John Byrne: Art and Life* (Farnham: Lund Humphreys, 2011).

Hinds, Donald, 'Busman's Blues' in Andrew Salkey (ed.), *Stories from the Caribbean* (London: Paul Elek Books, 1972 [1965]), pp. 98–103.

Hirsch, Afua, 'Meghan Markle's Wedding Was a Rousing Celebration of Blackness', *The Guardian*, 20 May 2018, www.theguardian.com/uk-news/2018/may/19/meghan-markles-wedding-was-a-celebration-of-blackness (last accessed 4 March 2020).

Hopkins, Peter, 'Politics, Race and Nation: The Difference That Scotland Makes' in Dwyer and Bressey (eds), *New Geographies*, pp. 113–24.

Hornby, Nick, *High Fidelity* (London: Victor Gollancz, 1995).

Huggan, Graham, *The Postcolonial Exotic: Marketing the Margins* (London: Routledge, 2001).

Hutchison, David, 'The Experience and Contexts of Drama in Scotland' in Ian Brown, *The Edinburgh Companion to Scottish Drama* (Edinburgh: Edinburgh University Press, 2011), pp. 200–10.

Ignatiev, Noel and John Garvey (eds), *Race Traitor* (London: Routledge, 1996).

Innes, Catherine Lyn, *A History of Black and Asian Writing in Britain, 1700–2000* (Cambridge: Cambridge University Press, 2002).

Innes, Kirstin, 'Renton's Bairns: Identity and Language in the Post-Trainspotting Novel' in Schoene (ed.), *Edinburgh Companion to Contemporary Scottish Literature*, pp. 301–9.

James, C. L. R., *The Black Jacobins: Toussaint L'Ouverture and the San Domingo Rebellion* (New York: Vintage, 1989 [1938]).

Jenkinson, Jacqueline, 'The Glasgow Race Disturbances of 1919' in Kenneth Lunn (ed.), *Race and Labour in Twentieth-Century Britain* (London: Frank Cass, 1985), pp. 43–67.

Johnson, Linton Kwesi, *Mi Revalueshanary Fren: Selected Poems* (London: Penguin, 2002).

Jones, Carole, *Disappearing Men: Gender Disorientation in Scottish Fiction 1979–1999* (Amsterdam: Rodopi, 2009).

Jones, Carole, 'White Men on Their Backs – From Objection to Abjection: The Representation of the White Male as Victim in William McIlvanney's *Docherty* and Irvine Welsh's *Marabou Stork Nightmares*', *International Journal of Scottish Literature* 1 (2006), n. pag.

Joyce, James, *Ulysses*, ed. Hans Walter Gabler (London: The Bodley Head, 1986).

Kay, Jackie, *The Adoption Papers* (Tarset: Bloodaxe Books, 1991).

Kay, Jackie, 'The Broons' Bairn's Black (A Skipping Rhyme)', *Off Colour* (Newcastle upon Tyne: Bloodaxe, 1998), p. 61.

Kay, Jackie, *Chiaroscuro* in Goddard (ed.), *The Methuen Drama Book of Plays by Black British Writers*, pp. 59–117.

Kay, Jackie, 'John Kay Obituary', *The Guardian*, 9 February 2020, www.theguardian.com/politics/2020/feb/09/john-kay-obituary (last accessed 30 March 2020).

Kay, Jackie, *Trumpet* (London: Picador, 1998).

Kelly, Aaron, *Irvine Welsh* (Manchester: Manchester University Press, 2005).

Kelman, James, *"And the Judges Said": Essays* (London: Secker & Warburg, 2002).

Kelman, James, *The Busconductor Hines* (Edinburgh: Polygon, 1984).

Kelman, James, *Dirt Road* (Edinburgh: Canongate, 2016).

Kelman, James, *A Disaffection* (London: Secker and Warburg, 1989).

Kelman, James, *How Late It Was, How Late* (London: Vintage, 1998 [1994]).

Kelman, James, *Mo Said She Was Quirky* (London: Hamish Hamilton, 2012).

Kelman, James, *Some Recent Attacks: Essays Cultural and Political* (Stirling: AK Press, 1992).

Kelman, James, *You Have to Be Careful in the Land of the Free* (London: Penguin, 2005 [2004]).

Kemp, Arnold, 'The Shame of Sighthill', *The Guardian*, Sunday 12 August 2001, www.theguardian.com/uk/2001/aug/12/immigration.immigrationandpublicservices3 (last accessed 27 September 2019).

Kidd, Colin, 'From Jacobitism to the SNP: The Crown, the Union and the Scottish Question', Stenton Lecture, 2013, University of Reading, www.reading.ac.uk/web/-files/history/From_Jacobitism_to_the_SNP.pdf (last accessed 20 August 2019).

Kidd, Colin, 'Protestantism, Constitutionalism and British Identity Under the Later Stuarts' in Brendan Bradshaw and Peter Roberts (eds), *British Consciousness and Identity: The Making of Britain 1533–1707* (Cambridge: Cambridge University Press, 1998), pp. 321–42.

Kidd, Colin, 'Race, Empire, and the Limits of Nineteenth-Century Scottish Nationhood', *The Historical Journal* 46:4 (2003), pp. 873–92.

Kidd, Colin, *Union and Unionisms: Political Thought in Scotland 1500–2000* (Cambridge: Cambridge University Press, 2008).

Killingray, David, 'Review: Black Writers in Britain 1760–1890', *Journal of African History* 35:1 (1994), p. 172.

King, Colin, 'Is Football the New African Slave Trade?' in Daniel Burdsey (ed.), *Race, Ethnicity and Football: Persisting Debates and Emergent Issues* (London: Routledge, 2011), pp. 36–49.

Knabb, Ken (ed. and trans.), *Situationist International Anthology*, 2nd edn (Berkeley: Bureau of Public Secrets, 2006).

Knox, Robert, *The Races of Man* (London: Henry Renshaw, 1850).

Kovesi, Simon, *James Kelman* (Manchester, Manchester University Press, 2007).

Kumar, Krishnan, *The Making of English National Identity* (Cambridge: Cambridge University Press, 2003).

Kundnani, Arun, 'The Rise and Fall of British Multiculturalism' in Gavan Titley (ed.), *Resituating Culture* (Strasbourg: Council of Europe, 2004), pp. 105–12.

Lambert, Iain, 'This is Not Sarcasm Believe Me Yours Sincerely: James Kelman, Ken Saro-Wiwa and Amos Tutuola' in Gardiner, Macdonald and O'Gallagher (eds), *Scottish Literature and Postcolonial Literature*, pp. 198–209.

Lavery, Hannah, *Finding Sea Glass: Poems from The Drift* (Edinburgh: Stewed Rhubarb Press, 2019).

Leask, Nigel, *Stepping Westward: Writing the Highland Tour c.1720–1830* (Oxford: Oxford University Press, 2020).

Ledent, Bénédicte, 'Black British Literature' in Dinah Birch (ed.) *The Oxford Companion to English Literature*, 7th edn (Oxford: Oxford University Press, 2009), pp. 16–22.

Lee, A. Robert, *Other Britain, Other British: Contemporary Multicultural Fiction* (London: Pluto Press, 1995).

Lentin, Alana, *Racism and Anti-Racism in Europe* (London: Pluto Press, 2004).

Lentin, Alana and Gavan Titley, *The Crises of Multiculturalism: Racism in a Neoliberal Age* (London: Zed Books, 2011).

Liinpää, Minna, 'Nationalism and Scotland's Imperial Past' in Davidson et al., *No Problem Here*, pp. 14–31.

Lindsay, Andrew O., *Illustrious Exile: Journal of my Sojourn in the West Indies by Robert Burns, Esq. Commenced on the first day of July 1786* (Leeds: Peepal Tree Press, 2006).

Loach, Ken dir., *Ae Fond Kiss* (Icon Film Distribution, 2004).

Low, Gail and Marion Wynne-Davies (eds), *A Black British Canon?* (Basingstoke: Palgrave Macmillan, 2006).

Maan, Bashir, *The New Scots: The Story of Asians in Scotland* (Edinburgh: John Donald, 1992).

McCrone, David, *The New Sociology of Scotland* (London: Sage, 2017).

McCrone, David, *Understanding Scotland: The Sociology of a Nation*, 2nd edn (London: Routledge, 2001).

McCrone, David, Angela Morris and Richard Kiely, *Scotland – the Brand: The Making of Scottish Heritage* (Edinburgh: Edinburgh University Press, 1995).

Macdonald, Graeme, 'Postcolonialism and Scottish Studies', *New Formations* 59 (2006), pp. 116–31.

Macdonald, Graeme, 'Scottish Extractions: "Race" and Racism in Devolutionary Fiction', *Orbis Litterarum* 65:2 (2010), pp. 79–107.

Macdonald, Kirsty, '"This Desolate and Appalling Landscape": The Journey North in Contemporary Scottish Gothic', *Gothic Studies* 13:2 (2011), pp. 37–48.

MacDonald Fraser, George, *McAuslan in the Rough* (New York: Alfred Knopf, 1974).

McLean, Duncan, *Bunker Man* (London: Jonathan Cape, 1995).

McLeod, John, 'Adoption Aesthetics' in Osborne (ed.), *Cambridge Companion*, pp. 211–24.

McLeod, John, 'Black British Writing and Post-British England' in Westall and Gardiner (eds), *Literature of an Independent England*, pp. 175–87.

McLeod, John, 'Fantasy Relationships: Black British Canons in a Transnational World' in Low and Wynne-Davies (eds), *A Black British Canon?*, pp. 93–104.

Maloney, Paul, *The Britannia Panopticon Music Hall and Cosmopolitan Entertainment Culture* (London: Palgrave Macmillan, 2016).

Marshall, Ashley, 'Defoe as Satirist', *Huntingdon Library Quarterly* 70:4 (2007), pp. 553–76.

Mbembe, Achille, *A Critique of Black Reason*, trans. Laurent Dubois (Durham, NC: Duke University Press, 2017).

Meer, Nasar, 'What Do We Know about BAME Self-Reported Racial Discrimination in Scotland?' in Davidson et al. (eds), *No Problem Here*, pp. 114–27.

Mercer, Kobena, *Welcome to the Jungle: New Positions in Black Cultural Studies* (London: Routledge, 1994).

Miles, Robert and Leslie Muirhead, 'Racism in Scotland: A Matter for Further Investigation?' in David McCrone (ed.), *Scottish Government Yearbook 1986* (Edinburgh: Unit for the Study of Government in Scotland, University of Edinburgh, 1986), pp. 108–36.

Miller, Gavin, 'How Not to "Question Scotland"', *Scottish Affairs* 52:1 (2005), pp. 1–14.

Miller, Gavin, '"Persuade Without Convincing . . . Represent Without Reasoning": The Inferiorist Myth of Scots Language' in Eleanor Bell and Gavin Miller (eds), *Scotland in Theory: Reflections on Culture and Literature* (Amsterdam: Rodopi, 2004), pp. 197–209.

Miller, Gavin, *R. D. Laing* (Edinburgh: Edinburgh Review, 2004).

Miller, Gavin, 'Welsh and Identity Politics' in Schoene (ed.), *Edinburgh Companion to Irvine Welsh*, pp. 89–99.

Modood, Tariq, *Multicultural Politics: Racism, Ethnicity and Muslims in Britain* (Edinburgh: Edinburgh University Press, 2005).

Modood, Tariq, 'Political Blackness and British Asians', *Sociology* 28:4 (1994), pp. 859–76.

Morris, Michael, *Scotland and the Caribbean c.1740–1833: Atlantic Archipelagos* (London: Routledge, 2015).

Morrison, Toni, *Playing in the Dark* (Cambridge, MA: Harvard University Press, 1992).

Moten, Fred, *In the Break: The Aesthetics of the Black Radical Tradition* (Minneapolis: University of Minnesota Press, 2003).

Muir, Edwin, *Scottish Journey* (London: Flamingo, 1985 [1935]).

Mullard, Chris, *Black Britain* (London: Allen and Unwin, 1973).

Mullen, Stephen, *It Wisnae Us: The Truth about Glasgow and Slavery* (Edinburgh: RIAS, 2009).

Nairn, Tom, *After Britain: New Labour and the Return of Scotland* (London: Granta, 2001).

Nairn, Tom, *The Break-Up of Britain: Crisis and Neo-Nationalism* (London: Verso, 1977).

Nairn, Tom, *The Enchanted Glass: Britain and its Monarchy* (London: Vintage, 1994).

Nasta, Susheila, *Home Truths: Fictions of the South Asian Diaspora in Britain* (Basingstoke: Palgrave, 2002).

Nasta, Susheila and Mark Stein (eds), *The Cambridge History of Black and Asian British Writing* (Cambridge: Cambridge University Press, 2019).

Niblett, Michael, 'Scotland' in Dabydeen, Gilmore and Jones (eds), *Black British History*, p. 433.

Niven, Alastair, 'New Diversity, Hybridity and Scottishness' in Ian Brown (ed.), *The Edinburgh History of Scottish Literature*, vol. 3: *Modern Transformations: New Identities (from 1918)* (Edinburgh, Edinburgh University Press, 2007), pp. 320–31.

Niven, Alex, *New Model Island: How to Build a Radical Culture Beyond the Idea of England* (London: Repeater Books, 2019).

Norquay, Glenda, 'Janice Galloway's Novels: Fraudulent Mooching' in Aileen Christiansen and Alison Lumsden (eds), *Contemporary Scottish Women Writers* (Edinburgh: Edinburgh University Press, 2000), pp. 131–43.

Nwonka, Clive James and Sarita Malik, 'Cultural Discourses and Practices of Institutionalised Diversity in the UK Film Sector: "Just Get Something Black Made"', *The Sociological Review* 66:6 (2018), pp. 1111–27.

Okojie, Irenosen, 'The Spirit of Harry and Meghan Can Revitalise Our Divided Nation', *The Guardian*, 20 May 2018, www.theguardian.com/uk-news/2018/may/19/markle-harry-royal-wedding-race-curry-family-britain-society (last accessed 4 March 2020).

Omi, Michael and Howard Winant, *Race Formation in the United States: From the 1960s to the 1990s* (New York: Routledge, 1994).

Osborne, Deirdre (ed.), *The Cambridge Companion to British Black and Asian Literature (1945–2010)* (Cambridge: Cambridge University Press, 2016).

Owusu, Kwesi (ed.), *Black British Culture and Society* (London: Routledge, 2000).

Parekh, Bhikhu (ed.), *The Future of Multi-Ethnic Britain: Report of the Commission on the Future of Multi-Ethnic Britain* (London: Profile Books, 2002 [2000]).

Parker, David and Miri Song (eds), *Rethinking 'Mixed Race'* (London: Pluto Press, 2001).

Paxman, Jeremy, *The English: A Portrait of a People* (London: Penguin, 1999).

Pearce, Lynne, Corinne Fowler and Robert Crawshaw (eds), *Postcolonial Manchester: Diaspora Space and the Devolution of Literary Culture* (Manchester: Manchester University Press, 2013).

Penrose, Jan and David Howard, 'One Scotland, Many Cultures: The Mutual Constitution of Antiracism and Place' in Dwyer and Bressey (eds), *New Geographies*, pp. 95–111.

Petrie, Duncan, *Contemporary Scottish Fictions: Film, Television and the Novel* (Edinburgh: Edinburgh University Press, 2004).

Phillips, Caryl, *A New World Order: Essays* (New York: Vintage, 2002).

Phillips, Deborah, Cathy Davis and Peter Ratcliffe, 'British Asian Narratives of Urban Space', *Transactions of the Institute of British Geographers* 32:2 (2007), pp. 217–34.

Pitcher, Ben, *The Politics of Multiculturalism: Race and Racism in Contemporary Britain* (Basingstoke: Palgrave Macmillan, 2009).

Pittin-Hedon, Marie-Odile, *The Space of Fiction: Voices from Scotland in a Post-Devolution Age* (Glasgow: Scottish Literature International, 2015).

Pittock, Murray G. H., *Celtic Identity and the British Image* (Manchester: Manchester University Press, 1999).

Pittock, Murray G. H., *Jacobitism* (London: Macmillan, 1998).

Procter, James, *Dwelling Places: Postwar Black British Writing* (Manchester: Manchester University Press, 2003).

Procter, James, *Writing Black Britain 1948–1998: An Interdisciplinary Anthology* (Manchester: Manchester University Press, 2000).

Reich, Howard and William Gaines, *Jelly's Blues: The Life, Music, and Redemption of Jelly Roll Morton* (Cambridge, MA: Da Capo Press, 2003).

Rewt, Polly T., 'Introduction: The African Diaspora and its Origins', *Research in African Literatures* 29:4 (1998), pp. 3–13.

Riach, Alan, 'Other Than Realism: Magic and Violence in Modern Scottish Fiction and the Recent Work of Wilson Harris', *International Journal of Scottish Literature* 4 (2008), n. pag.

Riach, Alan, *Representing Scotland in Literature, Popular Culture and Iconography* (Basingstoke: Palgrave Macmillan, 2005).

Rice, Alan, '"Heroes across the Sea": Black and White British Fascination with African Americans in the Contemporary Black British Fiction of Caryl Phillips and Jackie Kay' in Heike Raphael-Hernandez (ed.), *Blackening Europe: The African American Presence* (London: Routledge, 2004), pp. 217–33.

Richetti, John, *The Life of Daniel Defoe* (Oxford: Blackwell, 2006).

Robertson, James, *Joseph Knight* (London: Fourth Estate, 2003).

Robinson, Cedric, *Black Marxism: The Making of the Black Radical Tradition* (Chapel Hill: University of North Carolina Press, 2000 [1983]).

Rodríguez González, Carla, 'The Rhythms of the City: The Performance of Time and Space in Suhayl Saadi's *Psychoraag*', *The Journal of Commonwealth Literature* 51:1 (2016), pp. 92–109.

Ross, Jacob (ed.), *Closure: Contemporary Black British Short Stories* (Leeds: Peepal Tree Press, 2015).

Rushdie, Salman, '"Commonwealth Literature" Does Not Exist' in *Imaginary Homelands* (London: Granta, 1992), pp. 61–70.

Saadi, Suhayl, *The Burning Mirror* (Edinburgh: Polygon, 2001).

Saadi, Suhayl, 'In Tom Paine's Kitchen: Days of Rage and Fire' in Schoene (ed.), *Edinburgh Companion to Contemporary Scottish Literature*, pp. 28–33.

Saadi, Suhayl, 'Infinite Diversity in New Scottish Writing', Association for Scottish Literary Studies (2000), https://asls.arts.gla.ac.uk/SSaadi.html (last accessed 30 March 2020).

Saadi, Suhayl, *Psychoraag* (Edinburgh: Chroma, 2005 [2004]).

Said, Edward, *Orientalism* (New York: Pantheon Books, 1978).

Sassi, Carla, 'Acts of (Un)willed Amnesia: Dis/appearing Figurations of the Caribbean in Post-Union Scottish Literature' in Giovanna Covi, Joan Anim-Addo, Velma Pollard and Carla Sassi (eds), *Caribbean–Scottish Relations: Colonial and Contemporary Inscriptions in History, Language and Literature* (London: Mango Publishing, 2007), pp. 131–98.

Sassi, Carla, 'Sir Walter Scott and the Caribbean: Unravelling the Silences', *The Yearbook of English Studies* 47 (2017), pp. 224–40.

Schoene, Berthold, 'Alan Warner, Post-feminism and the Emasculated Nation' in Schoene (ed.), *Edinburgh Companion to Contemporary Scottish Literature*, pp. 255–63.

Schoene, Berthold (ed.), *The Edinburgh Companion to Contemporary Scottish Literature* (Edinburgh: Edinburgh University Press, 2007).

Schoene, Berthold (ed.), *The Edinburgh Companion to Irvine Welsh* (Edinburgh: Edinburgh University Press, 2010).

Schoene, Berthold, 'Going Cosmopolitan: Reconstituting "Scottishness" in Post-Devolution Criticism' in Schoene (ed.), *Edinburgh Companion to Contemporary Scottish Literature*, pp. 7–16.

Schoene, Berthold, 'Welsh, Drugs and Subculture' in Schoene (ed.), *Edinburgh Companion to Irvine Welsh*, pp. 65–76.

Schwartz, Bill, *The White Man's World* (Oxford: Oxford University Press, 2012).

Scotland's Census, 'Ethnicity, Identity, Language and Religion', www.scotlandscensus.gov. uk/ethnicity-identity-language-and-religion (last accessed 29 September 2019).

Scottish Government, *Scotland's Future* (Edinburgh: Scottish Government, 2013).

Scruton, Roger, *England: An Elegy* (London: Continuum, 2001).

Sesay, Kadija, *Write Black, Write British: From Postcolonial to Black British Literature* (London: Hansib, 2005).

Shaw, Jo, 'Citizenship and the Franchise' in Ayelet Shachar, Rainer Bauboeck, Irene Bloemraad and Maarten Vink (eds), *The Oxford Handbook of Citizenship* (Oxford: Oxford University Press, 2017), pp. 290–313.

Shukra, Kalbir, *The Changing Pattern of Black Politics in Britain* (London: Pluto Press, 1998).

Sivanandan, A., 'Race, Class and the State: The Black Experience in Britain', *Race and Class* 17:4 (1976), pp. 347–68.

Sivanandan, A., 'Resistance to Rebellion: Asian and Afro-Caribbean Struggles in Britain', *Race and Class* 23:2&3 (1981), pp. 111–52.

Smith, C. Gregory, *Scottish Literature, Character and Influence* (London: Macmillan, 1919).

Smith, Matthew, 'Most Conservative Members Would See Party Destroyed to Achieve Brexit', *YouGov*, https://yougov.co.uk/topics/politics/articles-reports/2019/06/18/-most-conservative-members-would-see-party-destroye (last accessed 30 March 2020).

Smith, Zadie, *White Teeth* (London: Hamish Hamilton, 2000).

Smithies, Bill, Peter Fiddick and John Enoch Powell, *Enoch Powell on Immigration* (London: Sphere, 1969).

Smout, T. C., 'Introduction' in Muir, *Scottish Journey*, pp. ix–xxxii.

Somynne, Robert, 'Scottish Nationalists Aren't Racists – They're Reacting against the UK's Bigotry', *The Guardian*, 1 March 2017, www.theguardian.com/commentisfree/-2017/mar/01/scottish-nationalists-racist-uk-bigotry-sadiq-khan (last accessed 4 March 2020).

Stein, Mark, *Black British Literature: Novels of Transformation* (Columbus: Ohio State University Press, 2004).

Stevenson, Randall, 'A Postmodern Scotland?' in Gerald Carruthers, David Goldie and Alastair Renfrew (eds), *Beyond Scotland: New Contexts for Twentieth-Century Scottish Literature* (Amsterdam: Rodopi, 2004), pp. 209–28.

Sulter, Maud, *As a Black Woman* (London: Akira Press, 1985).

Sulter, Maud, *Zabat: Poetics of a Family Tree* (Hebden Bridge: Urban Fox Press, 1989).

Sutherland, Luke, *Jelly Roll* (London: Transworld, 1998).

Sutherland, Luke, *Venus as a Boy* (London: Bloomsbury, 2004).

Taylor, Elly M. dir. *Angelou on Burns* (Taylored Productions, 1996).

Taylor, Paul C., *Black is Beautiful: A Philosophy of Black Aesthetics* (Chichester: Wiley-Blackwell, 2016).

Thomson, Alex, '"You Can't Get There from Here": Devolution and Scottish Literary History', *International Journal of Scottish Literature* 3 (2007), www.ijsl.stir.ac.uk/-issue3/thomson.htm (last accessed 30 March 2020).

Tutuola, Amos, *The Palm Wine Drinkard and His Dead Palm-Wine Tapster in the Deads' Town* (London: Faber and Faber, 1952).

Upstone, Sara, *British Asian Fiction: Twenty-First-Century Voices* (Manchester: Manchester University Press, 2010).

Upstone, Sara, *Rethinking Race and Ethnicity in Contemporary British Fiction* (London: Routledge, 2017).

Walker, Amy, 'All Hail Stormzy for Historic Glastonbury Performance', *The Guardian*, 29 June 2019, www.theguardian.com/music/2019/jun/29/stormzy-historic-glastonbury-performance (last accessed 30 March 2020).

Wardle, Huon and Laura Obermuller, '"Windrush Generation" and "Hostile Environment": Symbols and Lived Experience in Caribbean Migration to the UK', *Migration and Society* 2:1 (2019), pp. 81–9.

Watson, Roderick, 'The Modern Scottish Literary Renaissance' in Ian Brown and Alan Riach (eds), *The Edinburgh Companion to Twentieth-Century Scottish Literature* (Edinburgh: Edinburgh University Press, 2009), pp. 75–87.

Welsh, Irvine, *Filth* (London: Vintage, 1999 [1998]).

Welsh, Irvine, *Marabou Stork Nightmares* (London: Jonathan Cape, 1995).

Welsh, Irvine, *Trainspotting* (London: Vintage, 2004 [1993]).

Westall, Claire and Michael Gardiner (eds), *Literature of an Independent England: Revisions of England, Englishness and English Literature* (Basingstoke: Palgrave Macmillan, 2013).

Wester, Maisha L., *African American Gothic: Screams from Shadowed Places* (New York: Palgrave Macmillan, 2012).

Whyte, Christopher, 'Masculinities in Contemporary Scottish Fiction', *Forum for Modern Language Studies* 34:3 (1998), pp. 274–85.

Winant, Howard, 'Theoretical Status of the Concept of Race' in Les Back and John Solomos (eds), *Theories of Race and Racism* (London: Routledge, 2000), pp. 181–90.

Young Fathers, *Some White Men Are Black Men Too* (Big Dada Recordings, 2015).

Young, Carol, 'Changing the Race Equality Paradigm in Scotland's Public Sector' in Davidson et al., *No Problem Here,* pp. 180–98.

Young, Robert J. C., *Colonial Desire: Hybridity in Theory, Culture, and Race* (London: Routledge, 1995).

Young, Robert J. C., *The Idea of English Ethnicity* (Oxford: Blackwell, 2007).

Zagratzki, Uwe, '"Blues Fell This Morning" – James Kelman's Scottish Literature and Afro-American Music', *Scottish Literary Journal* 27:1 (2000), pp. 105–17.

Žižek, Slavoj, 'Multiculturalism, or, the Cultural Logic of Multinational Capitalism', *New Left Review* 225:1 (1997), pp. 28–51.

Index

Printed and bound by CPI Group (UK) Ltd, Croydon, CR0 4YY

18/03/2025

01834143-0001

—